"General Tommy Franks and Lieutenant General Mike DeLong were masters at warfighting, managing the sensitive relationships in the region, and holding together the complex coalition put in place to deal with the significant threats that faced us. General DeLong was the unsung hero of these efforts. His savvy, intellect, common sense, professional competence, and honesty come through in this book and give us a rare insight into critical events that have shaped our course at the beginning of this troubled century."

—General Tony Zinni, USMC, ret., former Commander in Chief of CentCom, and coauthor of *Battle Ready*

"DeLong is known as 'Rifle' DeLong, and not just because he was a crack shot with a rifle (and other common Marine Corps fashion accessories such as pistols and helo-mounted rockets). The nickname stuck because, as DeLong rose in rank, and he and his subordinates had to make life and death decisions, DeLong learned to be a tough grader. He gave his people just one shot to get it right. . . . When you have a president who is smart enough to turn Tommy Franks and Rifle DeLong loose on the bad guys, you have a president who can win the war."

—*National Review* Online

"From the point of the bayonet to the crisis of the conference room, General DeLong has spent a lifetime serving his country in war and peace, in combat and in preparation. His experience from Mogadishu to Tampa, from fighting terrorists to dealing with Washington (for a military man maybe even more terrifying) gives him a unique vantage point from which to help his fellow Americans understand the world they live in and the challenges they face."

—Newt Gingrich, former Speaker of the House

"[*A General Speaks Out* is] a deep look into the inner workings of the Central Command and America's war-fighting apparatus. . . . For anyone interested in the military's war on terror, behind-the-scenes, [this book] is essential reading."

—LateFinal.com

"General DeLong did an outstanding job on General Tommy Frank's behalf in dealing with Secretary Rumsfeld, chairman of the Joint Chiefs of Staff, General Richard Meyers, and the president himself. General DeLong was also the 'go-to' guy for the sixty-plus countries that participated in the Afghanistan and Iraqi campaigns. This is truly an insider's view of these history-making events."
—General Joseph Hoar, USMC, ret., former Commander in Chief of CentCom

"Lieutenant General Mike DeLong was General Tommy Franks' right-hand man in conceiving and executing the Afghanistan and Iraq wars. While Franks was in the field, former Marine combat pilot DeLong ran Central Command (CentCom), the nerve center of both wars—where he was an active participant in discussions involving President Bush, Donald Rumsfeld, Paul Wolfowitz, Franks, George Tenet, and many others. Now, General DeLong offers the frankest and most authoritative look inside the wars—how we prepared for battle, how we fought, how we toppled two regimes. . . ."
—*Human Events* online

"[Lieutenant General Michael DeLong] and General Franks are probably the most authoritative sources on the [Afghanistan and Iraq] wars. DeLong's book is exactly what one would expect from a Marine—clear, concise, and to the point. There is no fluff, and no sugar-coating. DeLong calls it as he sees it, and his viewpoint is one well worth paying attention to. DeLong's book is explosive in some aspects. . . . DeLong also lays out the reasons for a lot of the post-liberation chaos, and does so with honesty. . . . Ultimately, DeLong's book . . . provides a superb first draft of history for the initial part of the war on terrorism, far more accurate than much of the media coverage."
—*Strategy Page* (strategypage.com)

A GENERAL SPEAKS OUT

THE TRUTH ABOUT THE WARS IN AFGHANISTAN AND IRAQ

LT. GEN. MICHAEL DeLONG

USMC (RET.) FORMER DEPUTY COMMANDER U.S. CENTRAL COMMAND

with Noah Lukeman

ZENITH PRESS

Originally published in 2004 as *Inside CentCom* by Regnery Publishing, Inc. This revised edition is published in 2007 in cooperation with the authors by MBI Publishing Company LLC and Zenith Press, an imprint of MBI Publishing Company, Galtier Plaza, Suite 200, 380 Jackson Street, St. Paul, MN 55101 USA

Library of Congress Cataloging-in-Publication Data

DeLong, Michael, 1945-
  A general speaks out : the truth about the wars in Afghanistan and
Iraq / by Michael DeLong, with Noah Lukeman.
    p. cm.
  Originally published: Inside CentCom : the unvarnished truth about the
wars in Afghanistan and Iraq / Michael DeLong with Noah Lukeman. Regnery
Pub., 2004.
  Includes index.
  ISBN-13: 978-0-7603-3048-7 (softbound)
  ISBN-10: 0-7603-3048-4 (softbound)
  1. Afghan War, 2001—United States. 2. Iraq War, 2003– 3. United
States. Middle East Central Command. 4. United States—Armed
Forces—Afghanistan—History. 5. United States—Armed
Forces—Iraq—History. 6. War on Terrorism, 2001– I. Lukeman, Noah.
II. DeLong, Michael, 1945– Inside CentCom. III. Title.
DS371.412.D45 2007
956.7044'3—dc22
                        2006100087

Zenith Press titles are also available at discounts in bulk quantity for industrial or sales-promotional use. For details write to Special Sales Manager at MBI Publishing Company, Galtier Plaza, Suite 200, 380 Jackson Street, St. Paul, MN 55101-3885 USA.

To find out more about our books, join us online at www.zenithpress.com.

ISBN-13: 978-0-7603-3048-7
ISBN-10: 0-7603-3048-4

Designers: Jennifer Maass and Tom Heffron
Printed in the United States of America

Cover photograph courtesy of Lieutenant General Michael DeLong

Dedicated to the men and women who died during the attacks of September 11 and on the USS Cole, and to the men and women who fought and died during the Afghan and Iraqi wars.

To the three heroes in my life: my father (World War II Double Ace and Korean Hero), my mother (the strength of our family), and my wife—my inspiration and driving force.

CONTENTS

"I consider it no sacrifice to die for my country.
In my mind we came here to thank God that
men like these have lived rather than
to regret that they have died."

General George S. Patton, Jr.
speech at an Allied cemetery in Italy, 1943

FOREWORD

by General Tony Zinni, USMC, Ret., former CentCom commander

"My centre is giving way, my right is pushed back, situation excellent, I am attacking."

—Ferdinand Foch, Marshal of France
First Battle of the Marne, September 1914

AS BOTH THE COMMANDER AND DEPUTY commander of United States Central Command (CentCom) for four years, I knew firsthand that these positions were vitally important to our nation. This was also clear to Chairman of the Joint Chiefs of Staff General Hugh Shelton and Secretary of Defense Bill Cohen. Both asked for my recommendations for these posts and stressed their view that these were among the top few positions that demanded the very best and most competent selections. In their words: "We have to get these right."

As I was leaving command of CentCom in 2000, my recommended successor, General Tommy Franks, asked for my help and advice in getting the deputy commander he desired for CentCom. He said he wanted a Marine aviator and asked who I would recommend. Without hesitation I told him he needed General Mike DeLong.

I first worked with General DeLong in Somalia and was highly impressed by this square-jawed Marine who could quickly cut through the red tape and get to the heart of all the important issues we faced; he further impressed me with his seemingly effortless ability to get difficult things done well. When I was assigned as the commanding general of the 1st Marine Expeditionary Force, I was pleased to have General DeLong as my deputy commanding general. He reinforced every quality I had seen in him in Somalia and I recommended him to the commandant of the Marine Corps for future command and higher grade. To me he was clearly a superb leader, with a great future in our Corps.

Obviously, Tommy Franks and Mike DeLong proved to be a great team in trying times. We all saw firsthand the brilliant handling of the military operations in Afghanistan, Iraq, and elsewhere in the volatile area of responsibility assigned to CentCom during the three years that Franks and DeLong were there. They were masters at fighting wars, managing the sensitive relationships in the region, and holding together the complex coalition put in place to deal with the significant threats that faced us.

General Mike DeLong was the unsung hero of these efforts. He kept things together behind the scenes and saw all facets of the day-to-day operations firsthand. He had a unique position that enabled him to truly see how and why things unfolded as they did. His savvy, intellect, common sense, professional competence, and honesty come through in this book, and give us a rare insight into critical events that have shaped our course at the beginning of this troubled century.

PREFACE

AS DEPUTY COMMANDER OF UNITED STATES Central Command during the critical months between September 2001 and September 2003, I was in a unique position to witness both the political and military sides of the war to know what *really* happened, and to be an active participant in the major decisions. Throughout that time, it was frustrating for me to have to watch the onslaught of inaccurate reporting, and it has been even more frustrating for me since, as I continue to travel frequently in an Iraq that bears slight resemblance to what appears in the newspapers and on television.

Moreover, when it comes to books, I have yet to see someone tell the impartial, unbiased truth about what really happened during that time. It seems that nearly everyone who has written about the war has an agenda. I do not. I am a retired general with no political aspirations. My only motive is to air the truth about the wars in Afghanistan and Iraq from my perspective.

The truth is never absolute, and never as black and white as any of us might like. But that is the nature of the truth: serving none and serving all.

There will be many revelations in this book. You'll learn for the first time how our military reacted to September 11 at the highest levels; how the war was really waged in Afghanistan, and why we chose a unique combination of Special Forces and CIA agents to do the job; how we had been watching Saddam Hussein since 1991, the extent of information we had about him, and the many reasons he was, in fact, a threat; how we planned and executed the Iraq War, along with our thought process during the many manifestations the plan took over a year and a half; and how we knew that Saddam did, in fact, have WMD and where they likely are today.

In the wake of the Iraq War, America is wondering whether we did the right thing to attack Iraq, whether Saddam was really a threat, whether WMD really existed, whether our troops died for nothing and are dying today for nothing. If nothing else, *A General Speaks Out* will show, from an unbiased military perspective, that we absolutely did the right thing in attacking Iraq. If nothing else, I hope this book can help us to stop second-guessing ourselves and to feel good that we took the action we did, when we did, and that we did the right thing for the safety of America and the world.

Mostly, I want to take you along for the ride. Even after thirty-three years of service, my three years at CentCom were beyond anything I could have expected. I want you to see and experience what we went through to fight the War on Terror, the war in Afghanistan, and the war in Iraq. I'll show you the mistakes that were made and how we can (or have) overcome them. And I'll reveal some unheralded victories to set the record straight. I want you to know how hard America's military is working for America's safety, and to understand what that work entails. *A General Speaks Out* is that story.

INTRODUCTION TO THE PAPERBACK EDITION

It has been two years since the hardcover edition of this book (titled *Inside CentCom*) published, and a lot has happened in the world—and in CentCom's area of responsibility (AOR) in particular—since. Sectarian strife is gripping Iraq; the Taliban are regaining a foothold in Afghanistan; Hezbollah, backed by Syria and Iran, has attacked Israel; North Korea has tested long range nuclear-capable missiles (despite China's urging them not to) and even a nuclear weapon itself. And despite months of diplomatic efforts, Iran continues to enrich uranium.

Many things I wrote in 2004, which were greeted with skepticism at the time, have proven to be true. I warned that Iraq could head in the direction of a civil war. I stated North Korea would be an escalating problem. And I concluded the 2004 edition of *Inside CentCom* stating that Iran, Syria, and Lebanon were problems that had to be dealt with.

Approximately 30% of the book you are about to read has never been seen before, not even in the hardcover edition. Substantial portions of the manuscript had originally been cut due to time and space limitations. In preparing for this new edition, I have gone back and restored most of this material. I also took this opportunity to carefully examine everything I wrote in 2004, to see if there was any material that I might change, or that felt dated. The answer was "No." Everything I stated in 2004 still holds true now.

I'd like to take a moment, though, to address how the world has changed militarily since 2004, and to again offer insights into the current world situation, and my assessment for what's on the horizon.

Over the last two years, there have been many positive developments. To begin with, Central Command and the U.S. military have taken "jointness" to a new level. This practice of encouraging the branches of the U.S. armed services to proactively work together—instead of merely staying out of each other's way—was hammered home by General Franks, myself, and others, and has evolved to an art form under the leadership of Generals Pace,

Abizaid, and others. The U.S. military now works together as one well-oiled machine, which is perhaps the most significant development to occur in our military over the last decade—and which will have significant ramifications in the decades to come.

Our relationship with the international community in capturing terrorists has never been better. We now have true partners around the world in the fight against terrorism: Saudi Arabia has stepped up in helping capture terrorists, as has Kuwait. Jordan continues to be a leader. And Pakistan, under the leadership of President Musharraf, has gone above and beyond. Musharraf has helped the U.S. capture the bulk of al Qaeda prisoners today, while managing to balance anti-U.S. sentiment in his own country. He remains one of the unsung heroes in the war on terrorism.

If Bin Laden's alive, he's on the run, likely hiding in the caves somewhere in Pakistan's porous border region. While Bin Laden has not been captured yet, Musharraf and the United States are succeeding in keeping him off balance and on his toes. Al Qaeda's international sleeper cells may very well continue to execute nefarious murder plots in the years to come, but if so, it will not be due to the effective leadership of this one man.

There also remains cause for concern. Two years ago I mentioned North Korea would be a problem, and it continues to be one today. Waging a war against them, though, is a no-win proposition for us: while we would win, it could end up costing as many as five hundred thousand South Korean lives (who would be the butt of a North Korean retaliation). And in victory, we would end up owning a bigger problem than Iraq, a nation already devastated by years of famine, neglect, and lack of infrastructure. However, I don't lose sleep over North Korea. I still think it's mostly saber-rattling on their part. Ultimately, the brunt of policing them probably falls on China, and we need to keep the pressure on China to take a more active role in reigning them in.

The Taliban are, unfortunately, beginning to leave their hiding places in the hills of Pakistan and work their way back into Afghanistan. There has been a lot of criticism in the media recently about this, particularly about the U.S. withdrawing troops from Afghanistan and allowing NATO troops to take their positions. I believe this criticism is unwarranted. A massive ground presence of U.S. troops is not the solution to the re-emerging problem in Afghanistan. One has to look at the big picture, ask why the Afghan people have tolerated the Taliban's partial comeback.

Afghanistan remains a desperately poor country. There are few jobs, and in any such environment a government will be weakened, and a country will be more prone to infiltration by criminal and terrorist organizations. In Afghanistan in particular, the conditions are ripe for turmoil. The poppy fields of Afghanistan serve as the world's primary supply of opium: 90% of Euorpe's heroin still comes from Afghanistan. There is big money to be made from drugs in Afghanistan, and hardly any money to be made otherwise, and the Taliban take advantage of this. They're back into some of the major provinces and arguably now control two or three of them. Compounding the problem is that the Northern Alliance tribes—which came together so well under U.S. leadership to oust the old Taliban regime—disbanded after the victory, each returning to their own province. An Afghan national army took their place, but it is young, and does not yet have the same power of enforcement. The Taliban, perhaps sensing vulnerability, have in turn become more aggressive, using Iraqi IED (improvised explosive device) tactics.

Despite media reports, there are actually more troops on the ground now in Afghanistan than ever. When we waged the war, we never had more than ten thousand Americans on the ground (including coalition forces); currently there are about twelve thousand troops on the ground. Some of the U.S. military have been replaced by NATO forces, but this is an appropriate move (one which we'd been requesting for two years), since what we face now in Afghanistan is primarily a long-term, peacekeeping mission. Keeping a major U.S. troop presence—or refusing to substitute NATO troops—will not change the picture. The Russians kept an enormous troop presence in Afghanistan for years and met with disaster.

The path to a sustained victory in Afghanistan lies in improving their economy, creating jobs for the Afghanis, strengthening their government and national services, getting the provinces to trust each other and work together, and eliminating the opium trade. Previously, the United States' policy was to not get deeply involved in internal Afghani drug issues; now we've changed the policy and are actively working to eradicate the drugs. But nobody has yet to come up with a way to shut down the poppy fields and get the Afghani people back to work. Until that happens, the Taliban will inevitably creep back in.

xviii   A GENERAL SPEAKS OUT

Iraq today suffers from many of the issues that plague Afghanistan, but on a larger scale. Like Afghanistan, Iraq needs a stronger national government, supported by all the provinces; it needs a stronger national army; it needs a stronger police force; it needs its infrastructure rebuilt; it needs its sectarian groups to at least respect each other and work together; and it needs jobs. All of this takes time and hard work. Two years ago, I said it would take time. The same holds true now. If we pull out now, we will leave the nation vulnerable to civil war, and a terrorist haven. I believe we must stay the course until Iraq can provide its own security.

Partly what exacerbates the Iraqi situation is the media. Two years ago I said that for every piece of bad news from Iraq that plays in the media, there are fifty pieces of good news you will never hear about. This is even more so the case today. In my opinion, the media has not been helpful to the Coalition war effort. Is it the cry of the media or the cry of the American people that affects Iraqi policy? If America had had the same type of media coverage during World War II, we probably would have lost that war. They would have castigated FDR, Patton, McArthur, and others. These men made mistakes, lost battles, and people got killed. Back then, there was less of a rush to condemn.

In the mad rush for ratings, to get there first, the media is too quick to air stories on any accusation. Our troops need to have the same rights as anyone else. If something happens, it will be investigated, and the media should wait for the outcome. The media is sometimes going so far as to give away state secrets, exposing our methods of monitoring the enemy or our latest technology. We're at war, and the American media needs to be more circumspect. Don't they realize that the enemy is tuned to CNN?

During the two years since this book's publication, several retired generals have stepped forward and called for Secretary Rumsfeld's resignation. The media picked up on the story and ran it for weeks. Having worked so closely with him for such an extended period of time, I felt compelled to set the record straight on what he was really like to work with (as you will see I do throughout this book). To their credit, The Sunday New York Times ran my Op-Ed, which can be found in the appendixes of this edition. [Editor's note: Secretary Rumsfeld resigned on November 8, 2006, following the 2006 mid-term congressional elections.] Similarly, when Senator Kerry used his campaign to criticize the military for losing Bin Laden in Tora Bora, I wrote an Op-Ed for the *Wall Street Journal* which set the record straight regarding Senator Kerry's erroneous facts. That can also be found in the appendixes. I am apolitical, but I have little tolerance for the dissemination of false information to the American public.

During the last two years, even though a former Iraqi General has stepped forward and claimed Iraq definitely had weapons of mass destruction, we have yet to find any concrete evidence of WMDs in Iraq. As I said in 2004, I still firmly believe that Iraq had WMDs and that one day they will be found. I know that some of it was moved to Syria and Lebanon. At this point, though, even if found, it would be indistinguishable today, mixed with Syrian and Lebanese WMD systems. Along these lines, we cannot let Iran obtain nuclear weaponry. As I said two years ago, Syria and Iran are nations that must be dealt with. We need to apply greater pressure on Middle Eastern countries to take the lead and initiate sanctions against them.

In August 2006, General Abizaid, the current commander of CentCom (and my former co-deputy commander of CentCom), testified before the Armed Services Committee and stated that the greatest military threat facing our nation in the twenty-first century is "non-state enemies." I agree. At the dawn of this new century, a new type of enemy is rapidly emerging: terrorist and paramilitary organizations unaffiliated with their harboring nations. Hezbollah, for example, based in Lebanon, is a puppet of Syria and Iran. Al Qaeda, based in sixty-plus countries, used British citizens for their thwarted airline hijacking of August 2006. We were shocked when we invaded Afghanistan in 2001 and found ourselves fighting al Qaeda members who were American and Australian citizens. Hezbollah, a non-state entity, has arguably the fourth or fifth strongest military in the Middle East—stronger than a number of Middle Eastern countries . They are also one of the best-equipped militaries in the Middle East, thanks to Syria and Iran. They are certainly stronger than the Lebanese army of their host nation. Which, incidentally, raises another problem: a number of the members of the Lebanese army are Hezbollah by night . No wonder Israel is wary to accept a Lebanese Army "peacekeeping force" comprised of fifteen thousand Lebanese soldiers.

We are no longer fighting nations, but ideologies—in particular, Muslim fanaticism. Fighting them on the ground is a public relations nightmare, as Israel recently discovered. These terrorists hide among civilians and use cowardly tactics, and have no regard for human life. If someone is willing to blow himself up, there is little we can do to prevent it. We can keep coming up with ways to combat their tactics, but they will continue to be innovative, and one day they will catch us off guard and take down that vulnerable plane, or that crowded civilian marketplace. So how do we battle them for the long term? How does one battle an ideology?

In my view, the best hope is to attack the ideology itself. What the world needs today is for moderate Muslim leaders with great influence in the Arab world to step up and publicly—and repeatedly—denounce Islamic fanaticism. Our best hope of getting through to the young, impressionable fanatic and preventing him from going down that road is to offer him another viewpoint—and from a person he respects. If the world works together, we can surely find a way to offer protection to those who stand up against extremism. Once moderate Muslims see that it is safe to denounce fanaticism, there could be a steamrolling effect, and many more might come forward. Eventually, the momentum can turn. And we need to be even more aggressive about tracking and shutting down the financial networks of terrorist, even if it means more encroachments on our civil liberties. Money is their lifeline, and if we can shut it down, we can severely impair their ability to operate.

The military situation of the twenty-first century is rapidly evolving, and will no doubt be more complex than at any time in history. We need to evolve, too, and to learn to fight seamlessly on multiple fronts: militarily, diplomatically, financially, economically, covertly, and ideologically. The military is only as strong as the other institutions supporting it.

—Lieutenant General Michael "Rifle" Delong, USMC, Ret. with Noah Lukeman, October 2006

PROLOGUE

IT BEGAN AS A TYPICAL MONDAY MORNING at CentCom. General Franks was in the Middle East, so I was in charge of our headquarters in Tampa. I had already run the morning meeting, gotten briefed by my men, and now I had Secretary of Defense Donald Rumsfeld on the phone and was filling him in on the events of the day before. It was relatively uneventful.

Suddenly, one of my aides approached me. He handed me a piece of paper, not wanting to interrupt my conversation. I knew it must be important.

It was.

I held an "urgent" message from Current Operations, which meant that something was going down at that very moment in the battlefield and it was sensitive enough to require rules of engagement (ROE) approval. As I glanced over the paper, I realized the magnitude of the situation. I immediately knew that this was something I'd need to run by Rumsfeld. I interrupted him.

"Excuse me, Mr. Secretary, but something's just landed that you need to know about."

"Tell me."

"A speedboat has been spotted racing out of a Pakistani port. Our men hailed it on the radio, and it didn't respond. There are Coalition ships in the area and they chose not to fire any warning shots. As of this moment, it's speeding away, and it has already reached international waters."

Silence.

We both knew what this meant. From the beginning of the Afghan War, we had known that al-Qaeda operatives would try to flee. We knew they had only two real options of escape—small aircraft and speedboats—so we watched the skies and the ports very carefully. We were especially on the lookout for any small craft speeding out of Pakistan. This fit the description. If we let this craft go, it could very well be Mullah Omar or Osama bin Laden on that boat.

Additionally, the boat had already reached international waters, which complicated things infinitely. If the boat had been within twelve miles of the Pakistani shore, it would have been in Pakistani waters, and we could have easily forced it to stop. But once it crossed the twelve-mile mark the waters were international, and the rules were no longer clear. That meant we had to follow our ROE. These called for a warning by radio, and if that failed, a warning shot over the bow, and if that failed—nothing else. Our men would have to go to a higher authority in order to escalate the conflict. That's why they were calling me.

Every war and conflict that the United States enters has its own ROE. Contrary to what most people think, the U.S. military does not have a complete license to kill, even in wartime. We are not a barbaric state, and we do not enter any war with the intention of unilaterally killing anything in our path. We go out of our way to spare civilian lives, to keep those who are not in the war out of it—sometimes even at the expense of risking our own soldiers' safety. We do this by creating strict rules to which our soldiers must adhere. These rules govern when they can fire, when they cannot; what type of force they can use, what type they cannot; what they can do in particular situations, and what they cannot. The reason for this is that battles can become very confusing very quickly, and a common soldier needs simple rules to guide him, to know when he is or is not allowed to kill—and who is and is not the enemy.

The rules of engagement were drafted by our CentCom staff and approved by General Franks and myself. They were then sent to the Department of Defense for approval. Once approved, they were final. If we needed to override them, we needed approval from Rumsfeld. Rumsfeld, in turn, would need to get approval from the president, depending on the magnitude of the situation.

We also had our own lawyers at CentCom, advising us every step of the way. Beside me throughout the incident was Captain Shelly Young. She was there to constantly explain the subtleties to us. She would say, "Here's what the rules of engagement really mean." There are complex international laws that must be considered—the law of land warfare, the law of the sea—and the lawyer has to protect the command and ensure what you're doing has a legal look.

"Are you sure it's al-Qaeda?" Rumsfeld asked.

"No, we're not sure. But intel leads us to believe it could be."

My aide handed me another sheet of paper.

"Mr. Secretary," I said, "I have Admiral Moore on the other line. If it's all right with you, I'll talk to him, have him fill me in, and then call you right back."

"Do that."

I hung up and picked up with Admiral Moore.

Admiral Willy Moore was a three-star admiral, commander of the entire 5th Fleet, stationed in Bahrain. He was the best war-fighting admiral in the Navy.

"How reliable is this intel?" I asked him.

"Very," he answered. "One of my admirals called it in. His ship is 150 miles from the location. He has planes patrolling, one of which spotted it."

"What ships do we have in the vicinity?"

"French and Canadian Coalition ships, and one of ours. We have a four-teen-person Marine attachment on board the U.S. ship commanded by a First Lieutenant Zinni." That would be Zinni's son—Tony Zinni, that is, a four-star general and the previous commander of CentCom, whom General Franks had replaced.

"Do you think it's al-Qaeda?" I asked.

"Yes."

"Let me talk to the secretary."

I put him on hold and got back on the line with Rumsfeld.

"He confirmed it," I said to Rumsfeld.

There was a pause.

"What are our options?" Rumsfeld asked. "Can we stop them?"

"We can shoot out the engines. But they're moving so fast, we only have one shot at this. And it's an open-hulled craft. If we shoot out the engines, chances are someone might get hit."

Silence.

This was our first ROE incident in international waters, and we both knew the ramifications of a wrong decision. It couldn't have come at a worse time, or in worse waters. At that time, tensions were at a peak between

Pakistan and India—the two countries were literally on the brink of a nuclear war. We needed both sides to stay neutral, not only to help us fight in Afghanistan, but more importantly, to prevent a possible nuclear catastrophe. In fact, I had been spending nearly all my time in those days on the phone with Pakistani senior staff, doing what I could to calm the Pakistani side while the State Department worked India. Tensions were high, and making a mistake in these waters was the last thing we wanted to do.

Rumsfeld cleared his throat.

"Do what you have to do."

I picked up the phone with the waiting admiral. It was twilight in Afghanistan.

"Do it."

Chapter One

WELCOME TO CENTCOM

"If military art consisted of always taking a safe position, then glory would become the property of mediocre people."

—Napoleon Bonaparte

AN APPOINTMENT AS DEPUTY COMMANDER of United States Central Command is not something you ask for. You have to be nominated by the chairman of the Joint Chiefs of Staff, then approved by the secretary of defense, and then approved by the president himself. The nomination comes before the Senate, and it must formally take a vote. To get recommended in the first place, you have to be chosen out of a pool of several hundred decorated generals. It is one of the hardest spots to land in all of the armed forces.

CentCom is a crucial command center for our national security, and becoming commander or deputy commander at CentCom means a promotion. For the deputy commander it means moving from two stars (major general) to three stars (lieutenant general). For the commander it means a promotion from three stars to four stars. These are among the few military "desk" jobs that are not in fact desk jobs at all—being at CentCom, unlike other appointments, means you'll spend a lot of time out in the field. As such, appointments as commander or deputy commander are two of the most coveted positions in the entire military, positions that many military people spend a lifetime hoping to get.

In my case, I was recommended for appointment as deputy commander by the previous commander of CentCom, Marine Corps General Tony Zinni—which is ironic, because when I first met General Zinni, we didn't exactly get along.

We were in Somalia in 1992, where later campaigns would ultimately have disastrous results (later to be dramatized in the book and film *Black Hawk*

Down). General Zinni was then in charge of combat operations for the Coalition Joint Task Force, while I was in charge of air operations, an unusual position for a Marine. In fact, it was the first time a Marine had been given this coveted Air Force position.

When I first met Zinni, it was an argument. Flight operation plans—originating from our carriers at sea—were being delivered by air to our camp. These plans were crucial, and we needed to get them promptly several times a day, from ship to shore. We used S3 Viking planes, small two-engine planes normally reserved for submarine warfare, to take the plans from the ships and drop them over our embassy compound. The Vikings had to dump the plans at a high speed and thus with little accuracy. To give the papers weight, they were wrapped in a rubber package. Since they were dropped from the planes at 150 to 200 miles per hour, they had a tremendous velocity. We cleared an entire parking lot for them in the embassy area, but they kept missing the mark. Day after day, these rubber packages were putting holes in tents, knocking out radio dishes, and coming close to hitting people. They were a major—and dangerous—nuisance.

After one of these packages hit a (luckily helmeted) soldier on the head, I'd had enough. I stormed into Zinni's tent.

"This is bullshit!" I said.

In the room were several officers, who must have thought I was crazy. Colonels do not talk to generals that way. It was, in fact, probably the dumbest thing you could do in the armed services. It could easily mean the end of your advancement, which in turn could mean the end of your career.

But I just didn't care. When I feel something is unfair or unjust, I've always been one to speak my mind, regardless of the consequences. That, traditionally, has been the fault (and the pride) of many in the Marine Corps.

The room was silent.

"Get out," Zinni growled.

He escorted me out, away from the eyes of the others.

"Who do you think you are talking to me like that!" he barked as soon as we were outside.

"One of those flight plans hit one of my boys in the head today. This is dangerous. It's stupid. You need to stop it now."

"Who the hell do you think you are to tell me what to do?"

"You don't need to use the planes."

"Hell we don't. There's no other way to drop 'em."

"You can use the choppers. I can get you what you need, when you need it."

"They're not fast enough."

"I'll get them to take off early, land late. Work double shifts. It'll be just as fast."

"Bullshit."

We were face to face. He wasn't going to give in. I wasn't either.

Finally, for the sake of good order, I replied, "I've said what I came to say. You're two ranks senior to me. You'll do what you choose to do. This isn't going anywhere."

His demeanor instantly changed. He took a long look at me.

"We shouldn't argue like this," he said.

"True," I said. "It's a no-win situation for me."

He sighed, and looked into the distance.

"Those fucking planes," he said. "Driving me crazy." He paused. "You know what? You're probably right. We can find another way to do it." He paused again. "I'm going to do what you recommend," he said.

We implemented my recommendations. I had the choppers airlift the plans; I worked out the scheduling like I promised, and we never suffered for it. We got the plans just as quickly, and the menace from the skies stopped.

Zinni took note. He realized I wasn't out to make him look bad, or prove my bravado. I was just another butthead Marine trying to take care of the troops. After that, we worked together better than just about any other military relationship I'd had.

A year later, when I was a one-star general and he was a three-star, he was selected as the Marine Expeditionary Force commander at Camp Pendleton, in charge of fifty thousand Marines, and he asked me to be his deputy commander. I accepted.

Shortly afterwards, Zinni became deputy commander of CentCom, and after a one-year term he became commander, the first general to be promoted from deputy commander to commander at CentCom. When he retired, he had to make a recommendation for a new commander and a new deputy. At that time, as a two-star general, I was commander of the largest Marine air wing in the world, in Miramar, California. Under my command were 420 airplanes, 53 squadrons, and seventeen thousand Marines. It was the best job in the world for a marine aviator. After thirty-three years in the service, including two tours in Vietnam (where I was shot down three times), I was happy with my life at Miramar.

Zinni recommended Army General Tommy Franks as the new commander of CentCom, and then recommended me for the deputy slot. The deputy position, of course, requires presidential and senatorial approval, but the incoming commander has to first make the recommendation. So it was up to Franks.

I knew Franks, but not well. We had worked together in the past, mainly in field training exercises, massive joint armed forces exercises where each armed service is supposed to work together (although that is not always the case). Franks was the 3rd Army commander at Fort McPherson, Georgia, and in the exercise he had control of all the land forces defending a mock Kuwait. I was in charge of air support.

Franks had asked what I could do to support him. I had told him I could fly my fixed-wing aircraft over his troops and keep my Cobra helicopters up front to protect them. He was surprised with the plan I drew up, because it provided him with more support than he was used to getting. When the exercise was over, he told me he'd never had better cooperation.

But that was years ago, and I hadn't interacted with Franks since and had no idea whether he had another general in mind. CentCom is one of the few places focused on joint operations. Indeed, everyone who takes a position at CentCom must appear before the Senate and answer the question: "If you come before us, will you tell the truth and not have a service or Department of Defense bias?"

Nonetheless, when it came down to it, Franks was an Army man and I a Marine; it was very possible he might be inclined to choose one of his own. I had no idea how it would play out, and in fact had mixed feelings. Of course I would have liked to continue to be promoted, but had I been thinking of a new position for myself, I would have hoped for a command in the field, in the midst of the action. A job at CentCom, I imagined, might not be as exciting in comparison. (How little I knew.) Plus, joining CentCom meant walking away from thirty-three years as a Marine, with the Marine Corps, in a sense turning away from my family. It was a final decision, with no turning back.

Then one day the phone rang. My aide told me it was General Franks. I picked up the receiver.

"Okay, asshole, you're going to be my deputy," Franks said, and hung up.

With that, I was a three-star general (select). I was on my way to CentCom to what would be the most demanding thirty-six months of my life.

CentCom is a "regional command"—a command dedicated to watching over a certain part of the world: the Middle East, East Africa, and Central Asia. Prior to September 11, 2001, there were three additional regional commands, which covered Europe, the Pacific, and the Southern Hemisphere. There was also Joint Forces Command, which covered Iceland and the Atlantic Ocean. The Area of Responsibility (AOR) of each command ranges from ninety countries (for the European command) to twenty-five countries (for CentCom). Numbers, of course, are deceiving: Of the ninety countries under the European command, very few are "hot"; of the twenty-five countries under CentCom's watch, most are hot areas. CentCom's AOR includes the eastern horn of Africa, Egypt, Jordan, Lebanon, Yemen, Saudi Arabia, Kuwait, the Gulf states, Iraq, Iran, Afghanistan, Pakistan, Uzbekistan, and all the other central Asian states.

The regional commands provide security for their assigned areas, discourage hostilities, balance a military presence with diplomacy, and make sure that foreign aid goes where it's supposed to go. If one of the countries in a regional command's AOR is a potential threat, then the command develops contingency plans to deal with it.

CentCom was not formed until 1980, after the fall of the shah of Iran destabilized the Middle East and unleashed Islamic extremism under the support of Ayatollah Khomeini. CentCom was formed as a direct response, and as such, its primary focus has been the Middle East.

On my first day, I drove into CentCom pulling a four-horse trailer. I had taken the three-thousand-mile trip from California with my wife, Kathy, our four horses, and our four dogs, stopping every few hundred miles to board the horses. The guards were happy to see me, although they didn't quite know what to make of the horses. Dogs are not allowed to stay in temporary quarters on base—let alone horses—so this caused a bit of consternation.

I was shown my new quarters. They were the nicest I'd ever stayed in. The deputy commander, like the commander, has a large house at CentCom. It was on the base, less than a mile from the CentCom building, so my commute would be easy. And my wife was happy, which, after her twenty years of devotion and selflessness, was important to me.

CentCom is housed on MacDill Air Force Base in Tampa, Florida. MacDill is situated on the end of a peninsula, so there is only one way in or out. The water around it is patrolled for a wide radius with our boats, and there are multiple barbed-wire gates guarded by Air Force police. MacDill is also home to SpecialOps command, half a mile away, one of the U.S. Air Force's most secure bases.

The CentCom building itself is equally secure. To begin with, it would be impossible to approach it inconspicuously. There is no building within seventy-five yards of it; guards are at every door and all baggage is checked. The building has thick walls, few windows, and many of its rooms have vault-like security for highly classified meetings and for holding secure documents. The rectangular original building has been added on to over the years, and it's easy to get lost in its corridors.

The first person I met with was three-star general Mike Dotson, the former deputy commander, who would fill me in on what to do and what to expect. We sat down in one of the conference rooms.

"CentCom is divided into six directorates, known as 'Js' for joint," he said. "J1 is personnel. J2 is intel. J3, operations. J4, logistics. J5, plans and programs. And J6 is communications and information technology. It's the same J-layout as the Pentagon. Each of these has its own staff, headed by a one- or two-star general. The total staff numbers between nine hundred and one thousand. All of these people will now report to you.

"Every morning you'll get briefed on what's going on in our twenty-five countries, what happened the night before, the current status of all of our troops, planes, and ships, and where we are headed for the future. You'll have to break it all down, and figure out what needs to be dealt with. Every day there are often multiple issues, with different degrees of crisis. You're going to have to also work all the diplomatic and political issues in these countries—in conjunction with the State Department—which means you'll be on the horn with most of our ambassadors or deputy chiefs of mission nearly every day. You'll be talking to multiple assistant secretaries of defense daily. We're often called before Congress, on both routine and special matters, so part of your job is to prepare whoever is going to testify. And then there are the hot areas, of which we seem to have more than anyone else. War plans and contingency plans must constantly be kept up to date for each of these areas. Franks normally deals with the four-stars and above—you deal with everyone else."

Our conversation went on for hours: Here's who you work with in Washington; here's who you deal with in the services; the normal work week is ten to twelve hours a day, six days a week. He showed me around the halls, introduced me to the staff, and I quickly came to see that CentCom was a world in itself.

Dotson prepared to go. Before he left, he stopped and offered a final comment: "Good luck working with Franks."

"What do you mean?"

He didn't answer, but his eyes showed a combination of fear and bitterness.

Franks was in fact my next stop. Our meeting was short, and he was matter of fact.

"Here's how I want things done," he began, and took it from there. He knew exactly what he wanted, how he wanted it; he was detail-oriented and one of the most focused people I'd ever met. His mind grabbed onto a subject like a pit bull; God help you if you tried to deviate from it. He said he had absolutely zero tolerance for digressing from the exact topic he wanted discussed.

When our meeting was over, he paused.

"Mike," he reflected. "I know how to be professionally mean."

It was a strange statement, one I would grapple with in the months and years to come. Franks was a hard man to get to know. He didn't talk much, and he didn't necessarily like having people around him. He could be cold and distant. I like humor; Franks rarely did, except in private. Which is ironic, because he had a great sense of humor, but he wanted humor when *he* wanted it. For the most part he was rather somber, in sharp contrast to myself. He trusted few people, and trust came very slowly to him.

Over the next several days I was briefed by my staff. I went to their offices so that I could meet not just the officers, but also the people under them. There were dozens of generals reporting to me—many of them two-stars—representing the Army, Navy, Air Force, Marines, and SpecialOps. I was used to having many people under my command, of course, but not so many generals.

The more people I talked to, the more I observed that they were shell-shocked by Franks's aggressive new style. For the previous three years they had operated under the laid-back managerial style of General Zinni. Franks had taken command two months before my arrival, and had apparently given these people a rude awakening. Franks was rumored to be very, very hard; things had to be done the right way, no excuses. These fine officers had found themselves catching some flak. A huge transition had to take place.

I had worked for some of the toughest people in the Marine Corps and had never been intimidated by anyone, and wasn't about to be by Franks. Besides, Franks had chosen me, we had worked well together and liked each other, and on my second day on the job it was Franks whom I chose to "pin" my third star on me. When one is promoted, the officer who "pins" you (promoting you by physically putting your stars on your uniform) is usually someone from your own service. But I wanted to emphasize my commitment to joint operations by choosing Franks, in what was a large and wonderful ceremony.

Things wouldn't stay rosy for long. Our first heated exchange came as the result of a memo. Every day hundreds of memos for Franks crossed my desk. It was my job to lessen his workload, and to sign off on as many of them as I could. The logistical memos I could sign, but he had wanted to sign the policy memos. One day I initialed a policy memo and told my staff that Franks had to see it before it was sent out. The memo went through, with my initials, and was sent out without Franks seeing it. He noticed it the next day in a "sent" folder. He was livid.

In front of a large group of generals and colonels, Franks caught me off guard and laid into me, asking me if I thought I was the commander, if I thought I did policy, and so on. I asked the other officers in the room to leave, which they happily did. Then I turned to Franks.

"Don't you ever do that again," I snapped back at him. "If you want to chew my ass out, that's your prerogative. But don't you ever do it in front of anybody else. If you want me to support you and want me to continue to have the respect of these other generals, you cannot do this in front of them."

Franks stared back at me. I don't think anyone had ever talked to him like that.

"Screw you, DeLong," he said.

I walked out of the room. I had made my point. And he never did it again.

But Franks didn't let up on the staff. This issue was not Franks or the staff—it was change. And it would take a thousand people a while to change. Franks and Zinni were both effective managers, but in very different ways. While Zinni was more sociable, he was also more of a lone decision maker. He used the CentCom staff on a freelance basis, having each department submit information to him, which he alone processed and made decisions on. Franks, on the other hand, while having an autocratic personality, was a communal leader; he wanted the CentCom staff to process their information together and make decisions together.

Like so many brilliant men, Franks was paradoxical. He was hard on the staff, but he loved and respected them. He was a loner, yet he rarely made decisions alone. Trust didn't come easy to him, yet he delegated tremendously, giving myself (and others) responsibilities and positions of power that we never would have had otherwise. He was a tough man, but it was my job to make him and the command look good; it was in everybody's best interest that he be projected in the best possible way. I'm able to figure out just about anybody, but I just couldn't figure out Franks. Then again, nobody else had ever been able to either.

I tried—not always successfully—to act as a buffer between Franks and the staff. Many one- and two-stars wanted face time with Franks, which they didn't really need, and I tried to discourage them because I knew that Franks didn't like having people hang around. He could see through an agenda instantly, and God help the person who wasn't prepared. If the generals insisted, I let them enter. When they came out, time and again, they wished they hadn't.

It was August 2000, and Iraq was firing at our aircraft almost every day. Operation Southern Watch had us patrolling the no fly and no drive zone between Iraq and Kuwait. It was an internationally recognized zone, backed by the United Nations, intended to prevent Iraq from invading Kuwait again. Yet the Iraqis violated it nearly every day and fired at our planes patrolling the zone. Our ROE allowed us to fire if fired upon, so nearly every day there was an incident. Even in 2000, Iraq's aggressive behavior was escalating.

Iraq also was attempting to smuggle millions of barrels of oil out of the country, violating UN sanctions, and making a mockery out of the UN Oil-for-Food Program. Nearly every day our ships intercepted an Iraqi ship full of oil coming out of Um Qasr. Iraq was keeping us busy, yet things were relatively calm at CentCom. We were still only working ten to twelve hour days, six days a week. But all that was about to change.

October 12, 2000, began like any other day. Franks was in the Middle East, so I was left running the CentCom staff. I had just finished a routine meeting when I received a phone call from Admiral Willy Moore, the 5th Fleet commander. Moore said there had been an explosion on one of our ships in the port of Aden, in Yemen. It was the USS Cole. That was all the information he had. With four hundred–plus ships in the U.S. Navy, accidents and explosions can happen, so we didn't leap to any conclusions. But quickly, more reports flowed into CentCom. A second report said that seventeen American sailors were dead. A third report said the ship was taking on water and having trouble staying afloat. Then a fourth report came in, raising the possibility that it had been a terrorist attack.

That's when I moved into action. If there had been a terrorist attack on the Cole, I had to assume there might be some sort of coordinated global attack, that an attack on our other ships might be imminent. After a phone call to General Franks and in coordination with Willy Moore, we decided to put out an area order: "All ships currently in any port in the Mideast, go to deep water." Our ships were vulnerable in ports: Vehicles and men could be ambushed at piers, rocket-propelled grenades (RPGs) could be fired from shore, and speedboats could approach them. Out at sea, though, our ships were untouchable—nothing could get within miles of them without being spotted and stopped.

As we gathered information over the hours and days to come, it became clear that the Cole had been attacked by terrorists affiliated with al-Qaeda. A speedboat filled with an estimated seven hundred pounds of explosives had driven into the ship in a suicide attack. It was the worst attack on an American ship since World War II, and the worst terrorist attack on an American ship in history.

The irony here is that we had taken multiple precautions against precisely such an attack. To begin with, Aden was considered one of the safest of the Middle East ports—and there weren't a lot of safe ports in the Middle East. We had inherited the policy of refueling there (and of promoting friendly relations with Yemen) from General Zinni, and we thought it was a good one.

The Cole had refueled from a floating refueling dock, far out in the harbor, two thousand feet from shore. The refueling dock's high-velocity pump provided nearly 2,200 gallons per minute, so the entire ship could be refueled in only six hours, minimizing the risk-exposure time. We had shooters on the decks of the Cole, on the lookout for any suspicious water craft that might approach. As an additional precaution, we never refueled in Yemen on a regular, predictable schedule, but staggered the refueling at odd intervals; we had, for example, refueled in Yemen only a few times that entire year.

On that day, our shooters aboard the *Cole* had indeed spotted an approaching speedboat, but it had seemed to be a normal harbor patrol boat. But when our shooters fired warning shots over the bow and the speedboat didn't slow down, it was too late.

The plastic explosive the suicide bombers used had been molded into the frame of the speedboat itself, so it was impossible to detect. Our boys did all they were allowed to do, but what they were allowed to do was not enough to stop the *Cole* from being engulfed in flames.

In this situation, the soldiers on deck were adhering to the Navy's ROE, which demanded that they first shoot a warning shot over the bow. The problem was that they had time for only one shot. They did what they were trained to do, but their rules were not appropriate for terrorism in the Gulf. In this situation, if the soldiers aboard the *Cole* had adhered to CentCom's ROE (which were different and better geared to terrorist-fighting) instead of the Navy's, it *might* have made the difference. At that time, however, the Navy's ROE were the rule for all Navy personnel. After the *Cole* bombing, we changed the protocol: From then on, all craft entering CentCom's territory had to adhere to CentCom's ROE.

In the meantime, the *Cole* was sinking. It was a 505-foot boat, one of the largest in the service, with a complement of 249 men and 44 women. An Arleigh Burke–class guided-missile destroyer, it was a billion-dollar ship. Its complete destruction would have been disastrous—especially at the hands of terrorists in the Middle East, who could brag that America was so vulnerable that even one of its mightiest ships could be taken out by a speedboat. That boat could not sink.

We rounded up every ship in the area, as well as engineers and extra security, and rushed them to the *Cole*, where the sailors were battling to save their ship. They worked pumps, ran lines, and worked twenty-eight hours straight, sleeping standing up. They were without electricity, had little fresh food and water for three days, and only one toilet worked. It was 113 degrees on deck and 130 degrees below decks. We brought in fresh sailors to replace them, but the sailors of the *Cole* absolutely refused to leave their ship. The massive hole in the hull was too deep for their pumping efforts; they were losing the ship. Finally, in desperate ingenuity, they boldly cut a second hole in the hull, thinking the pumps might work more effectively then. It worked. These heroes saved the *Cole*.

Still, it was an embarrassment for the United States and yet another warning about al-Qaeda. We alerted the Yemeni president about the terrorist attack, and General Franks, who had been in the area, flew into Yemen the next day. We got on the phone with the U.S. ambassador in Yemen, Barbara Bodine—one of the toughest women I've met—and told her we needed to beef up security at the embassy, hotels, and other "American" locations. Ambassador Bodine accepted our sending over a CentCom SpecialOps unit, an elite eight-man team, under the direct control of CentCom. This unit secured buildings, put shooters on roofs, blocked entrances, and did whatever had to be done to make Yemen airtight for Americans. For the next several months, the Navy changed its ROE and required that all ships refuel offshore, which meant many more tankers and oilers in the area—a considerable, but necessary, cost.

Most importantly, we wanted to retaliate. But we just didn't know who or what or where to hit. Finding that out was a matter of investigation and intelligence. For that, we turned to the experts: the FBI and CIA. We brought them in, and let them take over the investigation; this was their domain, and we wanted the best. Nothing could be done without intelligence.

In the months and years to come, we would take a lot of heat for the bombing of the USS *Cole* and be sharply criticized for our failure to act on "credible intelligence" that we supposedly had in advance of the bombing. So many accusations were hurled by people who really had no idea what they were talking about, or what the facts were. The facts were this: we had received an intelligence report warning that "somewhere in the world there might be an attack in a port against a U.S. ship," and we kept our ships on guard as a result. Various intelligence indicated that the attack could happen in the eastern Mediterranean, in the Red Sea, in the Indian Ocean, or in the Gulf. And there was no telling when. The bombing of the *Cole* occurred *six months* after this piece of "intel." It is impossible to take action based upon such vague intelligence, and this is one of the reasons why Dick Clarke's book, *Against All Enemies*, in my opinion, draws wrong conclusions.

I met Dick Clarke when he came down to CentCom to brief us. He specifically told us how comfortable he was with all that President Bush was doing for the War on Terror. But he was not an insider. He was not included on any of the numerous video teleconferences I attended with President Bush. I suspect we might have had better knowledge of existing intelligence from the Middle East than Clarke did. I was given a daily breakdown of all the intel—including from the CIA, FBI, and our intelligence units—originating out of the twenty-five countries in our AOR. There was of course a lot of intel that warned in a general way that "something was going to happen somewhere." Our intel people were constantly doing "spider graphs" so that this vague intel might be pinpointed, but the spider trails almost always resulted in very few leads. It was frustrating and time consuming.

The bottom line is that, when it comes to intel, you're no better than the people you have in the field collecting the information, the technical intel you receive, and the analysts that you have interpreting that information. Intel is ultimately no better than the educated guess of an expert analyst—and there will always be some analyst somewhere who, like Dick Clarke, will step forward after the fact and hurl accusations of ignored intel. One thing we had learned in interpreting intelligence about possible terrorist attacks was that there would often be a spike in the sheer *amount* of intel warning of an attack, even if the who and where were unknown. This is precisely what happened in the months leading up to September 11, 2001. Again, the intel was frustratingly general, but a spike in al-Qaeda message traffic about a big hit somewhere made an attack seem imminent. We naturally assumed the attack would be in the Middle East, and in the weeks leading up to September 11, 2001, our AOR was kept in a high state of alert.

That summer I was at a dinner party with Dick Greco, the four-time mayor of Tampa. He asked me if I was worried about a terrorist attack.

"We're concerned," I answered. "Based on what we've been seeing, we think al-Qaeda is going to try to harm Americans somewhere."

Conversation around the table grew quiet.

"What do you think they'll do?" he asked.

"We expect an attack in the Mideast. Maybe an American embassy or hotel, maybe even something more fantastic, like the Eiffel Tower."

"What do *you* think they'll do?" he asked again.

The guests looked at me. I paused.

"If I were them, I'd go after the U.S. *in* the U.S. I'd do something to tear the fabric out of the American soul, something that would change our way of living. Maybe something to affect the financial markets.

"But that would also be the worst thing they could do," I continued. "Right now, Americans are basically comfortable and not overly concerned, and as a result, our enemies underestimate us. But God help the person who wakes us up. The way Americans are, all of us, is that once somebody does something to hurt us, we change. It brings us together, wakes up the core of America."

I prayed I was wrong. But in the months to come, I would be horrified to learn just how right I was.

Chapter Two

SEPTEMBER 11

"Our responsibility to history is clear: to answer these attacks and rid the world of evil . . . . This nation is peaceful, but fierce when stirred to anger. The conflict was begun on the timing and terms of others. It will end in a way, and at an hour, of our choosing."

—President George W. Bush
September 14, 2001

AT 7 A.M. ON SEPTEMBER 11, 2001, we were immersed in our weekly staff meeting in the Master Room at CentCom. The department heads—the generals of the J (Joint) sections—sat with me around the huge conference table, their assistants standing along the back wall. We were breaking down the previous night's intel from the Middle East. Franks was traveling, so I was running the show. I had just returned from Oman, where I had met with Omani defense officials, so we had a lot to cover.

At 8:45 a.m., my secretary came into the room and discreetly handed me a piece of paper, not wishing to interrupt the proceedings. The note read: "An airliner has just hit one of the World Trade Center towers."

I quietly rose from the table and walked down to my office with my executive assistant. We always have a television on at CentCom (on mute), tuned either to CNN, FOX News Channel, or MSNBC, so we turned up the volume and began to watch. I said to my assistant, "The weather must be bad and someone got lost. That must be the explanation."

But when I saw a second plane appear in the clear blue skies, I knew it was an attack. Before it hit, I was on the phone to the head of Operations, Major General Gene Renuart.

"Stand up the CAT," I said.

The Crisis Action Team (CAT) is used only in dire emergencies—usually ones necessitating force—and is designed to assemble instantly. The team is composed of about fifteen officers from all six directorates—personnel, intel, operations, logistics, plans and programs, and communications and information technology—and has its own situation room at CentCom where they can focus exclusively on the issue at hand and keep intel flowing to the rest of us.

"Are you sure?" General Renuart asked. Pulling officers for a CAT leaves the directorates undermanned, so you need to be damn sure you need it.

"Yes."

"Shouldn't we wait?"

"No."

I turned to my assistant.

"Get a hold of General Franks, the chairman of the Joint Chiefs, and the secretary of defense."

If coordinated attacks were occurring at the World Trade Center, attacks could be imminent or in progress against our boys in our AOR.

I called our regional commanders and told them to lock down their bases. When bases are locked down, guards are doubled, physical barriers are erected for a wide perimeter, no one is allowed out, entry is restricted, soldiers are made to put on battle dress (including flak jackets and helmets), and everyone is positioned to expect an attack. Transport airplanes often won't want to fly into a locked-down area.

It costs a fortune and obviously puts extreme stress on base personnel. You can't lock down bases for extended periods of time.

We then heard the Pentagon was hit, and that another plane was heading for the White House. Twenty-five thousand people work in the Pentagon, including our direct boss, the secretary of defense. I tried to get through on the phone, but the Pentagon went into a blackout and all their phones were down.

That's when my red phone rang.

The red phone—only Franks's office and my office had one—is a direct-dial secure phone to reach the president, the secretary of defense, the deputy secretary of defense, the chairman of the Joint Chiefs of Staff, the vice chairman of the Joint Chiefs of Staff, and the commanders of all the regional commands around the world. I picked it up.

"Do you know what's happened?" the voice asked.

It was Dick Myers, the vice chairman of the Joint Chiefs of Staff. He was calling from the Pentagon; somehow he'd found a working phone. He told me the Pentagon had been hit hard. We compared notes on what we knew, what we had done, and what we needed to do, especially regarding the lockdown of our bases. I told him we were tracking down Franks, and he said, "Rumsfeld will want to talk to you too. But I had a hell of a time getting through and don't have a working number here to give you."

As I hung up with Myers, I looked at the television and saw images of the burning Pentagon. Rumsfeld was on the screen, carrying bodies out of the building.

Myers's voice, usually emotionless, could barely contain his shock, anger, and thirst for retribution. All day long I was on the phone with leaders at the Pentagon and their voices conveyed the same intense anger. One even told me, "You don't sound angry."

"I am, but I have a job to do. I can't afford to let anger dictate what I'm going to do next."

Many CentCom staffers thought we might get hit next. We elevated security tenfold in and around MacDill Air Force base, erecting barriers outside and putting multiple shooters on the roofs.

My assistant had Franks on the phone from Cyprus.

"I'm coming home," he said.

"I'm not sure I can get you clearance," I said. "There's nothing in the air right now."

"I'm coming home," he repeated. "You find a way." He hung up.

Then Myers was back on the line, this time with Rumsfeld. We reviewed the actions we'd taken or were going to take in expectation of additional attacks. Myers assured me that Franks would be cleared for arrival.

Later, the mayor of Tampa called me, apropos of our conversation months before. He said, "My God, how did you know?"

The calls never stopped coming, and most of my day was consumed with logistical details. I discovered that rather than the brief retaliatory strikes that had been the Clinton administration's response to terrorist attacks, this administration would want war, and we immediately began preparing for that, requesting that troops on leave be recalled. I asked our J3 to review existing counter-terrorism contingency plans. I wanted to pinpoint known terrorist cells so that we could deploy SpecialOps as soon as we got the order.

Mostly, I was occupied with logistically helping get the CAT into place. It began with twelve people, but by day's end we realized this crisis wasn't going away, and the CAT grew to thirty-five people, which was enormous for a CAT and required substantial reshuffling of personnel. Indeed, this was just the beginning of what was to come: the CentCom staff, normally around a thousand, would triple to almost three thousand in the months to come. Not only that, but this incident would be the catalyst for a deployable (forward) CentCom headquarters, situated in Doha, Qatar. This is something I had set in motion months before, at Franks' request. He had wanted a second, deployable CentCom headquarters, in the region of our AOR, to be able to deploy wherever a war would be. (It was not used or needed during the Afghan War, but would be pivotal in the Iraqi War.)

All day long we watched TV and talked to our people. At some point the name "al-Qaeda" arose, and it seemed to stick. If that was the case, we had a target: al-Qaeda itself, and the Taliban government of Afghanistan, a terrorist-sponsored government which supported al-Qaeda and gave them sanctuary in the region. We also, of course, then had a location: Afghanistan.

I began to pull our information on Afghanistan, and in a short time realized we had very little. With no military presence there, no ambassador, little human intelligence, we had almost nothing to go on; it was largely a mystery. So I requested any and all information we could on Afghanistan. At CentCom we have a permanent political advisor who's a former ambassador, and we had him gather as much information as he could from the State Department; we also have a permanent CIA representative—we had him work with the CIA to get us everything he could. Throughout the day we turned to any and all sources to educate ourselves on the country, its military, its government, its terrain, its history of warfare. I knew that when Franks returned he'd want to have briefings ready on who was responsible, what our course of action should be, and how we were going to execute it. He would want thorough information, and he'd want a recommendation.

Sure enough, it wasn't long until Franks was back on a plane, heading for the United States. He called me from the air. He was in a more relaxed mood, maybe because he was heading home, maybe because he knew there would be action before him or maybe because he had been able to get through to Rumsfeld and Shelton in the past few hours. He told me how the pilot had summoned him to listen to his headset. "I don't hear anything," Franks had told him. "That's the whole point," the pilot had responded. "Right now we're the only thing in the air over the entire Atlantic."

Franks sighed.

"Mike, these are going to be some long, hard times," he said.

"We're not sleeping here yet," I answered.

He laughed; one of the rare times I'd heard him laugh that day.

It was true. I wasn't going to sleep yet, and wouldn't for a long time. On September 11th, I didn't leave CentCom until 2 a.m. of the 12th. All day long people were calling me from the CIA, the State Department, the Pentagon, the Department of Defense, constantly updating me with more and more information on Afghanistan. I already started to become the "answer man," as Rumsfeld and Wolfowitz would later come to dub me. By the end of the day I was drained—and there was no relief on the horizon.

War was on the horizon. And Afghanistan was the next stop.

President George W. Bush was staring at me. Franks and I were on a video teleconference with President Bush, Vice President Dick Cheney, Secretary of State Colin Powell, Secretary of Defense Donald Rumsfeld, Director of Central Intelligence George Tenet, National Security Advisor Condoleezza Rice, and others—the entire National Security Council. The president would be briefed on who was responsible for the attacks, what we'd done, and what action could be taken (our part).

"There's no doubt in my mind it was al-Qaeda," Tenet said, noting the recent spike in al-Qaeda chatter, including chatter claiming credit for the attacks, and the September 9 assassination of Ahmed Shah Massoud. Massoud had been an enemy of the Taliban, an Afghan hero and leader of the Northern Alliance in Afghanistan, and a possible U.S. ally in the event of war.

"The agency has some contacts in Afghanistan," Tenet continued. "We've been looking into that area for a while. We know al-Qaeda is there— under Clinton we threw missiles at them there. We've been working with some of the tribal leaders to support the Northern Alliance in a limited way. It was a small operation. But we have people in place. I think we can handle this thing."

Rumsfeld interjected, "This needs to be a military operation. And if it's going to be a military op, then it has to be run by the military, not the CIA. I'm not even so sure Afghanistan is the right place to start. What if Iraq is involved?"

"What are you talking about?" Powell said. "We have al-Qaeda to deal with. If Iraq's involved and we know they're involved, then they'll be a part of this war. All we know for now is that al-Qaeda is responsible—and they're in Afghanistan."

"Let's deal with one thing at a time," the president said. "Let's deal with what we know. We know al-Qaeda is responsible. Let's focus on al-Qaeda."

Rumsfeld called us shortly afterwards, with Hugh Shelton, the chairman of the Joint Chiefs of Staff, on the line.

"What about Iran?" Rumsfeld asked.

"What about them?" Franks replied.

"I want as much intel as we have on whoever we think was involved—whether it's Afghanistan, Iraq, Iran, or anyone else. Just because it was al-Qaeda doesn't mean they weren't working in conjunction with some state. I don't want to rule anything out until we know for sure."

"I need you to come back to us with a plan for Afghanistan," Shelton said. "It can be a preliminary one, but I want that ball rolling."

"Got it," Franks said.

"What's your criteria for picking targets?" Rumsfeld asked.

Franks paused. "Mr. Secretary, if you want me to run this war, then let me run it."

There was a pause.

Rumsfeld is a hands-on person, and tends to micromanage. Franks is a commander, and did not need any help picking targets. They were two senior people who didn't know each other very well yet and who were thrown into a crisis together; as in any organization, neither could know how the other would react. Eventually they would come to know and trust each other, and get along famously; but in the beginning, there were some tense times. They were like two powerful sumo wrestlers, testing each other, seeing how far the other would bend.

"Come on, Tommy," Rumsfeld said. "You're my guy."

"Good. Then trust me, and we'll get back to you soon with options for Afghanistan."

Franks and I—along with the entire CentCom staff—turned our attention back to Afghanistan. We sat down and studied everything we had. We could see at a glance that Afghanistan was a rogue nation. The nation did not sponsor terrorists—it was run by terrorists. Al-Qaeda helped the Taliban stay in power, and the two were inextricably linked, controlling about 80 percent of the country. The Taliban, backed by international powers, had risen to power in the mid 1990s, and held a firm grip on the country. Their only opponent was the Northern Alliance, a disparate group of warlords based in the northeast who controlled 5 percent of the country and were locked in a long-term fight for 15 percent more of it. The Taliban needed the muscle of al-Qaeda, and were essentially a front for al-Qaeda. Although al-Qaeda had cells in nearly sixty countries, Afghanistan was al-Qaeda central, a convenient and safe place for them to have harbor and a permanent base of operations.

We learned that Afghanistan is a remote country with extreme terrain and an extreme climate—ice-capped mountains rising over twenty thousand feet, and burning deserts that surpassed 120 degrees. It was also one large booby trap, littered with nearly eleven million mines—one of the largest concentrations on the planet. It was a haven for opium, one of the largest producers of the drug in the world. Completely landlocked, bordered by Pakistan to the south, Iran to the west, Turkmenistan and Uzbekistan to the north, Tajikistan to the northeast, and by China in a small region in the northeast, it would not be an easy country to reach with our armed forces. None of the bordering countries were reliable U.S. allies, and we needed at least one of them as a base of operations. It was clear there would be a diplomatic-political war ahead of us to make that happen.

We studied possible targets and collected information on Afghan airfields and runway lengths, on the Taliban's and al-Qaeda's lines of communications and supplies.

We spoke with those who knew the country best—academic specialists, historians, aid workers, former CIA agents, adventurers, and expatriate Afghanis. We studied Afghanistan's extensive history of war against the Mongols, the Huns, and the Brits, and also researched its civil wars. We studied the Soviet experience in Afghanistan, a debacle that deployed 620,000 Soviet troops. In a ten-year war that they lost, the Soviets suffered 15,000 dead and 55,000 wounded, and lost 115 jets and 330 helicopters. It didn't take us long to rule out the Soviet plan. If Afghanistan could defeat the Soviet army, it was no pushover. We had to begin by studying targets and asking questions: Do we go after the Taliban headquarters? Do we go after Mullah Omar (the Taliban leader) directly? What are the targets? How do we do this? We collected information on Afghani airfields, on runway lengths, on their lines of communications, on their capability of resupply. We had to be careful not to be hasty, not to set ourselves up for a potential disaster. We even brought in Russians and asked for their advice. They said, "If you'd just let us win in Afghanistan twenty years ago, you wouldn't be in this problem today." (We didn't respond to that.)

Before we could really get deeply into planning the war, we first needed to know what type of war the president wanted. Did he want, as Clinton had, a simple retaliatory strike? Or did he want a full-scale, prolonged war? Either of these options—or anything in between—would mean a radically different approach. So, as a first step, we came back to Shelton and Rumsfeld with three options.

The first was a simple cruise missile strike. We had ships, submarines, and aircraft that could hit al-Qaeda training camps with cruise missiles. The upside was instant retaliation and little risk; it was the sort of option the Clinton administration had favored.

The second option was option one plus manned bombers (B-52s and B-1s) to take out al-Qaeda camps and Taliban military bases in a three-to ten-day air war. The third option, which we favored, packaged cruise missiles and bombers with "boots on the ground," using Special Forces and possibly other Army and some Marine units. We would need at least ten to twelve days to get our forces in-country. If the administration wanted an instant retaliation, this was not the way to go. If they wanted substance and a real campaign, this was the best option.

Shelton and Rumsfeld got back to us quickly. They wanted option three. But they also wanted something else: an Afghanistan left intact for a quick reconstruction, and goodwill in the Arab world.

Achieving this would be a challenge anywhere, but it would be unprecedented for Afghanistan. *Before* the war, Afghanistan was in dire straits, destitute and war-torn. We were given the task of waging a war and then walking away leaving the country better than it had ever been.

Franks and I and the CentCom staff worked twenty-four hours a day, studying and planning. The question which we all obsessed over: How do we do this? We hardly left the building. In fact, we couldn't even if we tried: in those first few days following September 11, a hurricane hit CentCom, trapping us inside. The building was strong enough to withstand it, and we weren't going anywhere anyway, so it was business as usual. When I returned home the next day, though, I found my house partially flooded. I asked my wife why she didn't call me; she answered that she thought I was busy enough, and didn't want to burden me with anything else. She got some help, but most of it she had taken care of herself.

After all of our studying and planning, we decided that we'd need two elements to be successful in Afghanistan: a coalition of Arab allies to maintain good relations with the Arab and Islamic world, and a leading role for the Afghans themselves in overthrowing the Taliban. We wanted *them* to be the heroes and liberators, while we played a supporting role. We thought this was crucial for rebuilding the Afghan government on a solid foundation.

To enlist the Afghans in our fight, we needed to work with the main organized opposition to the Taliban, which was the Northern Alliance. The key questions were: Could we trust them? Would they cooperate with us? Were they skilled enough?

We would learn that Tenet had people in Afghanistan and a CIA agent in CentCom. Through him we arranged a secret meeting between Franks and the tribal heads of the Northern Alliance in a remote area outside of Afghanistan.

Franks landed on a remote runway in a C-17 in the middle of the night, accompanied by his personal security people and several CIA agents. The tribal leaders were waiting for him. It was a diverse group, brought together only by necessity. Among them were General Abdul Rashid Dostum, an Uzbek; General Karim Khalili, a Hazara Shi'ite; and General Ismail Khan and General Fahim Khan (head of the Northern Alliance), both Tajik Sunnis. They represented all the tribes and religious sects, which was crucial for success in Afghanistan.

They were not only diverse, they were tough. General Dostum, for example, was known as the "Butcher of the North." They had each been fighting every day for the last twenty-five years; fighting, and killing without remorse. They were possibly the most hardened fighters in the world, each having personally killed close to fifty men. They were the sort of men who could smile at you and slit your throat at the same time. That was just the way of life. These, theoretically, would be the generals of Franks's ground army. They were brought aboard the plane.

Franks wasted no time.

"Here's the plan," he said. "You'll provide the army. I'll provide the firepower. The United States will fund your armies. We will pay for your weapons and salaries for you and your troops, in cash." Franks gestured with his hand and the CIA agents removed a cloth hiding a stack of cash, a fortune's worth.

The Afghans looked amazed. It was indeed a fortune. But from our perspective, it was still less than it would have cost to put even one U.S. battalion on the ground. In that sense, it was a bargain—and more important, it would help keep thousands of U.S. soldiers out of harm's way.

"This is for you," Franks said. "If you're successful in taking Mazar-e-Sharif, there will be another equally large payment for you."

The Afghan generals consulted briefly.

"That's fine for us personally," they said. "But how are you going to pay our troops?"

Like so many Afghanis, these tribal chiefs were masters at the art of bargaining. But they didn't know who they were dealing with. Franks's tolerance for haggling was zero.

"Bullshit," he said.

He stood up, grabbed a cigar, and walked off the back of the plane. He walked to the runway, lit up, and stood there smoking, his back to them.

They didn't know what to make of him.

Five minutes passed, then ten, twenty, thirty. The Afghan leaders debated about what to do. Franks was one of the toughest sons of bitches on the planet. He wasn't going to negotiate—they would have to come to him and say yes.

The leaders finally realized who they were up against. After forty-five minutes had passed, one of the leaders came out and put a hand on Franks's shoulder.

"I think we can work something out," he said.

Franks looked at him. He threw out his cigar, turned around and went back in. And that was the beginning of Franks's army.

Nothing is as important in war as chain of command and unity of command. If Franks had let the tribal leaders run over him at the start, or dictate how things were going to be, it would have been over. Instead, Franks made it clear: You play by my rules or not at all.

Winning the cooperation of the Northern Alliance was not enough. They had been fighting the Taliban unsuccessfully for years. We would have to provide them with close, coordinated air support—jets, cruise missiles, and bombers—and support on the ground in the form of our elite SpecialOps forces, who could pinpoint targets for our airpower, provide tactical command support, gather information, and act as trigger pullers if necessary.

We would need the CIA's help too, and Franks and I got along well with George Tenet. Tenet was a real team player and knew a hell of a lot about Afghanistan. He wanted to be a part of this thing, and increasingly, we realized how much we needed him, and could use each other. The CIA also controlled many Predators (unmanned aerial vehicles, on loan from the Department of Defense), which could shoot Hellfire missiles, and it had agents on the ground who could help us with the Northern Alliance.

We decided to embed SpecialOps forces and CIA agents in each Northern Alliance unit. It was an unprecedented union, and would be the first time in the history of warfare that CIA agents and SpecialOps agents would be fighting side by side. It was a remarkably bold plan, one that to this day the American public knows little about.

Another peculiarity to this war was that many of our troops would be on horseback. The mountainous Afghan terrain, lack of paved roads, and difficulty in delivering vehicles to landlocked Afghanistan made horses a better choice than Humvees; horses were also better for assimilating our men with the Northern Alliance fighters. Ironically, at CentCom we were set up to monitor this war with some of the most sophisticated technology in the world: high-tech, flat-screen plasma TV sets covering the action from GPS devices in most of our major military equipment and multi-million-dollar unmanned drones. It would be a spectacular combination of the old and the new, of ancient war-fare and modern technology. It would be a truly new type of war.

On September 13, 2001, we scored another political victory when NATO agreed to support any United States military action with troops, equipment, and other assistance. Things were falling into place. There was only one stop left on the war path, and it was one we were not looking forward to: briefing the Joint Chiefs of Staff.

The Joint Chiefs of Staff are the heads of each branch of the U.S. military. The chairman of the Joint Chiefs is the principal military advisor to the president, secretary of defense, and the National Security Council, and is the senior ranking member of the armed forces. The purpose of the Joint Chiefs is to act as a balance of armed forces power: they are there to make sure that each force is represented. They offer objective, balanced feedback on war plans, and give their recommendations to the chairman of the Joint Chiefs, who in turn advises the president and secretary of defense directly. In reality, though, each of the Joint Chiefs is there to look out for his own service—to raise money for supplies and weapons, and to recruit and train his forces.

Franks needed to go before them because CentCom had no assigned troops of its own; in order to get troops (other than a small number of rotating forces for one of its missions or wars) CentCom had to "borrow" them from the other services. This was always a challenge for us. We wanted to move forward with our Afghanistan plan quickly and secretively. The last thing Franks wanted to do was go to D.C. and possibly jeopardize our plan by briefing the Joint Chiefs. There were always a lot of people in the room, which meant things could easily leak.

For Franks, briefing the Joint Chiefs was merely a formality. Our plan, developed in the highest secrecy to guard against leaks, had already been approved by Secretary of Defense Rumsfeld and President Bush.

But the majority of the Joint Chiefs didn't see the briefing as a formality. They saw it as their chance to criticize our war plan. This particularly irritated Franks, as we had been studying Afghanistan 24/7, and they had not. Most of them thought it was risky and too unconventional; they thought there were too few troops on the ground; they thought we put too much trust in the Northern Alliance; they thought that our plans for air support were insufficient. And then there was inter-service rivalry. The Air Force representative insisted that the Air Force, not the Navy, should provide the main bombing support. The Navy insisted that more carriers were needed. The Army insisted we needed more ground troops. (The Marines, at least, were basically supportive.)

Franks didn't want any of this. He wanted a scaled-down operation, relying mainly on Northern Alliance Afghan troops, enough air support, and SpecialOps missions.

One of the chiefs said: "No one's ever fought a war using an indigenous rebel force, reinforced only with SpecialOps, agency people, and fire support. What you're proposing is completely unprecedented."

"I'm fighting this war—you're not," Franks said.

"We don't think it will work."

"Bullshit," Franks answered, standing up. "It's my plan. And I am responsible for its execution."

And with that, he walked out.

When it came down to it, the Joint Chiefs each wanted what was best for his service and truthfully what he thought was best for the country. Franks wanted what was best for the country, regardless of which service was or was not included. To his credit, Franks was one of the most joint-oriented commanders I had ever met; he never once favored his Army background.

The Joint Chiefs might have been outspoken partly in order to impress Rumsfeld, their new boss, who was in attendance, or to protect themselves if things went wrong. But Rumsfeld liked Franks's lean, mean plan. He trusted Franks. Bush trusted Franks. Our plan was a go.

As we sat down and studied the maps, the first thing that became clear was that we'd need a lot of help from other countries. Afghanistan was landlocked. To get close to it, we'd need to either access Iran from the west, Pakistan from the south and east, Uzbekistan from the north, or Tajikistan from the northeast. We'd need to use their air space, their ports and seas, their border lands for bases of operations. We'd need to run flights over Pakistan and Uzbekistan; we'd need to position our naval carriers in Pakistani waters; we'd need forward bases for our troops in Uzbekistan for the northern front and Pakistan for the southern front; and, first and foremost, we'd need to station air and rescue operations in these surrounding countries. And we'd need to seal Afghanistan's borders so al-Qaeda terrorists couldn't escape

We'd need any help we could get from other countries in the area, too: Kyrgyzstan, United Arab Emirates, Qatar, Kuwait, Oman, the Gulf countries. If nothing else, as Arab and Central Asian nations, they could be helpful in enlisting the support of the other Arab and local nations on our behalf. We also asked ourselves what countries we could have trouble with as a result of attacking Afghanistan, or having a presence in that area. Russia had controlled the surrounding area for years. China and India had a strong presence in nearby countries. We would have to ensure their leaderships that we had no designs on any of their territory.

We made a list of world leaders we needed to talk to, along with their ministers of state, ministers of defense, and ambassadors. Working closely with the Department of State and the Department of Defense, we decided who should talk to whom, and what should be said. Some calls were handled by Bush, some by Cheney, some by Powell, some by Rumsfeld, some by Franks, and some by myself, depending on the level of the person being called. Normally, calls like these would be handled entirely by the State Department; but these were unusual circumstances. There was a sense of urgency in getting our operations off the ground, and these were ultimately military matters that needed to be discussed; having our State Department make all the calls would waste time since ultimately we'd be the ones who'd need to get on the phone and explain—militarily—exactly what we needed.

A big part of my job was working the diplomatic front to win cooperation from these countries. At this point, I was dealing mainly with ambassadors and deputy chiefs of mission. On the whole, I found that the U.S. ambassadors tended to be very intelligent, slightly liberal, and favored diplomacy as their weapon of choice. Political and diplomatic by nature, their first choice in solving problems was not force. They had a certain way of doing business; they had their own rules of engagement. You would call them first, then they would set up the appropriate call with the appropriate contact in the foreign government. *Appropriate* was always the key word. Proper channels must always be gone through and the foreign government's customs respected. And they'd always prime you on how to deal with certain people, what to say, and what not to.

After September 11, there was a pressing sense of urgency in America for retaliation; many people thought the launch of our attack on Afghanistan was taking too long. We were planning the war carefully, but when it came to slow, bureaucratic foreign diplomacy, we couldn't waste any time. We had immediate requests to make, and we couldn't afford to go through a million proper foreign channels and wait for a response. We were going to talk to who we wanted to, when we wanted to, and get answers immediately. For most of our ambassadors overseas, this was a culture shock. I would call and say we needed to talk to a certain foreign minister, president, emir, or appropriate head of state. I'd tell them to go directly to that president and tell him that in two hours he would be talking to Vice President Cheney or Secretary Powell, and to be prepared to discuss issues such as runways, overflight rights, access to ports and transportation systems, fuel at airports, security at airports and seaports, and help with air defense.

We talked to who we needed to, got the answers we needed, and got the job done. Our requests were granted by foreign leaders, although not without a quid pro quo: We bought what we needed in their countries, sometimes gave them weapons systems they weren't getting before, and often ended up also relieving some of their debts. It was a good deal for them monetarily, although politically some countries put themselves at risk. President Pervez Musharraf of Pakistan, for example, supported the Afghan War effort despite tremendous political opposition.

We began to realize the importance of international cooperation not just in our AOR but around the world. We were fighting an enemy unlike any other fought in history; it was an enemy not confined to one nation or territory, but spread throughout the world in small, anonymous cells. To fight al-Qaeda well, we needed to fight it everywhere at once, which meant international cooperation to help us freeze bank accounts, seize assets, seal borders, share intelligence, and work with police forces around the world. It was truly one war we were all fighting, and we needed to fight it together. We needed a permanent coalition.

Franks and I sat down with the CentCom staff, and we all talked about the need for a permanent coalition. At the same time, within days of the attacks of September 11 our State Department was receiving calls from around the world offering support; not just abstract well wishes, but concrete support from nations truly wanting to join us in our war. The State Department would call us at CentCom every day and tell us of more calls, more offers. Finally, it reached a boiling point. They said, "So many people are calling us. How are we going to deal with this?"

To his credit, Franks didn't hesitate. He made an instant decision to take action.

"Just send them down to CentCom," he said. "Cut through all the red tape. We'll take care of them."

Franks turned to me and said, "You got this."

And with that, the Coalition was born.

Within hours, British, French, and Canadian two- and three-star generals showed up with their staffs. We brought in trailers to house them, and before long we had twenty trailers in the CentCom parking lot. We declassified as much intelligence as we could so that they could join us at our daily briefings every morning.

In the Afghan War, our allies wanted a highly visible role—they wanted their troops on the ground. It would mean good PR for them in their countries; every world politician could use the popularity of having soldiers in combat for a popular war. But flooding the ground with Coalition troops was exactly what we did not want to do. Yet they persisted.

The French were especially vocal that they wanted to get their troops in early for an Afghan ground campaign.

"Chirac needs these troops in there now," the French liaison officer said.

"We don't want anybody in there that doesn't need to be there," I replied. "We don't want anybody to be a target."

"This has to happen."

"And it will, but on our timeline. I'll look at it again and see if we can help you politically, and we'll do all we can, but we cannot jeopardize the operation."

The Russians offered to help early on; they offered to fly combat search and rescue teams and to build hospitals inside Afghanistan. We were grateful for the offer, but also hesitant. We knew that a Russian presence in Afghanistan could turn the Afghans against us, and we had our own highly trained search and rescue teams that would do that job.

Everybody wanted to help, but everybody also had political agendas. To appease them, we assured them that they would have a land role later in the war, after we'd taken certain objectives. Some countries brought carriers to the Pakistani coast, to be ready. The Italians brought their carrier, the *Garibaldi*; the French brought theirs, the *De Gaulle*; and the British came as well. The waters off the coast of Pakistan became a carrier parking lot. All of this put added pressure on Pakistani President Musharraf, who had to keep a lid on the Islamic extremists in his own country sympathizing with the Taliban and al-Qaeda.

Where we could use help, we got it. After twenty-three years of war—with Russia and in civil wars—there was hardly a place you could go in Afghanistan without having to worry about getting blown up by a landmine. We had mine-clearing gear, but most of it was affixed to the front of our tanks, and since we couldn't get any tanks in Afghanistan, we had to find alternatives. Poland, Norway, Britain, and Italy jumped in right away with extra mine-clearing gear, along with infantry. And when we asked our Coalition partners to help us shut down al-Qaeda's financial networks, they did.

We knew we'd need hospitals. In any war, you want to be prepared to set up fixed hospitals as soon as you can for your own troops and for humanitarian reasons, since it is inevitable that civilians get wounded. In Afghanistan especially, hospitals would be crucial; the country was so poor, and so poorly taken care of, that there were few hospitals to begin with. And since the Taliban took over the government and imposed their brand of the Islam faith upon the country, women and children hadn't been allowed in hospitals at all. Not a single woman had received hospital care in Afghanistan since 1996.

At the end of the day, the Coalition would turn out to be more than useful—it was critical. The Coalition countries always wanted to help, and there were many crucial support functions for which they stepped up and filled the gaps. Every morning we would have our meeting and I'd tell them what we needed, and we would always have it by the end of the day. In turn, I had to make sure that they were taken care of. I made a point of spending at least one hour each day with them. Each country had its own day at CentCom, a day devoted to celebrating and honoring the traditions of that country. Sometimes the country would bring in a unique beer; sometimes candies. We'd give a speech detailing a short history of the country and its contributions. As time went on, we started to realize that more than half of the countries celebrated their independence from the United Kingdom (including us). I turned to the U.K. representative and said, "We wouldn't have any days to celebrate if it weren't for you!"

While we were putting the Coalition to work, I was preoccupied with putting together another coalition: Bright Star. Operation Bright Star is the largest field training exercise in the world, conducted biannually since the early 1980s, with sixty-five thousand coalition troops attending from thirty-five countries. Much more than a training exercise, it is a highly symbolic show of strength and solidarity among coalition nations. Diplomats and soldiers from Europe, the Middle East, and Central Asia attend the exercise. They want to see what they're up against.

To skip Bright Star would have been disastrous—it would have sent a clear message to every nation of the world that the United States is so overextended in Afghanistan (and by being "locked down" in a state of terror alert around the world) that it can't also manage Bright Star. It would have showed we were vulnerable. In a telephone call, Rumsfeld told us directly that we were to resume such training exercises that made operational sense—and Bright Star was the model.

Franks and I sat down shortly after Rumsfeld's call. "I want you to run this thing," he said.

I was disappointed. Running Bright Star meant leaving for Egypt on October 7—the very day we'd kick off the war in Afghanistan. It meant being in Egypt for the first three weeks of the war, when I would rather have been in the thick of the action at CentCom, or even better, in Afghanistan.

But I was a good Marine and never objected.

"Bright Star is just as important as Afghanistan, Mike," Franks said, as if reading my mind. "You know that."

I did know that. Conducting such a massive operation is difficult to begin with—conducting it in a state of lock down—*and* while at war—is nearly impossible. No one thought we could do it, and to skip it would have confirmed their guesses. In the days to come, leaders from every attending nation called and asked if we would really go ahead with Bright Star. Were we truly able to handle it?

There was another, secret, reason that Bright Star was so crucial, which until now has not been revealed: We used it as a cover to get troops and support to the Middle East.

Getting Bright Star ready to kick off in just a few weeks' time was a monumental task. We had to get thousands of troops to Alexandria, Egypt, and assure their security. Egypt was especially worried that we wouldn't be able to make it. I was on the phone with Mohamed Hussein Tantawi, Egypt's minister of defense, constantly. He assured me Egypt would protect the exercise with extra forces, including air defense and port defense. Egypt desperately needed the event to go on as planned. Not only was it a boost to their revenue, but it was also a great honor for them to host the exercises, and they provided nearly half the forces involved. They had as much at stake in making it happen as we did.

Meanwhile, preparations for Afghanistan never ceased. As October approached, our preparations became more furious. As things heated up, we started increasing the size of CentCom. We brought in hundreds of liaison officers from foreign countries. We examined what the Navy already had in the region: 2 carriers, 25 ships, 177 aircraft and eighteen thousand military personnel.

One of the first things we did was deploy a CentCom Air Force commander, a three-star general, to the Gulf with a quick reaction package of about fifty people. He was instructed to set up a twenty-four hour command control in the region, a control center that could coordinate all the planes from all of our forces. These guys would run the air war. They would dictate where the bombs were dropped, who dropped them, where the air refueling tracks would be, how the transports would come in, how many planes we'd use, what kind of planes, and where to put them. They would have to handle all the traffic and sorties (flights) on and off the carriers; would coordinate the jets, choppers, and bombers so that we didn't have all these craft crashing into each other; and they would coordinate air traffic between our own forces and between Coalition forces of different nations, so that there would be no inadvertent crashes or friendly fire incidents. We got them over there early so that if something were to happen quickly, they would be able to run a small war. Over time this control center got to be bigger, and we used it for Afghanistan.

As war drew closer, we examined our ROE for Afghanistan. We asked ourselves what they should be, how they should be modified. Were the standing rules good enough, or should we change them? If so, how? We also considered what our collateral damage level would be. When planning a war, one of the first things you have to decide is the acceptable level of collateral damage: high, medium, or low. This decision is based on many factors, including the number of civilians in the area, the number of religious institutions (such as mosques), the number of hospitals, the number of women and children in the vicinity, the number of Red Cross facilities, and the sheer number of people. Whether you choose a low, medium, or high collateral damage war has a great impact on the way you plan, strategize, and execute the entire war.

Our decision for Afghanistan was that it had to be a low-collateral-damage war. That meant that every time we wanted to hit a medium or high-collateral-damage target, we would have to get personal clearance from the secretary of defense. That would be extremely time consuming.

This forced us to mitigate targets, which meant going through our list of targets and asking how we might take a high- or medium-collateral-damage target and convert it to a low-level target. There are many ways to do this: hitting a target at a different time of day, when there were fewer people inside; hitting it with a different type of weapon, or from a different angle of attack, which would force the blast to go in a different direction and minimize damage and civilian exposure; or using a more precise weapon. Figuring out how to mitigate each of these targets took time, and we scrambled as the days drew closer.

Of course, we had to have a target list to begin with. With most countries, this is easy. They have obvious targets: key government and military buildings, energy and utility plants, highways, bridges, railroads, dams, tunnels, runways. Afghanistan, though, was an anomaly. There were no major government or military buildings and no major communications systems—and not even a centralized enemy. There were few bridges, dams, tunnels, or railroads; no ports or ships; hardly any utility or energy centers; few paved roads and no major highways; and no fuel depots, as the Afghans mostly used horses. Ninety percent of the buildings were made of mud. Al-Qaeda members were spread out, living in caves, and we had no idea where bin Laden was.

Coming up with a target list had us all scratching our heads. The only things we could target were Taliban armor (though these were old tanks and there were not many); a few al-Qaeda training bases, a few leadership buildings, a few tactical aircraft, and some anti-aircraft guns and surface-to-air missiles. But that was it. We wanted to kick off the war with a major bombing campaign, but there just wasn't much to focus on. We were exasperated.

So was Rumsfeld. "You need more targets," he'd say.

"We don't have any."

"Find them."

We had to put our hope in "targets of opportunity," hitting the enemy when they moved, especially when they fled the early air campaign. Rumsfeld still didn't like it, but it was all we could do. Finally, we had to create a campaign plan—we had to decide where we would focus our strength, what the initial goals would be, and in what direction we would move. Our war plan was to begin with a three- to five-day bombing campaign across key parts of the country (but mostly in the north). Then the Northern Alliance armies could begin their attack on the key city of Mazar-e-Sharif, the Taliban and al-Qaeda's northern stronghold. From there, they could push south; later we could fly SpecialOps and Marines into the south to help secure Kandahar, the Taliban stronghold.

Our three basic objectives for the Afghan War were to completely wipe out al-Qaeda in Afghanistan, rid the country of Taliban leadership, and help the Afghan populace by setting up infrastructure, hospitals, and providing humanitarian aid.

As the eve of the war approached, we scrambled to put last-second things in place. We put our Combat Sea Air Rescue teams into Uzbekistan; in Oman, we took selected teams from our large SpecialOps base there and moved them to carriers off the coast of Pakistan; in Pakistan, we positioned our Predator unmanned aerial vehicles and urged the Pakistani army to seal off its border with Afghanistan; and we had our airplanes pre-positioned in the Gulf. And finally, we thought of America. Vice President Cheney was particularly vocal that the United States be prepared for a possible terrorist attack here. There were jets flying over D.C., Disneyland, New York, and other major metro areas, and additional jets were on a five- to thirty-minute ready status.

On October 6, 2001, President Bush gave Mullah Omar, the leader of the Taliban, a final warning to turn over Osama bin Laden or face the consequences. We all knew he would not respond.

He did not.

On October 7, 2001, the Afghan War was under way.

Chapter Three

THE WAR IN AFGHANISTAN

"Death is nothing; but to live defeated and without glory is to die every day."
—Napoleon Bonaparte

GEORGE TENET WAS ON THE LINE. He had called CentCom, asking for Franks. "We have a target that we strongly believe is Mullah Omar," he said. "We picked it up on the Predator."

The Predator was our state-of-the-art, unmanned aerial vehicle, able to be remote-controlled from thousands of miles away. It had caused a stir in recent months because it could be armed with two Hellfire missiles. Now we had armed, remote airplanes at our disposal, complete with video cameras, which relayed visuals to our screens back at CentCom. The CIA had several of them, too (on loan from the Department of Defense), under their direct control. If Tenet thought he had bin Laden or senior al-Qaeda leadership targeted, he had unique authority to strike without further authorization. But he always checked in with CentCom first. Our relationship had become so strong that he wanted to involve us, and extend us the courtesy; we also shared our information with him. We shared Predators, and often worked together in the controlling of them.

"We think Omar just got into an SUV," Tenet continued. "There's a caravan of about six of them. We're tracking them with our Predator now."

Omar was number two on our hit list after bin Laden. If Omar was taken out, the Taliban might capitulate and surrender bin Laden. It was possible that the entire war could be avoided.

"What do you want me to do?" Franks asked.

"We want you to use your air power. He's getting away right now."

We pulled up the visuals on our screen. The SUVs appeared, racing into the desert. We had a good fix on them, and were able to zoom in, but their occupants still couldn't be identified.

"I'm not convinced that's him," Franks said, "and the collateral damage issues are significant."

"We think it is him," Tenet said.

CentCom's ROE were strict: You had to be sure. Franks wasn't sure, and neither were the CentCom staff or the CentCom lawyers. Omar was a big fish, but we did not want to kill innocent civilians.

Franks answered. "We're going to wait."

As we watched, the SUV caravan broke up and the vehicles scattered in multiple directions.

So began the war in Afghanistan. If this incident was any indication of what was to come, it would be a complex war, unlike any other, and a very long game of cat-and-mouse.

Operation Enduring Freedom kicked off on October 7, 2001, less than one month after the attacks of September 11. The campaign began with massive air bombardments at targets throughout the country. We hit everything on the target list, including targets in Herat in the east, Kandahar in the south, Kabul and Jalalabad in the west, and Konduz and Mazar-e-Sharif in the north. We dropped one bomb on every known tank; we took out air defense; we took out fuel depots; we took out training camps and the tunnels around the camps; we cratered runways so they couldn't get their planes off the ground. (No airplanes made it into the sky, and even if they had, their air force was so pitifully outdated that we could have shot them down with ease.) We used B-1s, B-2s, and B-52s, our heavy-duty bombers, which we flew in from Gulf countries and from an island in the Pacific. We used F-18 and F-14 jets, which we launched from our aircraft carriers in the south, and Air Force F-16s and F-15s from the Gulf region. We fired Tomahawk missiles. We began at midnight and pounded them until dawn.

And then we did it again the next night. And the next. We continued the bombing for five days. As we had expected, the bombing caused some enemy movement and we bombed targets of opportunity as they presented themselves.

At the same time, we dropped tons of humanitarian aid. By day two we had already dropped 210,000 rations to hungry civilians. It was the right thing to do, since most of the international relief and charitable organizations had left Afghanistan before the bombing. The Brits joined us in flying sorties, as well as with intel, surveillance, recon, and refueling missions. Our bombing campaign softened the way considerably for the ground forces, and by the time we were through, the Taliban forces and al-Qaeda were deeply shaken. The pounding from our planes kept them from assembling in large groups and made it impossible for them to mount an attack against our ground forces.

Our air campaign was not without its problems, though: On the second day, a JDAM bomb (Joint Defense Attack Munitions) accidentally landed in a residential area near Kabul. These bombs are very reliable, but that still means that if you drop a hundred of them, a few will inevitably miss. We also accidentally dropped a thousand-pound bomb on a Red Cross building in northern Kabul. We heavily damaged it, destroying wheat and humanitarian supplies In this case, though, the fault wasn't ours; we had asked the Red Cross to tell us where their stations were, and they just gave us bad information. (They admitted it.) Oddly enough, though, several days later we would go back for another bombing campaign and this time, by our error, we hit the same building again. For some reason it had not been taken off our target list.

Another complicating factor was the exodus of civilians before the war began. One million Afghans fled the country days before the war (following the other half million who had fled in the preceding weeks). We had anticipated this and with the help of private volunteer organizations helped set up refugee camps in advance in Pakistan, Iran, Uzbekistan, and Tajikistan, offering the refugees food, shelter, and medical care. Still, it was a tremendous challenge for our planes to verify that civilians on the roads were "friendlies" and to keep them out of harm's way (another reason we did not hit the suspected "Omar convoy" earlier). Those convoys were relatively easy to spot, but verifying who was in the vehicles was a never-ending challenge.

On the morning of October 20, U.S. Special Forces linked up with the Northern Alliance, and on November 5, they began their ground assault against the key city of Mazar-e-Sharif. It was the most important city in the north, strategically and symbolically. Situated one hundred miles south of the Uzbekistan border, it is the largest northernmost city in Afghanistan and in many ways the crossroads of the north. Highways intersecting it lead to the city of Herat in the west (and into Iran), Kabul in the southeast, and

Kandahar in the south. Even in Alexander the Great's time it was a crucial city to capture.

If we could capture it—and capture it quickly, before the brutal northern Afghan winter set in—we could establish a land bridge to expedite the delivery of food, clothing, and other humanitarian aid to civilians, as well as military supplies and equipment for the Northern Alliance.

Most importantly, taking Mazar-e-Sharif would be a major blow to the Taliban and al-Qaeda. If we took it, the Taliban would be cut off from the north. Victory in Mazar-e-Sharif would greatly influence the Afghan warlords and people, who have a tradition of siding with the victors. On the other hand, if we lost, it meant that the Alliance would remain pinned in the north, and the entire northern campaign could collapse. General Dostum, an ethnic Uzbek, had ruled Mazar-e-Sharif for more than ten years when the Taliban displaced him in 1998. This was *his* city, and he had ample motivation to take it back.

But Mazar-e-Sharif would not come easy. It was a major city surrounded by layers of ringed defenses. Fighting our way *to* the city would prove to be as hard a battle as taking the city itself. Every step of the way the troops met fierce resistance. This is where the Taliban and al-Qaeda positioned some of their best forces, the toughest, most hardened killers. The al-Qaeda in particular would fight to the death.

Additionally, the Northern Alliance forces were outnumbered eight to one. To take a city such as Mazar-e-Sharif, the invading army should have at least a three to one ratio in its favor. A ratio of one to one is a formula for a losing battle, and a one to eight ratio is unheard of. In this case, though, we were counting on close air support and vastly superior firepower. Nonetheless, manpower is manpower, and for the soldiers fighting on the ground, there were still eight enemy soldiers for every one of theirs.

And it had an effect. Mazar-e-Sharif was not falling. Days passed, and the Northern Alliance forces couldn't get close to the city. They fought for every inch, apparently locked in a stalemate. The buildings were made of mud and the Taliban and al-Qaeda had positions dug in deep, masking their armor and artillery. They were too hard to see for our planes to hit effectively, too expert at spreading out and hiding. We couldn't call in air strikes with laser precision, or at the precisely appropriate targets; to do this, we'd need our Special Forces, and they were just joining the Northern Alliance units.

Calling in a precise, tactical air strike requires training and skill, and only trained forward air controllers (Special Forces in this case) could handle it. Without them, the bombs dropped were dropped mostly in general support, on preplanned targets that had been sent in seventy-two hours earlier, or on stationary emerging targets.

There was a sense of urgency for retribution after 9/11. But we took the time we needed to, planned carefully, lined up a coalition, and triple verified that we were going after the right culprits in the right way. But weeks passed, and America wanted action. Bush wanted action. We wanted action. We delayed the Afghanistan action until October 7, but we really couldn't hold off much longer. There was no ultimatum for any given time, but the feeling in the air was that we had to move quickly, and it was implicitly understood, since 9/11, that we would. We couldn't delay Afghanistan any longer.

But we also couldn't get our SpecialOps in before October 20. Logistically, we just couldn't get them in place in Uzbekistan that quickly; we couldn't get the SpecialOps carrier down to the coast of Pakistan before October 19, and from there we couldn't get them into the theater of combat for an additional twenty-four plus hours. Moving troops into a landlocked territory surrounded by semi-hostile nations is not an easy thing to do. It just takes time, and we didn't want to hold up the war because of it. We were digging in for a long war (no one thought the country would fall as quickly as it eventually did), and as such, we didn't think that if the SpecialOps came in a couple of weeks later it would make a major difference. We also wanted to give our planes time to destroy everything they had to, and we also wanted to wait a couple of weeks to see how things progressed. The Northern Alliance was still an unknown entity, and we had never worked with embedded CIA agents before. There were a lot of unknowns, and we wanted to take it slow. Plus, the war wasn't exactly on hold without SpecialOps: we had agency people on the ground and we could still bomb fixed and emerging targets, and force movement.

Days turned into weeks. Operating Enduring Freedom was going nowhere fast; we were making virtually no headway, and our first objective remained a distant sight. If it hadn't been for our incessant bombing campaign, the Northern Alliance might even have been overrun.

All the critics popped up: from their armchairs retired generals, colonels, and majors took to the airwaves in droves—along with the press and the pundits, many of whom lacked current military experience—offering evaluations and predictions, most based on outdated or faulty information. They criticized us for not having U.S. troops on the ground, for not having artillery and tanks, and for not fighting a different type of war. None of us at CentCom expected a short campaign, but the media demanded one, catering to the desire for instant gratification. In our age of information overload, the dissemination of wrong information was widespread. America's anger was rising. Did General Franks have it wrong?

We hung in there. And we knew the Northern Alliance would, too. They were tough and loyal (at least to whoever could pay them the most), and soon they would have the support they needed. SpecialOps were on the way.

On day one of the Afghan War, I was on a plane to Egypt for Operation Bright Star, which with its two years of planning and sixty-five thousand troops from twenty-five countries was, ironically, bigger in scope than our operation in Afghanistan. More world leaders would be attending than ever before—they still didn't think we'd be able to pull it off. All eyes were on us.

I was met in Egypt by General Hussein Amin, an Egyptian two-star, who, technically, was my deputy. However, the first thing I did upon arriving in Egypt was make him joint commander of Bright Star.

General Amin was an amazing man. With his gray hair and blue eyes, he looked like the movie star Errol Flynn and had the presence of a star, too: flamboyant and magnetic. Yet he was also a humble, religious Muslim. He spoke excellent English, and we spent ten hours a day together every day for the next three weeks. We made a point of having lunch and dinner with representatives from a different country each day. By the end of Bright Star we had become fast friends.

General Amin gave me his personal copy of the Koran. He said, "The more you understand the Koran, the more you'll understand the Muslim people." I read for an hour each night, and every day we would have a two-hour discussion about what I'd read. He was right: By the time we were through, I had a much deeper understanding of Islam, and even of CentCom's AOR. In all my years of service, nothing helped me understand Muslim culture and our AOR better than those three weeks.

Bright Star took place in a huge training area at the Mubarak Military Center outside of Alexandria, Egypt. Each of the attending twenty-five countries brought tanks, artillery, attack helicopters, and jets. We used live ammunition—live bullets, live tank fire, live mortar rounds, live bombs—so there was no room for error. Coordination had to be precise. For the first two weeks, each country trained separately, warming up for the finale, which would be a massive joint exercise.

For the finale of Bright Star, we simulated a massive land war. On one side we had a Marine tank battalion, reinforced by an expeditionary unit, including airplanes, tanks, artillery, and a battalion of Marine infantry, about twenty-two hundred people. They were pitted against a division of Egyptian and other countries's tanks, with air support. All of the forces fought together; in any given unit you might find dozens of soldiers from different nations. The coordination was excellent. They truly fought as one, which was the entire purpose of Bright Star. By the end of the operation they could be called upon to fight a joint coalition war and do so smoothly.

Bright Star was successful in more ways than one: we began with sixty-four thousand troops and finished with fifty-five thousand. These nine thousand troops didn't disappear; halfway through the exercises, we quietly funneled some of our Navy forces to Afghanistan. It got our boys in the area, warmed them up, and enabled us to get them where they needed to be without raising too many eyebrows.

In addition, Bright Star built a tremendous amount of goodwill among the twenty-five countries in our AOR, as they appreciated how much work we put into helping them, and they felt included. The exercise also strengthened our image around the world. After Bright Star, for example, North Korea's saber-rattling grew suddenly quiet.

After three long weeks, when I returned from Bright Star, I got off the plane and went directly to CentCom. I hadn't been there forty minutes when Franks came into my office through the back doorway. (The commander and deputy commanders' offices at CentCom are linked by a private hallway.)

"I got more reports on how well Bright Star went than I can tell you about," he said. "Thank you. You have done a tremendous service for our country."

With that, he walked off.

I was shocked. It was more praise than Franks had given me in the entire time I'd known him. I think he finally realized that I was on his side, loyal, and would go where needed. From then on, his attitude toward me changed:

We became friends, and his trust was unreserved and genuine. But, as usual at CentCom, the rosy mood didn't last very long. My returning to CentCom gave Franks the chance to leave it. Before my chair was warm, he told me he was flying to the Middle East.

"You've got to brief the secretary of defense in the morning and the afternoon from now on, until I get back," he said offhandedly.

I had spoken to Rumsfeld on only a couple of occasions, and I had no idea what he expected from Franks's briefings. I had been away for three weeks; I wasn't prepared to brief the secretary in only a few hours' time.

"I'm not up to speed," I said to Franks.

"Tough shit," he answered. "You will do fine. Suck it up, Marine."

Needless to say, my first briefing with Rumsfeld did not go well.

On the line were Rumsfeld; the new chairman of the Joint Chiefs of Staff, four-star Air Force General Richard Myers; and the new vice chairman of the Joint Chiefs of Staff, Peter Pace (who happened to be an old classmate of mine from the Naval Academy).

My briefing had forty minutes of information in it.

"Okay," Rumsfeld said, "you've got two minutes."

"I can't do this in two minutes, sir," I said.

"You're wasting time."

I started to rattle off highlights from yesterday's intelligence. He cut me off.

"This isn't the way we normally do this."

"This is the information I have, sir."

"Okay, keep going."

I began again.

"Faster," he said.

I sped up.

"Slow down," he said.

After ten minutes I was sweating. I said, "Sir, I thought you said we only had two minutes."

"I need more information."

I continued.

"Where's your verb?" he asked.

"Sir?"

"I didn't hear a verb in that last sentence. When you speak to me, speak in complete sentences."

On and on it went. Almost immediately after it ended, my phone rang. It was Pace.

"That didn't go very well," he said, barely suppressing his amusement.

"No shit."

"Let me go over the format that the secretary is comfortable with. I know this was your first briefing to him, but relax, speak slower, and brief him on what's *not* in the memo—he's already read the memo himself. Only brief him on something that you believe would be worthwhile to the president and only give him details when he asks for them. If you're briefing him before 7 a.m., he doesn't do well—it means he's in a bigger rush because the president has called an earlier brief. Your briefing is the basis for his briefing of the president."

I went home that night madder than hell; it was the first time in my life that I had not been on top of everything from the start. But from that bad beginning I recovered and built a strong relationship with Rumsfeld, which was important, because we talked at least once a day every day for the next two years.

It was early November, and our troops had just arrived in Afghanistan. It was time to take Mazar-e-Sharif. The Special Forces we sent into Mazar-e-Sharif were the elite of the elite, handpicked for high-altitude operations because they could fight at heights over ten thousand feet. At that altitude, you lose oxygen more quickly. The air is less dense. Our choppers could barely operate at that altitude, and landings were essentially controlled crashes. And it was cold as hell. In a few weeks it could reach negative fifty degrees Fahrenheit in the mountains.

We sent in five- to twelve-man teams, who wore winter-ready uniforms—a combination of our own uniforms and Afghan tribal uniforms—to blend in. We wanted them to look like their Northern Alliance comrades, to dress like them, eat with them, ride with them—we even let our soldiers grow long beards. After a while, it was hard to tell them apart.

One of our big fears in entering Afghanistan was a chemical or biological attack. We thought the Taliban probably had chemical weapons (we later found evidence they were attempting to develop them). We also thought they had biological weapons and couldn't rule out the possibility that they had a dirty nuke. All of our troops carried chemical suits and gas masks, and were prepared for any contingency.

Except the horses.

The biggest initial impediment to our Special Forces was not the cold, not the rugged terrain, not chemical weapons, and not the altitude—it was learning how to ride a horse. We didn't have the luxury of hand-picking SpecialOps who were expert on horseback—we had to work with who we had, and there was no time to train our boys to ride. They would have to teach themselves and learn from the Afghans.

But it wasn't working. The Afghan saddles were in bad condition, and we desperately needed long-distance saddles. Somehow we found them in Australia; we rounded up a hundred of them and shipped them into Afghanistan. Still, there were problems. After a day or two of riding, our troops were terribly saddle sore, to the point of serious disability.

To ease the friction, we sent in a hundred jars of Vaseline. But in Afghanistan the dirt is a fine dust and it's everywhere; it lingers in the air and covers you from head to foot. This fine dust collected on the Vaseline; instead of helping, it converted the Vaseline into sandpaper. Now their legs were being cut up. What they really needed were chaps, like cowboys wear. But there wasn't time to measure them for chaps. So we decided on pantyhose. We sent over two hundred pairs. If it worked for Joe Namath in Super Bowl 1969, why not for our troops?

Lo and behold, it worked like a charm. The pantyhose saved the day.

On the more high-tech side, Special Forces were equipped with custom radios, laser designators, and global positioning system (GPS) designators that could give six- to eight-digit coordinates for bombing sites, which was what our planes needed in order to fix a target accurately. Without those GPS coordinates, our JDAM bombing couldn't be effective. This would be the firepower of the Northern Alliance.

Our Special Forces were also critical in giving us "ground truth," far better intelligence than we could expect from the Northern Alliance, and were invaluable in directing and training the Afghan forces.

Dug in behind the city walls of Mazar-e-Sharif were numerous tanks and anti-aircraft missiles that the enemy used as artillery, well positioned and hard to spot. The problem in charging the city was this hidden firepower—

THE WAR IN AFGHANISTAN 47

we'd get blown to hell if we came within a thousand yards. A vital task of SpecialOps units was to eliminate this artillery and armor by pinpointing the GPS coordinates of all of the major Taliban weapons—which they did—so we could coordinate air strikes and put an end to the stalemate

The day had come. Mazar-e-Sharif was surrounded by hills, and General Dostum and his Northern Alliance forces had slowly positioned themselves on the city's outskirts. From the top of one of those hills, Dostum sat in conference with our SpecialOps troops. Behind him, arranged in three rows, were his thousand troops, mounted on horses. In their traditional garb, they looked like Genghis Khan's army. The twenty-first century had met the thirteenth century. The day had come.

"I want tanks and artillery taken out as we begin our charge down the hill," General Dostum said to our Special Forces.

Our men stood by, ready.

At the designated time, Dostum charged, his thousand screaming soldiers following behind him. Our Special Forces called in the fire. Dostum's men rode bravely toward the city walls, exposed in the open, counting on our air support.

It didn't come.

Instead, pounding fire came from the walls of Mazar-e-Sharif: tank fire and artillery. One by one, Dostum's troops started to fall. In no time at all, one hundred of his men were either killed or wounded. Dostum realized what was happening and rallied his men. He was able to turn them around and return to the safety of the hills.

He was madder than hell. He strode over to our SpecialOps sergeant and captain.

"I don't know what happened, sir," our Special Forces guy said. "We called it in."

To this day, we still don't know what happened. Our planes received the transmission, but somehow there was a mixup in the timing; they thought they were supposed to come later.

"Call it again," Dostum said.

"When?"

"Now!"

Our Special Forces guy went to work.

"All right, General," he said. "Watch these bad guys disap—"

Before he could finish the word "disappear," hell poured down from the sky. The city blew up like a minefield.

The general turned back to his men.

"Charge!"

The Northern Alliance troops charged again for all they were worth. In minutes, they were through the walls and into the city itself.

The Taliban was in shock, and within an hour, eighty-five hundred Taliban troops surrendered to Dostum's nine hundred.

But the al-Qaeda terrorists didn't. They fought for hours, until we eventually killed or captured them all. In keeping with Afghan tradition, the eighty-five hundred defeated Taliban troops now joined forces with us. We charged into Mazar-e-Sharif with nine hundred men and came out of it with an army of more than ninety-four troops.

At that moment, we knew this war was ours.

Back at CentCom, we were ecstatic. It was one of the high moments of the war for us. For the first time in years, Mazar-e-Sharif was in the hands of the Northern Alliance. The Taliban and al-Qaeda were on the run. We now had a foothold in Afghanistan and controlled most of the north, including the highways leading east, west, and south. It was a major boost to our own forces and to the Alliance. Not to mention we now had an additional eighty-five hundred troops.

Even the Joint Chiefs were happy. As soon as Mazar-e-Sharif fell, they called and congratulated us. They had to admit we had been right. They loved the new tactics. Rumsfeld was also thrilled. Franks had validated Rumsfeld's trust in him. From that moment, their relationship went straight uphill and never wavered. They had a long, private conversation, after which Franks said to me, "I really respect Rumsfeld. I like that he questions me. There's just a point where I need to get on with it and do what I do. When we disagree, though, it's never personal."

Their only point of contention—which wasn't even truly a point of contention—was that Rumsfeld wanted Franks to be out there, talking to the press, putting a public face on things. Franks preferred not to. He is not the kind of guy who seeks the limelight, and more importantly, he wanted everything we did to be kept secret. He did not want to risk endangering our troops. Rumsfeld would say, "Tommy, you need to get up there." Franks would say, "I prefer not to." Rumsfeld would answer: "Tommy." Franks knew it had to be done.

The excitement over Sharif ran all the way up to the president. In our weekly video-teleconference he was happier than usual, and expressed his gratitude for our efforts.

But there was little time to reflect. The rest of Afghanistan lay before us, and we were incredibly busy running the war. Franks was traveling most of the time to the Mideast, visiting kings, prime ministers, and their ministers of defense. He was keeping in constant touch with our allies in the region, making sure no one reacted in an unexpected way to our military campaign. I was talking to Rumsfeld at least twice a day, dealing with the Joint Chiefs of Staff, the director of staff for the Joint Chiefs (my good friend General John Abizaid), talking to our key CentCom commanders in the Air Force (in Qatar), in the Army (in Kuwait), and in the Navy and Marine Corps (in Bahrain). Later, when we took Bagram and established a base there, I dealt with our generals inside Afghanistan, Generals Buster Hagenbeck and Dan McNeil, and received daily briefings from them. And whenever I talked to Rumsfeld I got a homework assignment: "I need you to talk to Franks"— Franks was usually traveling in the Middle East—"and see what direction we're going as far as prisons," or "How's Karzai going to be elected?" or "How's the Afghan National Army going to be paid for?" Not easy questions. And when he asked a question in the morning, he expected a complete, definitive answer by 4 p.m. No exceptions. He kept us scrambling.

I would work all day, go to my home (a few hundred yards away) around 11 p.m., then work out of my home office for a couple more hours. The military, in their wisdom, had replicated the deputy commander's office in the deputy commander's home, so that when I went home it was like going back to the office. It made it easy to work more. The phone rang from the moment I got home, and kept ringing every few minutes. When I finally got to bed around 1 a.m. or so, it kept ringing. It never stopped. We had people engaged in important activities all around the world all the time, which meant all hours of the night for me. They knew they could call me anytime, and it was my job to give them answers I rolled over and answered that phone throughout the night. If I got two hours of sleep, I was happy.

It stayed that way for nearly three years. I was so tired during the day that if there was a rare moment when I looked down at my computer screen and there was nothing going on, I would nod off. I slept in my chair. Sometimes I'd catch ten minutes (a "fighter nap"), or if I was really lucky, fifteen. That was just life at CentCom.

Our AOR was a sensitive region; the stakes were always high. Most of the peoples of most of the nations were at best neutral towards our presence. The stakes were also high between countries in the region; some of them were hostile towards one another. That was their business, but we could get caught in the middle of it. If we needed to use one of the countries as a surrogate, its first order of business would often be to drag us into the middle of a regional conflict. In no case was this truer than the conflict between Pakistan and India, which was growing from a minor nuisance into a potential catastrophe.

The problem was the Indian territory of Kashmir. For more than forty years, Pakistan had claimed that Kashmir's six million Muslims should be incorporated into Pakistan. The result was perpetual conflict between the two countries and long-running Islamic terrorism.

In January 2002, India decided it had had enough. Both countries mobilized troops along the India–Pakistan border and were threatening to use nuclear weapons. Unfortunately for us, this was all happening in the middle of the Afghanistan war.

At stake here was not just a conventional war that would inconvenience us in the region. There was an even bigger concern: Pakistan and India both had nuclear weapons, and from the way they were talking, they were prepared to use them. Pakistan felt bullied by India; they were much smaller, and didn't think that they had an army that could defend themselves conventionally from India's might. Just as China was the menacing force for India, India was the menacing force for Pakistan. Pakistan felt insecure, and might very well use their only option for defense: a nuclear weapon. If that happened, India would launch one, too, which could result in the death of thousands of our troops in Pakistan and the devastation of the region.

This border buildup also caused another, more immediate, problem for us: at our request, Pakistan had stationed many of their battalions on the Pakistani-Afghani border. We needed them there to prevent al-Qaeda from fleeing across the border. We couldn't position our own troops on the Pakistani side because the local tribes would not permit anyone in the area except the Pakistani Army's frontier forces—and it would have been untenable for Musharraf if we forced our way in. So, they had to do it for us. If they went to war with India, or even prepared to go to war with India, they would have to take these battalions away from the Afghanistan border and move to the Indian side. This would leave the Pakistani border wide open for al-Qaeda to cross. And once the al-Qaeda fighters were inside Pakistan they would disburse and blend in with the local population, and it would be up to the Pakistanis to catch them. We would lose hundreds, if not thousands of them. We would be routing them from Afghanistan only to move them, intact, somewhere else, where we couldn't wage war on them. Those borders had to stay as sealed as we could possibly keep them, and those Pakistani battalions had to stay in place.

I had been spending most of my time in those days on the phone with Pakistani senior staff, doing all I could to calm the Pakistani side, while the State Department and the Pacific Command worked with India. Powell and Cheney dealt with Musharraf, while I was dealing with Pakistan's equivalent of the vice chairman of the Joint Chiefs of Staff. He was not happy

"We know you know where the Indian forces are," he said. "We need you to tell us where."

"I can't do that," I said. "What I can do is tell you that we have somebody working with the Indian forces, trying to defuse this."

"If you can't tell us, then I may have to pull our forces from the Afghan border."

"For the good of all of us, that would not be a good thing to do," I said. "It would increase the risk of war with India. And we will do everything humanly possibly to prevent a war between you two—especially a nuclear war. For our sake, we can't have you at war with India. For the sake of the War on Terror, your border cannot be left unprotected. And for the sake of mankind, nuclear weapons cannot be launched."

"We'll do what we have to if it comes to war with India," he said.

India was in the Pacific Command AOR, which was a good thing as both India and Pakistan could feel they had independent advocates within the U.S. government trying to resolve the dispute.

"If you can keep Pakistan from going to war," the deputy commander of Pacific Command told me, "we think we can keep India from going to war."

And that's what we did, for hours, days, weeks.

Finally, Pakistani President Pervez Musharraf traveled to India and met with its parliament, convincing them of his peaceful intentions.

India trusted him, because every time he said he would do something, he did it. Plus, it was costing India a lot of money to deploy so many troops. Under a mutual understanding, within days of each other, they both finally pulled back. Another crisis averted.

After Mazar-e-Sharif fell, we thought we'd have long, hard battles ahead of us for the remaining cities. We were happily surprised to find out how wrong we were. The taking of Mazar-e-Sharif sparked a domino effect: On its heels, one Afghan city fell after another. Most of the remaining cities took a day or less to capture. Often, the Alliance would just walk into a city and the Taliban would be ready to surrender. Cities were taken with little more than handshakes.

The remaining fighting that occurred in cities was always with the al-Qaeda holdouts. The Taliban who had surrendered were on our side, although we were not entirely sure of their allegiance. Additionally, the winter months were fast approaching and the temperature was dropping radically. So, while heavy Afghanistan fighting was mostly over, it was far from being a cakewalk. We never stopped dropping bombs. We pursued al-Qaeda everywhere we could. For the first time since the Vietnam war, we dropped a BLU-82 (a fifteen-thousand-pound bomb) over the Shir Har valley. That got their attention.

In the west, Northern Alliance General Ismail Kahn was in charge of taking Herat. Herat is the major Afghan city of the western part of the country and the gateway to Iran. General Kahn had been held prisoner by the Taliban for nearly five years, so he took this war very personally: he was not kind to any Taliban, or to any sympathizers. He was a Tajik, and the city of Herat comprised mostly Pushtuns (the Taliban and al-Qaeda were mostly Pushtuns). General Khan did not have a soft spot in his heart for Pushtuns. Numerous complaints filtered in that he was not even-handed with his people. But we needed General Khan. He was by far the strongest anti-Taliban leader in the west, he had devoted followers, and he ruled the west with an iron fist. He was also a great tactical general. His battle for Herat was not easy; it took him as long to take Herat—about thirty days—as it had taken General Dostum to take Mazar-e-Sharif. But his victory combined with our victory at Mazar-e-Sharif and smaller Alliance battles in the south set the stage for our converging on the Taliban and al-Qaeda's southern strongholds from all directions.

On November 13, General Dostum joined forces with southern generals—some of whom were Pushtun—and approached the Afghan capital of Kabul. The Taliban surrendered the city within two hours. Then came the hard part. Maintaining the city was much harder than capturing it. The people were happy to be liberated, but euphoria segued into looting. We had to act fast.

This was where the Coalition nations were especially helpful. The Brits volunteered to put a brigade into Kabul, in an International Security Armed Force (ISAF) joined by sixteen other nations, which would operate under NATO.

The Brits were excellent at training police and putting up police stations, but even at top speed, it would take them three weeks to deploy their men. The roads were in bad shape and the runways were too small for transport planes. We set to work opening a major runway at an airfield north of Kabul, in Bagram, for C-130 operations. It was our first large runway inside of Afghanistan, a major accomplishment.

But in the meantime, the Kabul security force needed five thousand people. So the Northern Alliance had to maintain order until ISAF showed up. We positioned our troops outside the city so that it couldn't be retaken, but we couldn't tie them up in the city to act as security guards. The Taliban and al-Qaeda still had control of the south of the country, winter was fast approaching, and we needed our troops available to take the remaining cities, including Kandahar.

On November 14, shortly after Kabul fell, Jalalabad, a city to the east, fell. Within two weeks of that, Konduz, the last Taliban stronghold in the north, fell. This was significant, because many al-Qaeda terrorists had escaped to Konduz after we had taken Mazar-e-Sharif. Now the north was finally ours.

The big prize now was the final Taliban stronghold: Kandahar. It would be the Taliban's last stand, and we knew the city would not fall easily. They would fight to the death, and anything could happen—they could, for all we knew, have chemical weapons, and be ready and willing to use them. They also had miles of the intricate caves of Tora Bora to fall back on in the east, and many holes in the huge Pakistani border to sneak through. This war was far from over.

Hamid Karzai, a Pushtun general, was the Afghan commander focused on Kandahar, and the man we saw as the leader of liberated Afghanistan. Karzai, an exile who had had a large following, reentered Afghanistan at the beginning of the war, crossing the border from Pakistan on a motorcycle, with no security.

Once inside Afghanistan, Karzai quickly reestablished himself as a leader against the Taliban. He asked for our help and we airdropped him equipment, weapons, food, and supplies.

He fought small skirmishes on his way to Kandahar, but we wanted him spared from the major clashes. Ironically, the greatest danger he encountered came from us: One of our B-52s accidentally dropped a bomb near him and he took a piece of shrapnel across the face. He was mad as hell, but otherwise okay.

By the time General Karzai reached Kandahar on December 7, he had little to do but walk in, fight for a few hours, and then accept the Taliban's surrender. Officially, that was the battle of Kandahar.

The real battle for Kandahar took place a couple of weeks before, starting in mid-November, and was waged by our elite Special Forces and a Marine Expeditionary Unit.

Before the war began, we knew Kandahar would be tough. We didn't want to launch a simple, expected attack from the north and get mired down in urban warfare and potential hand-to-hand combat. If not waged properly, the battle for Kandahar could be very costly. So we set the stage weeks in advance.

In a secret mission, we took a small number of Special Forces troops and flew them to a spot in the desert sixty miles south of Kandahar. They built a sand runway that had to be repaired constantly but enabled us to fly SpecialOps troops and Marines into a base we established and dubbed "Rhino." By the end of November, using C-130s, C-17s (out of Oman), and H-53s (off our carriers), we flew in a thousand-man Marine Expeditionary Unit.

Rhino was not a safe landing, and not a safe place to be. At that time many al-Qaeda and Taliban were fleeing in that exact direction, hoping to get out of Kandahar before the action started. Indeed, that was one of the main reasons we established Rhino—to catch al-Qaeda members fleeing south before they could reach the border with Pakistan. We were dropping our boys right smack into the middle of the action.

We didn't sit back and wait for the bad guys to come to us—we went out and looked for them. Our patrols, ranging from ten to a hundred men, lay in wait for al-Qaeda terrorists to come tearing down the highway from Kandahar at night. Our boys, waiting in the dark with night vision goggles, blew their trucks to hell from the side of the road before they could come within fifteen miles of Rhino.

As more and more Marines landed, we began attacking the areas around Kandahar. We would go out at nighttime (Marines, SpecialOps, and other Coalition special forces), in dozens of small groups, fanned out in different positions. Our troops never entered the city itself; they would take up positions on the roads leading to and from the city. Every night a convoy of Taliban or al-Qaeda would come out, either on their way to attack them, or seeking to flee, and our troops, waiting, would take them out, either from their positions on the ground, or in conjunction with our waiting attack helicopters. The Taliban and al-Qaeda had no other choice: they had to stick to the roads, because at that time of year the desert was too wet for normal vehicles. And they couldn't stay in the city; they needed to make it east or south to Pakistan, or west, to Iran. They couldn't go north because of the Northern Alliance forces. We had all the exits, all the major highways covered. We watched them with our Predators at night and our troops by day. This kind of warfare had to be done with fast-moving vehicles, without a lot of support. It had to be done at night in small groups. It was very high-risk. And it was exactly what SpecialOps and Marines were best at. They performed outstandingly, constantly surprising and weakening the Taliban and al-Qaeda forces. After a week of this, the enemy was so demoralized that Kandahar was ripe for surrender.

On December 7, after Karzai accepted the surrender of Kandahar's leaders, all of Afghanistan's cities were ours. We had accomplished in eight weeks what the Russians couldn't accomplish in ten years. Technically, we had won the war.

And yet the war was not over. Afghanistan is a large country—the size of Texas—and al-Qaeda knew how to hide and had the perfect infrastructure in which to do it.

Afghanistan is riddled with caves, complex enough to rival Saddam's billion-dollar underground tunnels. The caves of Tora Bora, twenty miles south of Jalalabad, stretch for hundreds of miles and have multiple exits in Pakistan. The al-Qaeda fighters could leave the country without seeing daylight. In the caves they had fresh water, electricity, food, weapons, ammunition, and even a ventilation system. They could live there for years, and they could escape very easily. It was a labyrinth. And the labyrinth was based in the mountains of Tora Bora.

There was never any question that Tora Bora, a region in eastern Afghanistan twenty miles south of Jalalabad, would be the next stop on the campaign. For us, it was like taking another city, and until the caves were destroyed, the major hostilities would not be over. We knew Afghanistan would never be safe until we completely wiped out al-Qaeda, which in any case was our primary goal. The only question we debated—and for which we have been criticized retrospectively by John Kerry and others—is how we decided to accomplish the mission of destroying al-Qaeda in Tora Bora. Do we put our troops on the ground, or do we do an extensive bombing campaign and rely on troops of the newly created Eastern Alliance? We chose the latter.

The simple fact is, we couldn't put a large number of our troops on the ground. The mountains of Tora Bora are situated deep in territory controlled by tribes hostile to the United States and any outsiders. The reality was, if we put our troops in there, we would inevitably end up fighting Afghan villagers—creating bad will at a sensitive time—which was the last thing we wanted to do. So, instead, using the CIA, our Special Forces, and friendly Pushtun generals, we created Eastern Alliance forces. The plan was to force al-Qaeda and the Taliban from the high ground of the mountains and into the caves, and then bomb the hell out of the caves.

Tora Bora began as a ground campaign (not, according to popular belief, as an air campaign). It is some of the roughest terrain in the world, at an elevation of around thirteen thousand feet, covered in snow and ice. Our choppers had trouble getting in there because of the elevation, so our Special Forces boys were without much support. Taking the high ground from the enemy was slow going—slower than a lot of people wanted, including Rumsfeld.

"Jesus Christ, can't you get them moving any faster?" Rumsfeld said to me one morning. "Hell, I've been up in that altitude skiing before. And I'm sixty-nine years old."

"Mr. Secretary, let's put this in perspective," I said. "They're each carrying 130 pounds on their backs. They're climbing straight uphill, on a wall of ice. They're getting shot at as they go. They're moving as fast as they can—and there are no ski lifts."

He laughed.

"Okay," he said. "Point made."

That was the great thing about Rumsfeld: He could be demanding, but if you gave him an explanation that satisfied him, he always accepted it and moved on.

We finally took the high ground and forced the enemy into the caves. Then we started bombing. We used "bunker buster" bombs and other classified bombs that could penetrate deep into the caves. Despite what some have said, no caves were too deep for our reach. We bombed nonstop for three weeks.

We were hot on Osama bin Laden's trail. He was definitely there when we hit the caves. Every day during the bombing, Rumsfeld asked me, "Did we get him? Did we get him?" I would have to answer that we didn't know. In the military, the burden of proof is tremendous, and we would not answer until we knew for sure. We'd get tons of leads on his whereabouts, run operations, and then troops would rush in and find dry holes. Credible intel told us that he had badly injured an arm or a leg. We're certain that he's alive today, and we're almost certain that he's in Pakistan. The trouble is that the caves have hundreds, if not thousands, of possible concealed exits, and we had no way of finding and closing all of them—especially along a fifteen-hundred-kilometer border.

We knew this could happen, and we implored the Pakistani military to be prepared. Between Afghanistan and Pakistan there is no set, defined border; it is a gray area that changes day to day. Anyone can cross freely from one country to the other. And the border runs about fifteen hundred kilometers, so that even if they tried to seal it, it would be nearly impossible. We wanted the regular Pakistani army to be repositioned from the north and put on the border near the Tora Bora area, so that we had real reinforcements. But Pakistani president Musharraf couldn't do that. Pakistan's border near Tora

Bora is remote and consists of tribal areas over which the government has little control. The tribes don't like outsiders, and they won't even allow the regular Pakistani army into their area. In that area, the loyalty wasn't to country, but to the tribe. And they were very territorial. Musharraf could not send
in his regular troops without sparking a civil war.

The most the tribes would allow into their territory were Pakistani "fron-
tier forces" (the equivalent of a militia) who were already positioned there.
These were the forces we'd need to depend on to capture the fleeing al-
Qaeda terrorists—including bin Laden—as they crossed the Pakistani bor-
der. To make matters worse, this tribal area was sympathetic to bin Laden.
He was the richest man in the area, and he had funded these people for years.

It was an impossible situation. We couldn't send our own troops into
Pakistan because if we did that, we'd have to fight with the tribal Pakistanis,
and that would make Musharraf—whose position was already precarious—
so unpopular that he could get overthrown by his own people. That was not
our objective.

The best we could do was work with the Afghans and Pakistanis. That
meant enlisting the help of the Pakistani Inter-Services Intelligence (ISI),
their equivalent of the FBI. The problem was, the ISI had long been friendly with al-Qaeda. At the onset of the war, we put tremendous pressure on
President Musharraf to clean up the ISI and weed out al-Qaeda sympathizers. Musharraf listened, and fired General Mahmoud Ahmad, the ISI's
leader, who had been working both sides. Symbolically, that was one of the
most important events in our hunt for al-Qaeda: it sent a clear message to the
ISI that sympathizing would no longer be tolerated. It transformed the ISI
into an effective force in carrying on the hunt for bin Laden within the cities
of Pakistan.

We're convinced that bin Laden's in there somewhere, likely moving to a
new location every night. In any case, he's on the run and thus not nearly as
effective as he was before the onset of the war. And while we haven't found
him, we have, with the ISI's help, rounded up hundreds of al-Qaeda operatives. In fact, about 80 percent of our al-Qaeda captures have happened with
the Pakistanis' help. Soon we were receiving prisoners by the handful. The
question quickly arose: What do we do with them?

With the bulk of major hostilities concluded for Operation Enduring
Freedom, it was time to turn our sites to other complex issues. How do we

help set up a successful Afghan government? An Afghani national army? How do we continue to weed out and round up al-Qaeda? To continue the War on Terror in other nations? And what do we do with all the prisoners?

We would deal with all of these issues in good time. But the latter issue— the prisoners—we would be forced to deal with right away. Just when we thought we could take a deep breath, we were to learn the violence wasn't over. Just when we thought it was winding down, we were about to take our worst casualties yet.

By the time we took Kabul, we had enough prisoners that we had to do something about it. The hastily erected POW camp in Sherbergan, about twenty miles north of Kabul, was the first. As a Northern Alliance prison, it was run by General Dostum. There were more than three thousand prisoners at Sherbergan, mostly al-Qaeda terrorists. The Northern Alliance wasn't really prepared for a prison of this size, and didn't have the security manpower in place for such an operation. We asked Dostum to be very careful when processing the prisoners, to do thorough checks and keep the security tight within the prison, but it would take time to get some of those measures in place. Such are the vagaries of wartime. No one could have imagined that prisoners might be sneaking weapons into the camp underneath their clothing.

On November 25, 2001, the al-Qaeda prisoners at Sherbergan attacked the prison guards with smuggled weapons and surprised one of the two CIA interrogators we had at the prison, killing Johnny "Mike" Spahn, a former Marine, and dozens of Northern Alliance troops. It took air strikes and twenty-four bloody hours of fighting to subdue the al-Qaeda revolt.

We were equally surprised the following day to find an American citizen among the group of al-Qaeda soldiers. As it turned out, among them were Pakistanis, Saudis, Egyptians, Australians, and many other nationalities; al-Qaeda had a coalition of nations as diverse as ours. We had been underestimating their international makeup; no one had ever thought we would find Americans and Australians fighting against us.

As more and more Taliban and al-Qaeda prisoners streamed in from all over Afghanistan, we knew had an issue on our hands. We needed our "own" prisons, not run by the Northern Alliance. We needed to establish something more permanent. Franks and I wanted to look outside of Afghanistan for the answer, but Rumsfeld initially wanted to keep the prison inside Afghanistan

"We need to build a more permanent place inside the country," he said.

I disagreed. "We have to put them somewhere else."

"What's wrong with Afghanistan?"

"We want to keep our number of troops down, and the ones that are there need to be out looking for al-Qaeda, fighting, not guarding prisoners."

From the start, we had designed our war plan for Afghanistan with a small number of troops; keeping our presence down was key to keeping the people's goodwill. If we brought in more soldiers (we would need thousands to provide proper security for all the prisoners), it would increase our presence, breed ill will, and make our troops sitting ducks for al-Qaeda suicide bombers. Additionally, keeping al-Qaeda prisoners in their own country was just a bad idea. It made them an easy target for renegades to attempt a jailbreak, and they could easily spark a riot.

"So where do you want to put them? There isn't a country in the Coalition that's going to want these guys in their backyard."

It was an excellent question, one we grappled with for a long time. Rumsfeld was right—none of the Coalition countries wanted these men, and most of them didn't have the death penalty. That option had to be there. We didn't want to rule out that possibility if we held terrorists who were involved in the September 11 attacks, the USS Cole bombing, or other atrocities.

The answer we eventually settled on was Guantanamo Bay, a small piece of U.S. territory separated from Cuba by only a fence line and guard towers, far away from the Middle East and with excellent security. While we waited for our facility in Guantanamo to be built, we built prisons near Kandahar and Bagram, limiting the numbers of prisoners held at each camp to one hundred. But some of the prisoners were so dangerous or so high-profile that we wanted them out of the country immediately. So we decided, as a short-term, temporary measure, on something that has never before been reported. We held some "special risk" al-Qaeda prisoners on a floating prison—a helicopter aircraft carrier. This did not last long, because we needed the carrier other places and, fortunately, Guantanamo opened up.

After we finally got the prisoners to Guantanamo and the FBI and CIA interrogated them, we received reams of invaluable information, which we shared with our Coalition allies and which stopped dozens of al-Qaeda terrorist operations cold.

The prisoners we had in Guantanamo were not prisoners of war (POWs). They were terrorists—unlawful combatants. POWs have rights under the Geneva Conventions that terrorists do not have. Guantanamo is Southern Command's (SOUTHCOM) territory, so they ran the show, in conjunction with the CIA.

On December 22, 2001, an interim government was established in Afghanistan with General Karzai as its head, but real authority was still with the tribal warlords. We had to unify the country, to institute national programs that would bring them together and make them rely on one another. Our first focus was to build the Afghan National Army. We asked for twenty-five thousand dollars to train its first battalion. Amazingly, we couldn't get it. We asked Rumsfeld and Deputy Secretary of Defense Paul Wolfowitz. They were embarrassed, but they had to say no. Technically, by law, Afghanistan was not a country to which we were allowed to give money. Like so many laws of the pre–September 11 era, it had to be changed, but there wasn't time for that. It was easy to get hundreds of millions of dollars from the U.S. government when we had to wage a war, but now that we needed twenty-five thousand dollars for the immediate, crucial aftermath, it was impossible.

So I went to our French liaison in the Coalition village at CentCom and asked him if they would pay for it. They did in a second. The French were instrumental in getting the new Afghan army off the ground. Not only did they fund it, they even trained every third battalion. They didn't let us forget it, either. Later, whenever France was publicly criticized by anyone in the U.S., I'd get a call from the French chairman of their Joint Chiefs.

He'd say, "You recall that we helped you with the Afghan army, don't you?"

I would answer, "Yes, sir, I do. And we love you."

He would laugh.

To help reconstruct the country, we assigned territorial regions to our Coalition partners, giving each full authority for the region, and sent provisional reconstruction teams tailored to the needs of each region. On each team were specialists—doctors, lawyers, engineers—who led our humanitarian efforts. In addition, dozens of humanitarian organizations sent representatives to CentCom so that we could work together on reconstruction projects.

A main focus was hospitals. As soon as we cleared an area, we brought in a team to set up a hospital, usually converting an existing building into a medical facility. We did this in Mazar-e-Sharif, where we quickly established full medical capability, including twenty surgeons imported from Jordan. (Whenever possible, we wanted Arabs running the hospital and an Arab medical staff.) The Afghans were so desperate for medical care that they came on foot from hundreds of miles away. Women and children had had no care for years, and they were desperate. We had to set up extra tents to keep them overnight. We treated tens of thousands of people.

It also worked out well because early on we were finally able to indulge the French request for troops on the ground. We had them come in as a security force for the Jordanian hospital. Of course, they ended up sending in substantially more troops than we'd asked. They got their photo-op. They stayed a short period of time and then left. On the one hand, it seems opportunistic, and perhaps it was, especially in light of how they would later respond to our action in Iraq; on the other hand, though, overall the French helped us a lot in Afghanistan, so any criticism has to be tempered by a large dose of gratitude.

The Russians, too, kept pressing to have a presence. We were wary of how the Afghanis would react, but we indulged them, let them come in and build a hospital near Kabul. The Russians were smart: they trained Afghani doctors and nurses, and left within a few short weeks, leaving behind their equipment to be used by the new Afghani hospital.

Going into the war, we knew that one of the measures of our success was going to be how many refugees returned to the country. In the aftermath of most wars, it takes a while for the indigenous people to return—months, even years. In this case, we were thrilled to see that they started to come back immediately. By December 22, nearly 750,000 refugees had already returned. Each region reacted differently, of course. In the north and west, people came back quickly. In the southeast, an area heavily sympathetic to the Taliban and al-Qaeda, they were reluctant to accept the change; in some of the border areas, they wouldn't accept the new government at all. Overall, though, it was highly unusual for as many to come back as quickly as they did, and this told us we were doing something right.

We continually kept up raids, weeding out Taliban and al-Qaeda wherever we could. In multiple raids we found armored personnel carriers, thousands of rounds of ammunition, artillery ammunition, mortar ammunition, small arms, rocket propelled grenades, and several filing cabinets full of documentary evidence. We were making the country safer with every operation.

Franks visited Afghanistan, and the mood was positive. Overall, while there was still much to do, it felt as if the major hostilities were over and Afghanistan was winding down. We thought maybe there would be a chance to relax. Of course, we couldn't have been more wrong. Franks hardly had time to return to America when he was summoned to Crawford, Texas. President Bush wanted to talk to him. It was December 2001, and he wanted to know all about the Iraqi war plan.

Chapter Four

BUILDING TO H-HOUR

"A good plan violently executed *Now* is better than a perfect plan next week."
—General George S. Patton, Jr.
War As I Knew It, 1947

"I'VE BEEN SUMMONED TO THE RANCH," Franks told me shortly after he returned from Afghanistan. "We need to pull our current Iraq plan out."

We both knew the invitation was unusual. Historically, presidents rarely, if ever, spend extended time with their senior military commanders. There had been a lot of rumors in the press at the time that Rumsfeld and Franks were at odds, that Rumsfeld might fire Franks—none of which, of course, could have been further from the truth. Nonetheless, the pundits took to the air every night and extolled it as if it were imminent, and it started to become a nuisance. So in part we thought Bush summoned Franks to make a public display of support for him, silence the media, and let everyone know they were all on the same page.

The mention of Iraq both did and did not surprise us. On the one hand, CentCom had been carefully watching Saddam Hussein since the close of the Gulf War in 1991. Iraq had been very aggressive of late, and we figured the president wanted to know where we were. On the other hand, we were still surprised that the president was inquiring about Iraq at this particular time. An Iraq plan was nothing new. We'd had a plan on the books for years to stop Iraq, if Saddam mobilized his divisions near Kuwait, launched a Scud missile at Israel, or used weapons of mass destruction (WMD). It was a defensive plan, and few people knew about it.

In fact, one of the errors in Bob Woodward's book *Plan of Attack* is his assumption that we didn't have such a plan already on the books. Woodward says Franks lied when he denied that Bush asked him to create an Iraqi war plan in December. Franks didn't lie. Rumsfeld asked every regional commander to update the on-the-shelf contingency plans—and asking a regional commander to update a plan is not the same thing as giving him an order to prepare to attack a country. Our plans needed updating. In fact, Franks had had earlier discussions with Rumsfeld on the Iraq plan prior to his summons to Crawford.

"I'm going to take Gene," Franks aid. "I need you here, running CentCom."

"Gene" was Gene Renuart, the two-star general in charge of operations at CentCom. When Franks returned, he told me what happened at the ranch.

When Franks got to Crawford, Bush sat him down, and he quickly found out that the meeting would be all substance.

"Show us what war plans you have on the shelf for Iraq today," Rumsfeld said from his video teleconference room in New Mexico.

Franks presented the plan—which called for the deployment of three to five hundred thousand troops.

They looked them over. Finally, Rumsfeld said, "This is old think."

"I agree," Franks said.

"We need something much more flexible. Fewer troops. And we need to be able to move on short notice."

"Flexibility and fewer troops, yes. Short notice is not possible. It takes time to get things in place."

Franks and Renuart took them through all that would be involved, logistically, to mount a war on short notice. Bush and Rumsfeld wanted more.

"Update the plans," Rumsfeld said. "We want this ready to go if need be."

"Rumsfeld is making all the regional commanders update their plans," Franks told me. "He wants a focus on speed and flexibility, and I agree."

There was nothing particularly unusual about updating a war plan; in fact, an entire department of CentCom was devoted to nothing but perpetually keeping all of our plans up to date.

Although we wondered about the timing, we never wondered about the rightness of removing Saddam from power. As military professionals, Franks and I spent many hours examining the reasons for attacking Iraq, and asking ourselves if they were sound. Our conclusion was that they were.

Here's why:

- Over the past several years, Saddam had been increasingly aggressive towards us, firing almost daily at our jets in
the no fly and no drive zones of southern and northern Iraq
while we enforced the U.N. sanctions. As time progressed,
the chances of our having a plane shot down were increasing dramatically. If that happened, then what? We could
end up in an extraordinarily difficult position. Indeed, Iraq
was the only country in the region that was being openly
hostile towards us and escalating the violence.

- It appeared Iraq was gearing up for war. It was openly
testing L-29 unmanned aerial vehicles with chemical
sprayers, something the Iraqis hadn't done for years. They
were openly testing maximum-range Scud missiles that
exceeded the range set by U.N. sanctions and had the ability to reach Israel, Jordan, Turkey, and Kuwait. These
Scuds could be armed with chemical and biological agents.

- Iraq was using Chinese fiber optic cable to build an air
defense system, which meant that if we waited a year or two,
a war with Iraq would be much harder. China was working
with the Iraqis to put in an underground system that would
tie all the air defense systems together. Once this was completed, the Iraqis would be able to talk via underground land
lines (instead of talking over the air) and that meant we would
no longer be able to intercept their transmissions.

- Saddam had a history of using WMD, including the
killing of thousands of Kurds with chemical weapons in
1988. (He still kept two divisions in the north, which could
attack the Kurds.)

- The Iraqi military remained the most powerful military
in the Arab Middle East. Despite the findings of the Senate

Select Committee on Intelligence in July 2004, Iraq's military was not "crumbling." It was smaller than it had been (due to our weakening it), but nonetheless Iraq had a very capable army and air force.

• We had credible intel from multiple sources that senior leaders in Saddam's regime had been meeting with the senior leadership of al-Qaeda over a ten-year period.

• We also had credible intel that there was an al-Qaeda base in Iraq, near the Iranian border, and that the Iraqis might provide al-Qaeda with WMD. (Saddam had a long, well-documented history of supporting terrorist organizations. Perhaps the most famous example is that every time a Palestinian suicide bomber blew himself up in Israel, Saddam paid twenty-five thousand dollars to the family of the "martyr.")

• Intel indications were that there was a chemical and biological weapons-testing compound in Iraq, close to the Iranian border, that was cooperating with al-Qaeda and housing al-Qaeda terrorists.

• We were 100 percent sure that Iraq had WMD. We had human and technical intel that claimed Iraq still had chemical weapons, and there were reports that Iraq had hidden some WMD components in Syria or Lebanon. These types of weapons are easy to move in different types of trucks and vans. Saddam knew we were watching, so he was careful about how and when he moved it. Whenever he let the U.N. inspectors in, they always had to give one week's notice, and that was always ample time to move whatever he needed to. We knew he had hidden materials related to weapons of mass destruction in the past. The intelligence was strong enough that everyone at CentCom felt 100 percent sure that he had WMD somewhere. There was also evidence that Iraq was again pursuing a nuclear weapons troops. It would also take a lot more time. The first Gulf War employed five hundred thousand troops, and that buildup took six months. It was not possible to achieve a buildup of five hundred thousand troops in only a few weeks. We could, of course, begin the war with fewer than eighty thousand troops and then add troops as we went, but in that case, we risked leaving them open to being initially outnumbered and flanked.

We kept going back to Bush and Rumsfeld, saying we couldn't give them an exact number of troops until we knew what they wanted us to do. In the early stages of the planning, all that could be decided was that we'd need a sliding plan, a plan that allowed for several contingencies and could accommodate anywhere from sixty thousand to three hundred thousand troops. The key word was flexibility. Since President Bush and Rumsfeld were insistent on being able to kick off any conflict with Iraq on short notice, it became clear that no matter what route we took, we would need to have troops in place in advance. We had to begin the buildup, even if the war didn't ultimately happen.

Because Bush and Rumsfeld insisted on not having an obvious early deployment of troops, we would have to find a quiet way to bring massive numbers of troops, equipment, weapons, and supplies close to Iraq, and keep them there.

So over the next year and a half, whenever we had a field training exercise in the region, we brought over more troops than we needed, masking their presence as part of the exercise. And when the exercise was over, we would keep some of them there, and if we were asked why, we told the truth: We needed a bigger military presence to counterbalance Saddam Hussein's increasing belligerence.

All of this meant money. In those days, not a lot of money was allocated to CentCom, and we were still operating on the basic infrastructure installed in the early 1990s. For example, the CentCom commander's plane was a 1961 EC-135. It shook and rattled so loudly that you could hardly hear yourself think. The air quality was poor, and it required six maintenance men to travel with it, taking up the few extra seats. If President Bush and Rumsfeld wanted us to get serious about Iraq, we would need to build up CentCom's infrastructure. We'd need to expand airports in our AOR; we'd need to help our allies in the area build deeper ports; we'd need more warehouses in Qatar to store additional armored vehicles and tanks. It was a long back and forth, and a very professional discussion.

Around this time, my two-year term as deputy commander at CentCom was set to expire. At CentCom, when your term is over, you leave. No deputy commander in the history of CentCom had stayed more than two years.

Franks approached me.

"What do you want to do?" he asked.

"I want to retire," I said, "But not yet. If there's another war ahead of us, I'd just as soon finish out with you."

"We started this together, and I would like us to finish it together," Franks said.

"I agree," I said.

Franks talked to Myers and Rumsfeld, and it was a done deal. I was officially extended for one more year as deputy commander.

In the meantime, the War on Terror never let up. We had to prepare for Iraq, but that didn't mean we could forget Afghanistan or the War on Terror in other countries. It just meant we had to work two or three jobs. And the terrorists never let us rest. Every morning we gave Rumsfeld a report that showed the number of al-Qaeda captured, killed, and on the loose.

For months we had been on the trail of Qaed Salim Sinan al-Harethi ("Abu Ali"), the leader of al-Qaeda in Yemen and one of the most determined al-Qaeda members anywhere. Ali had been behind the bombing of the USS *Cole*, the September 11 attacks, and a host of other atrocities. He was one of the most wanted al-Qaeda members in the world.

Finally, we had found him. Ali was spotted in a compound in Yemen in the northern province of Marib, about one hundred miles east of Yemen's capital, San'a. Our SpecialOps had the compound under surveillance—a Predator was watching from the sky—and were preparing to storm in when Ali exited with five of his associates. They got into SUVs and took off. Now we were involved in a high-speed Predator chase.

I pulled the Predator's visuals up on our screen. The two SUVs raced across the desert, showing up as glowing spheres in the desert night.

At that moment, Tenet called.

"Where's Franks?"

"He's in Qatar."

United States Central Command

MacDill Air Force Base, Tampa, Florida   **February 6, 2002**

Lt. General DeLong meets with the U.S. ambassador to Afghanistan, Dr. Zalmay Khalilzad.

Left to right: Lt. General DeLong; Admiral Edmund Giambastiani Jr., commander in chief of U.S. Joint Forces Command; Secretary of Defense Donald Rumsfeld; and Major General Gene Renuart. General Tommy Franks is in the background.

All photos courtesy of Lt. General Mike DeLong

Deputy Secretary of Defense Paul Wolfowitz with Lt. General DeLong.

Left to right: European Command (EUCOM) commander General Jim Jones, Lt. General Harry Blot (ret.), Lt. General Fred McCorkle (ret.), Lt. General Robert Magnus, and Lt. General DeLong.

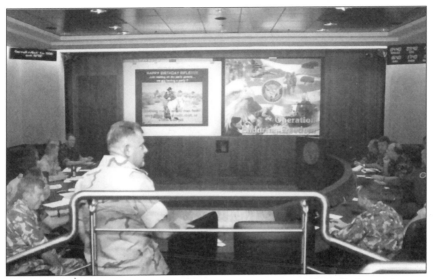

The Coalition members in the CentCom Tampa headquarters threw Lt. General DeLong a birthday party.

General Tommy Franks (left) with Ambassador Marty Cheshes (in light suit) and Lt. General DeLong (standing).

Former Washington Redskins players Sonny Jurgensen (left) and Sam Huff toss the football with Lt. General DeLong after a briefing.

President George W. Bush shakes hands with Lt. General DeLong.

Lt. General DeLong congratulates Brig. General Sachau, German liaison officer to CentCom, at Sachau's going-away party.

Lt. General DeLong with Brig. General Hosam El Dien-Anwer.

Former New York mayor Rudolph Giuliani with Lt. General DeLong.

Australian chief of defense Admiral Chris Barrie with Lt. General DeLong.

Lt. General DeLong shakes hands with former New York mayor Rudolph Giuliani while Rear Admiral Jim Robb and Kathy DeLong look on.

Secretary of Defense Donald Rumsfeld presents a special award to Lt. General DeLong.

Lt. General DeLong with the CentCom Italian liaison officer, Major General Armando Novelli.

Left to right: First Lady Laura Bush; Florida governor Jeb Bush; General Peter Pace, vice chairman of the Joint Chiefs of Staff; Lt. General DeLong; and an unidentified airman.

Left to right: Captain Van Mauney, General Tommy Franks, and Lt. General DeLong.

"Are you watching the same thing we are?"

"Have it right in front of me."

"We think it's a good hit. The intel is excellent. What do you think?"

"Our intel says that's him. We've got a positive ID on five out of six of them. One of them is an American—the fat guy. But he's al-Qaeda. The only question mark is the sixth passenger."

"Do we take them out?"

"Looks good to me, and General Franks will be comfortable with your call."

"I'm going to notify Saleh. Then we're going to do it," said Tenet.

Saleh was President Ali Abdullah Saleh, the president of Yemen. Saleh was in a precarious position. Yemen was (and still is) a transit country for terrorists and a center of al-Qaeda activity. If President Saleh appeared to be aggressively taking action against terrorists—especially in conjunction with the United States—it could make his position untenable.

Tenet told him what we were about to do. All Saleh asked was that we keep the operation secret. Tenet agreed. We didn't want publicity either. If questions did arise, the official Yemeni version would be that an SUV carrying civilians accidentally hit a landmine in the desert and exploded. There was to be no mention of terrorists, and no mention of missiles fired.

I watched the Predator get into position. Before it released its Hellfire missile, it climbed and pointed its nose downward, taking aim. The CIA was controlling these Predators; they had some operators in Pakistan, some in the Gulf region, and some in Langley, Virginia, at CIA headquarters.

At that moment, the two SUVs split up. Perhaps they'd heard the drone of the Predator and knew they were spotted. They were getting away.

Just then, a bright light lit up the screen. Missiles streaked from the sky to the ground. It was a direct hit. Our target SUV was blown to hell, a glowing image in the desert night.

As I watched, I saw one body fall out, badly injured. He began crawling across the desert floor, showing up as a glowing heat source on our screens. He crawled about twenty-five yards, then stopped. As I watched, the glow signifying his body heat slowly faded to black. It was a strange way to watch a person die.

Soon thereafter, an article appeared in the *Washington Post*. Somehow, the story had leaked. The article reported that CentCom had fired on an SUV in

Yemen, killing innocent civilians, among them an American citizen. It said that CentCom had used unilateral authority it didn't have to order the attack. It insinuated that CentCom used its weapons to fire on whoever it wanted, whenever, wherever, for its own purposes. It demanded to know how we got permission to fire at an unarmed vehicle.

President Saleh called Franks. He was livid.

"This wasn't supposed to get out," he said. "This is going to cause me major political problems."

Franks said, "Somebody leaked it—in Yemen or in D.C."

The heat in the press was getting worse. The CIA was keeping quiet, and Rumsfeld wasn't happy; he didn't like that CentCom was taking the heat. Finally, he had Wolfowitz appear to confirm that the attack was a legitimate U.S. operation and to set the record straight. In an interview with CNN, Wolfowitz called it "a very successful tactical operation." He confirmed that the agency fired the missile and that the passengers were terrorists, including the American. The president of Yemen, too, acknowledged that the targets were terrorists, but he stopped there, never saying he gave approval. Eventually, the hubbub died down.

Sometimes it was like that. But the important thing was that Franks, Tenet, John McLaughlin (Tenet's deputy), Rumsfeld, Wolfowitz, and myself were tight. The six of us never let anyone or anything get in the way of our working relationship. The relationship between the CIA and the military was the best it had ever been, and the six of us were a strong team. Tenet was a remarkable guy—he had managed to be successful in two administrations, and not many men can do that. And Tenet and McLaughlin were the perfect complement to each other: Tenet was always chewing on a cigar, hair disheveled, looking like he had been working all night. McLaughlin was always dapper in shined shoes. Tenet was the workhorse, and McLaughlin was the diplomat. No two guys worked harder to combat terror than these two.

The War on Terror had many branches. The Abu Ali strike would never have been possible to begin with if not for CentCom's joint task force in the Horn of Africa and the incredible work of its leader, two-star Marine Corps General John Sattler, one-star Army General and SpecialOps Commander Gary Harrell, and others.

Based out of Camp Lemonier in Djibouti, the Horn of Africa Task Force, with its nine hundred troops, ran the War on Terror in that area. They worked with the governments of Yemen, Ethiopia, Eritrea, Djibouti, Kenya, Sudan (which was unprecedented), and the tribes in Somalia to fight terrorists. They assisted police forces, provided military and agency backup for raids on al-Qaeda terrorists, and offered training and equipment to the police and military helping us. We patrolled their coastlines with Coalition ships and helped them capture many al-Qaeda terrorists, especially off the coast of Somalia, where al-Qaeda was trying to create a safe haven. We also (as an unintended consequence) stopped a lot of drug smuggling. By helping make these countries safer, we built great regional goodwill, and they became strong members of our Coalition. On purpose, we kept this low key. These countries didn't want to advertise they were going after terrorists using U.S. forces, and we didn't want to advertise it either. We could catch more people if they didn't know our methods, partnerships, or tactics. But silently, these people were all doing great work, were all heroes on the war against terror.

Operation Anaconda kicked off in March 2002. It had been five months since the end of major hostilities in Afghanistan, yet intelligence reports indicated that al-Qaeda was building up again, moving freely, and getting ready for a counterattack. They were operating with impunity, moving about in the open and doing whatever they wanted to do. We were not surprised; we knew they wouldn't go away so easily, and we had been prepared for such a scenario. We put together an operation to go into the Shah-i-Kot valley, dead south of Kabul in eastern Afghanistan, and weed them out. We called this Operation Anaconda.

Throughout the war, the Coalition ground forces had taken a back seat in Afghanistan; although we had done most of the work behind the scenes, we let the Afghans lead the way and take the credit. But now the Northern Alliance was officially disbanded and the Afghan National Army was still being built. They were producing only one new battalion of about six hundred soldiers every seven weeks—they weren't ready yet. So the task fell on us. Thus, strangely enough, Operation Anaconda would be the first major U.S.-led operation in Afghanistan.

We assembled troops from the 10th Mountain Division, the 101st Airborne Division, the Marine Corps, and Special Forces. We also included special forces from Australia, New Zealand, Canada, Germany, Denmark,

France, and Norway, as they were particularly good in this sort of fighting. From the Navy we included F-18s and F-14s; from the Army 105 Howitzer cannons and helicopter gunships; from the Marines F-18s, Harriers, and helicopter gunships; and from the Air Force F-16s and A-10s. It was truly a joint operation, commanded by Major General Frank "Buster" Hagenbeck of the 10th Mountain Division.

We prepared to attack from Bagram in the north and Kandahar in the south, and stationed the AC-130s, A-10s, Harriers, and Apaches there. Unfortunately, however, we couldn't fly all of our planes out of airbases in Afghanistan. Some of our jets were flying their missions from the Middle East, and some of our bombers still had to fly from the Pacific. Although we owned the Afghan runways, the Kandahar and Bagram runways were hard to maintain; the Russians had built them in the late 1970s, and they were falling apart and always in need of repair.

We hadn't wanted to make the same mistake the Russians had made (they'd kept hundreds of thousands of troops in Afghanistan, who became easy targets), so we kept our force presence small—around nine to ten thousand men. That meant nearly one-third of our forces would be deployed for Operation Anaconda.

The first thing we did was cordon off the area, which was no easy feat.

The area covered about seventy square miles of rough terrain. The altitude reached twelve thousand feet, and the nighttime temperature was fifteen degrees Fahrenheit. We put blocking forces in the mountains, the valleys, and other escape routes. The plan was to drop a battalion on a plateau to the northwest and put a Special Forces team on the twelve-thousand-foot northern ridge line and force the enemy down the ridge, into the main body of our forces. The Special Forces unit, carried by two choppers, was supposed to have a quiet landing; our intel had told us the al-Qaeda terrorists were much farther down the ridge.

Instead, in the midst of the covert operation at midnight, they were spotted by al-Qaeda insurgents who unleashed a barrage of RPGs and small arms fire. There was nowhere for the choppers to land, and no way to safely drop the SEALs they had on board. The incoming fire was too heavy.

An RPG lit up the night and hit one of the choppers, rocking it violently. It tore out of there, just in the nick of time.

But not before one of its passengers fell out.

Navy SEAL Petty Officer 1st Class Neil Roberts had unstrapped himself in preparation for the insertion. When the chopper took the RPG hit, he was thrown from the aircraft. Roberts hit the ground hard from a height of about ten feet. He lay there injured, expecting his buddies to come down for him.

But it was pitch black, and in the darkness, noise, and confusion, no one saw him fall. Enemy forces closed in on him as his buddies unknowingly took off.

He did what every great soldier is trained to do: He took a knee, locked and loaded his weapon, and prepared to defend his life. He wouldn't go down without a fight.

The chopper, badly shot up, had barely made it to a safe area when the crew realized that Petty Officer Neil Roberts was missing. They had no idea where he had fallen out.

At the same time, General Hagenbeck picked up some activity on his Predator monitor. He saw a firefight in the middle of the mountains, miles away from where our troops were stationed. It wasn't making any sense; he wondered if perhaps al-Qaeda terrorists were fighting each other. Then he was informed that a SEAL had fallen from a chopper somewhere. Suddenly, it all made sense. Special Forces immediately loaded up a new chopper to rescue him.

General Hagenbeck watched the drama unfold. Our trooper was firing in all directions, taking out many al-Qaeda terrorists. He got hit, but kept firing, while the terrorists moved in, closer and closer. Then he was down. General Hagenbeck watched helplessly. The blurry shapes on the heat-screen showed the terrorists move in closer, grab his body, and drag him away.

The rescue chopper started taking fire in a landing zone just down the ridge, and was also shot down. Al-Qaeda members moved in to attack the twenty Special Forces troopers, who set up defensive positions. Our boys were trapped. We had to bring in support, but at that altitude, attack helicopters were having trouble flying, and given the steep, jagged, mountain face, the withering enemy fire, and the broken helicopter already cluttering the only safe landing zone, there was no way to lift them out. We couldn't bring in a force from below—they were twelve thousand feet high and it would take hours of climbing just to reach them. And we couldn't drop any big bombs, because the al-Qaeda terrorists were only fifty yards from our troops.

All we could do was use the guns in our jets. We brought in A-10s and AC-130s and strafed the area around our troops. It was difficult, because the enemy was so close and there were only a few yards of margin. But they strafed all night, and our boys fought all night.

At daylight, we were able to mark our lines and bring in more firepower. By then, only three of our Special Forces troopers on the ground were unharmed: Six were dead and eleven were wounded. There were hardly any al-Qaeda left.

It was clear that we needed more men for Operation Anaconda. We brought in more troops to push the al-Qaeda down the ridge toward our blocking force, which had grown to five thousand. We had an intel indication that bin Laden or Mullah Omar might be there, and we didn't want to take any chances. The al-Qaeda fought hard, but we pushed them down the valley. Among the al-Qaeda were Chinese and Uzbeks who had been living and fighting in the mountains their entire lives. For us it was the heaviest and bloodiest fighting yet, with eight American and three Coalition soldiers killed in the first week. But in that same week we killed hundreds of enemy soldiers. Those we didn't kill melted into villages or found other escape routes. On March 8, six days later, Anaconda was over. It was a success, but we still didn't have bin Laden.

At the beginning of the war we had offered a $25 million reward for information leading to the capture of bin Laden. With $25 million, you could practically buy the entire country of Afghanistan. Well, we soon learned a valuable lesson on the deprivation of the Afghani people. No one came forward.

Coalition forces on the ground asked the Afghans, "Do you know how much money $25 million is?"

The Afghans responded that they did. With $25 million, they said, they "could buy twenty balloons" for their children's birthdays "and enough food to feed my family for a year."

This amount of money was clearly beyond their scope of knowledge. And the truth is, an Afghani with $25 million would have nowhere to spend it.

The hunt would continue.

"The deputy secretary is taking a trip to Dearborn, Michigan," Wolfowitz's assistant said, "to talk to a group of expatriate Iraqis. Would you like to join him?"

It was an odd request. I called Franks.

"What do you think?"

"Can't hurt."

I like Wolfowitz. He was unlike almost anyone I had ever met. First of all, he worked more than anyone: anytime, anywhere, he could always be found. I wondered if he ever slept. He's very personable; he looks you in the eye when he talks. When you talk to him you have to be prepared to spend a long time, because he's always asking questions, but he's never offensive. He's always a gentleman and very scholarly, and in many ways he reminds me of a professor. Franks and I both called him "Mr. Secretary" out of courtesy. He liked that.

We got on a C-9 and flew to Dearborn together. On the way, he explained to me how he had managed to round up five hundred or so Iraqi expatriates he thought could help us understand Iraq and its regime. They were Iraqi professionals—including doctors, lawyers, bankers, and former generals. They were waiting to greet us in the Fairlane Club, in one of the old Ford theaters in Dearborn.

We walked into the room and were shocked. It was like walking into Iraq. There, before us, in the middle of Dearborn, Michigan, were five hundred Iraqis in native dress. It was one of the strangest sights I had ever seen. Wolfowitz and I exchanged a look.

Wolfowitz quickly took the stage.

"If Saddam does not concede," he told the crowd, "we may have to take action against him. This is what we need to know: If that happens, will all the different tribes and all the different religious sects work together?"

They all, to a man, said YES. They all insisted that once Saddam was gone, Iraqis would put aside their differences and come together, and there would be immediate peace in the country.

"I've got General DeLong here from Central Command," he said. "Those of you who think you can be of help in postwar Iraq and would like to volunteer, please see him."

About a hundred people approached me, giving me names, cards, titles. They said if there was a war, they wanted to be a part of it. We put together

a list, and when war came, we did indeed contact these people to be inter-
preters and translators. Most said no; they wanted only positions of power or
leadership in the new Iraq.

Wolfowitz, I believe, put too much weight on the promises of Iraqi exiles,
Ahmad Chalabi most all. Few people know that Chalabi had been in gradu-
ate school with Wolfowitz. Wolfowitz trusted him, which was unfortunate,
because most of Chalabi's information has turned out to be suspect, and the
CIA and State Department never thought highly of him. Chalabi was also
responsible for another Wolfowitz-recommended venture that turned out to
be a waste of time and energy for us: the Iraqi "freedom fighters."

At CentCom, we knew that Iraqis would not be fighting at our side the
way the Afghans did, because there was no equivalent of the Northern
Alliance to latch onto in Iraq and because the war needed to be waged on a
much larger, more conventional scale. Nonetheless, we welcomed any native
support we could get. Chalabi had claimed there was a large group of well-
trained expatriate Iraqi fighters who could join us; some were in exile in
Europe and a large number were available in Iraq. He pushed the Defense
Department to incorporate them into our order of battle. Wolfowitz and others believed him, and put great faith in this force. Franks and I weren't so
sure.

So we set up an operation in Eastern Europe that weeded through the proposed Iraq "freedom fighters." Of the approximately five thousand men,
only about five hundred could pass the initial security check. They were sent
through a six-week boot camp and then assigned to units to act as translators
and advisors on how to help the Iraqi people.

Another story that the press glossed over is that these "freedom fighters"
were not the panacea they were promised to be. While some of them were
helpful in small battles, we received many reports of their looting and thievery in Baghdad. When the city fell, they melted into the local population.
Chalabi allegedly used some of them as his personal security force.

As the clock ticked down, it seemed increasingly likely we would go to war,
and our preparations never ceased. Saddam was still denying the UN inspectors full access, and was still firing at our aircraft protecting the no fly zones
in Iraq. We continued to quietly build up our troops in the region and under
the guise of military exercise, we were able to station nearly eight thousand

troops in Kuwait, Qatar, and Bahrain, and keep them inconspicuous. We also stocked up on bombs, bullets, food, and other supplies, storing them in massive warehouses in Kuwait and Qatar. We were constantly updating our Iraqi war plan, refining it, changing it, "what-ifing" everything, asking ourselves everything what could go wrong. We must have changed it sixty times. Also at this time, Saddam's son-in-law defected. He gave us all kinds of information, which was very helpful, including the fact that there were definitely WMD, and where they were. Saddam implored his son-in-law to return, claiming he would be welcomed back peacefully. Oddly enough, he believed him. Of course, upon his return he was executed.

In planning the Iraq War, we were charged with a difficult task: Entering the warped mind of Saddam Hussein in an effort to anticipate his moves and remain one step ahead. We asked ourselves: What would we do if we were him? Launch chemical and biological Scuds into Israel and Jordan? Torch the oil fields? Attack and massacre the Kurds in the north? Flood the plains? Let the U.S. troops come close, then spray them with chemical or biological weapons? Circle the Republican Guard forces in and around Baghdad and force prolonged, hand-to-hand urban combat? The answer was all of these and more. If Saddam wanted to, he could do a tremendous amount of damage, and cause such disaster that he could turn world opinion completely against the United States, possibly even forcing us to withdraw. How could we prevent all of this from happening?

The answer became clear: We might have to preempt him and act before he had a chance to. As such, more so than any other war in modern history, our plan, if executed, would begin before the war began. We would have to rely heavily on covert SpecialOps missions, on InformationOps ("psy-ops") to take key objectives in advance and to turn the minds of the Iraqi leaders and generals against Saddam. Our plan called for attacking Saddam simultaneously on five fronts. They were:

1. THE NORTH. Northern Iraq was important for many reasons. First, we needed to protect the Kurds, who occupied a large portion of northeastern Iraq. We did not want them to be massacred by Saddam as they had been in the wake of the first Gulf War. We owed them that.

We also wanted absolute control of the battlefield. We needed the Kurds to stay out of it, especially because Turkey was highly sensitive about armed

Kurds.

The huge Kurdish area in northeast Iraq spills over into southeast Turkey. The Kurds want their own state—Kurdistan—an idea that the Turks hate.

At first, we implored Turkey to allow us to use the country as a base. As a backup plan—while Turkey wavered for months—we decided to place an airborne brigade in Italy, to keep the 4th Infantry Division floating off the coast of Turkey in the Eastern Mediterranean sea, and to drop between twenty and fifty Special Forces "A Teams" into the north, with the Kurds. If Turkey refused us permission, with the help of human agents, we would attempt to convince the Iraqi government that Turkey's refusal was simply a ruse, that we would indeed be using the country as a base while publicly denying it. We would play on Saddam's paranoia. If it worked, this would keep eleven Iraqi Army divisions and two Republican Guard divisions frozen in the north.

2. THE WEST. We made it a priority, both diplomatically and militarily, to ensure that Israel did not enter this war. We were on good terms with Jordan (in the first Gulf War we had not been), Saudi Arabia, the Gulf States, Kuwait, and Turkey, and we had to ensure that Saddam did not try to attack them either. This made control of the Scud missiles on Iraq's western edge a strategic necessity. With a second's notice, Saddam could fire all of his Scuds, sparking a disaster heretofore unseen. The west was also significant in its own right, as it comprised a quarter of Iraq's land. It was crucial that we blinded Iraq's eyes in the west; we did not want them to see us approaching when the time came. We decided the best way to achieve this would be to drop another twenty to fifty Special Forces teams, along with special forces from three other nations, into the west before the war began. We would have them in position near Scud sites and border watchtowers, so that when we gave the order, they could take out the Scuds and blind the Iraqis to our approach. Nobody could know that we were invading Iraq before the war began.

In preparation for writing this book, Brigadier General Gary Harrell, in charge of SpecialOps for Afghanistan and Iraq, generously sat down with us in his secure headquarters in SpecialOps Central Command (SOCENT-COM) and gave us a two-hour interview, lending his perspective and expertise about some of the Special Forces missions. Much of it was too sensitive to put into print, but here is part of what he told us:

The area in western Iraq was huge: one million square miles. You would think that it would be easy to hide people there. But I learned a long time ago that there are very few places left in the world that are truly empty or barren. I remember one time I pulled up in the middle of nowhere, somewhere on the Sinai Peninsula. I said, "You know, there's just nothing out here. This is as far away from anyone as it gets." All of a sudden, I hear this weird music. I turn around, and an Arab rides up on a camel, carrying a boombox!

During the first Gulf War, we thought our men were isolated. The next day, a shepherd comes out with his flock, and he notices the dirt is a different color. It's hard to deceive folks who live close to the land. In Special Forces operations, you have to be very aware of this or it will get you in big trouble. In societies with repressive regimes, if the shepherd does *not* report, he and his family are in mortal danger.

Special Forces troops need to analyze the terrain and pick the best location to hide. It takes a great deal of effort and planning to pull it off. You have to assume there will always be somebody somewhere. If you're moving by jeep, for example, and leave tracks, how do you cover them? How do you stay undetected for days or weeks at a time, especially if your assignment is to hide near a strategic (and heavily guarded and patrolled) site?

There are huge implications if you cross the border early and are discovered. If you're a private in a conventional army force and make a mistake, it often doesn't have huge ramifications. But with the missions we have, if a guy makes a mistake, it's normally at the national level, and a very big deal. What would have happened if one of our guys was caught in Iraq days before Bush publicly gave Saddam his ultimatum? Special Forces carry a lot of political baggage. It's a big burden to put on the guys, which is why we have older, more experienced folks in Special Forces— because they know that what they do (or do not do) has an impact at the highest levels, in the United States and in other countries.

Which raises a good philosophical question. What do they do if they're discovered by the shepherd? Lots of folks think we would kill them, so as not to compromise the mission. That's a myth. That's not the answer. You can't kill a ten-year-old boy. If you kill a civilian non-combatant, you've just broken the law. Once you start breaking the law, you have huge problems. We don't knowingly break the law of land warfare.

If our guys are caught, they have to move. A shepherd boy runs back to his father who runs back to the local sheriff, who comes at you with a local mob or a small militia. It could be a big problem. That's what happened during the first Gulf War. We had teams compromised, and we had to extract them. In one case, we had a team compromised and a sizable force came after them—they were engaged in a three- or four-day battle before they could break contact. Of course, if you're fired upon, it's different. Then you're within your ROE to fire back. There is a difference between a shepherd boy and a mechanized rifle company.

In western Iraq, we could not afford for anything to go wrong because of the danger from the Iraqi Scuds.

3. AIR. We would bombard Iraq with air strikes. We would strike in every corner of Iraq, supporting our ground troops and taking out key leadership targets, air defense targets, and Republican Guard and regular Iraqi army divisions. We planned an air campaign that incorporated jet fighters, bombers, and Tomahawk missiles. It had to be flexible enough to either kick off the war or to follow on the heels of a ground war. During World War II, it could require three thousand air sorties to eliminate a single target. During the Gulf War, it took only ten. In the Iraq War, one plane was capable of tak-

ing out ten targets. Using GPS and laser-guided bombs, this would be the most precise bombing campaign in the history of warfare, with the fewest civilian casualties. We would also set aside numerous assets (such as Stealth Bombers) for time-sensitive targets of opportunity, if they should happen to emerge.

4. GROUND FROM KUWAIT. We planned to position nearly our entire ground force in Kuwait—hundreds of thousands of troops—and from there have them race on different paths to Baghdad. Speed was the main factor. If we could beat them there, there could be no battle of Baghdad. As such, our ground forces were told to, whenever possible, avoid long protracted fire-fights and keep driving for Baghdad. Our plan called for a timeline for victory in as quickly as sixty days.

Ideally, we would have had ground assaults from Turkey, Jordan, and Saudi Arabia. But we were going back and forth with Turkey until the last minute, and eventually we had to assume they wouldn't give us permission to launch ground troops from Turkish territory. We couldn't put ground forces in Saudi Arabia or Jordan because, while these governments were friendly, their people were neutral at best. We were able to use Jordan for Special Forces, but we couldn't push for any more of a ground presence there. That left us with a ground front only in Kuwait.

Logistically, this put more pressure on us to race to Baghdad. It meant not only a large number of assault vehicles but also a large number of tanker trucks. Hundreds of gas trucks would have to roll alongside and dash back and forth to our vehicles to keep them gassed up and moving at all times. We weren't marching to Baghdad—we were sprinting there. Franks's message was clear: Go faster, boys, because speed kills the enemy.

There was much talk in the media about an "invisible red line": If we crossed it, Saddam would supposedly use chemical weapons. But we were prepared. We had plenty of decontamination units in place, and we made sure our troops had at least two sets of nuclear biochemical suits. Additionally, our troops were moving at top speed: if they did get hit, they would be moving so fast that whatever hit them would be mostly behind them. Still, of course, we worried. We had intel that Hussein had fixed his L-29s UAVs with chemical sprayers, and we knew they had a range of five hundred kilometers. Another threat was that he could flood the plains in the south. We were concerned about this, so we did a hydrology study. The result showed that, even if he did, it wouldn't likely affect us very much. Still, it was one more reason to stress speed.

5. INFORMATION OPERATIONS. CentCom has teams devoted to information operations and psychological warfare. A bloodless front, this is the battle for the psyche of Iraq. If we could win this war without a shot, so much the better. We decided to try to convert key leaders in Saddam's regime, along with key generals and even common soldiers. We would find a way to get to them, then create a psy-ops campaign building on their fears of American military might and their impending doom. We would create twenty-five million leaflets and drop them en masse on the Iraqi people and soldiers.

Any war is a war of perception. We would attempt to make the Iraqis think we were using Turkey; to make them think our forces in Kuwait were there only for defensive purposes; to make them think we'd lead with an air campaign first. We would leak word that if we couldn't use Turkey, we wouldn't really attack at all, or just drop a few bombs. We would get them so confused, they wouldn't know where we were attacking from, when, or why. We would use electronic warfare. We would sever the regime's lines of communication (but not destroy them, because then we would have to rebuild them). We would destroy the fiber-optic nodes and repeater sites, forcing the regime to use their high-frequency radio and satellite phones, which meant we could intercept their transmissions. We would also take control of the radio and airwaves as soon as we could. We would broadcast on Iraqi radio to tell the people to stay away from our Army units and stay indoors and that we would liberate them from Saddam's tyranny. In broadcasts to Iraqi divisions, we would tell them that we had no quarrel with the Iraqi Army and that they should not die for Saddam's hated regime, that they should surrender peacefully. We also made it clear that if they chose to fight, we would fight. Saddam and his administration were furious about these broadcasts. They tried to shut them down, but there was nothing they could do.

In addition to these five fronts, we remained focused on two key objectives:

1. THE OIL FIELDS. There were one thousand oil fields in northern Iraq, and fifteen hundred more in the south. It was imperative that we reached

these before Saddam could blow them up. If he got to them first, their destruction would mean an environmental disaster and a battlefield disaster, as the choking smoke would limit our ability to conduct operations. It would also cost the liberated Iraq billions of dollars to repair—and that would ultimately fall on U.S. taxpayers. To beat Saddam to the wells, the plan was to send in SpecialOps units in the north and to use the 1st Marine Division in the south, whom we trained for this scenario. The SpecialOps, dropped in before the war, would work with local friendly forces, including the Kurds. The Marines would have to surprise the Iraqis and capture the wells the first day of the war. But that would still capture the Iraqis by surprise, since the ground assault would begin at the same time (or earlier than) the air assault, which the Iraqis would never expect.

2. BAGHDAD. The last thing we wanted was a pitched battle for the Iraqi capital. House-to-house, door-to-door warfare was to be avoided at all costs. Baghdad was a major city, with a population of five million, and if we got mired in urban warfare, it could take months. Worse, we'd be fighting on their ground, where our air superiority would be mitigated— we'd be unable to use our major firepower. And Iraqi civilians could join the fight, which would make the fighting much more messy, and turn Iraqi and world opinion against us. We knew that Hussein would try to circle the wagons, bring his forces in to draw us into Baghdad or Tikrit. Again, we decided to use SpecialOps before the war began, dropping them into Baghdad beforehand. Undercover, their mission was to seek out Shi'ite sympathizers—we knew where they were—and recruit people to our cause.

We also knew we'd have to cut off the Republican Guard divisions before they could make it back to Baghdad. When the time came, we'd cut them off using airpower by dropping bombs—we knew their positions in advance—and we'd also cut them off on the ground. We'd use massive numbers of troops to race to Baghdad before the Republican Guard knew what hit them.

Overall, it was a brilliant and unconventional plan, relying heavily on SpecialOps, misperception, psy-ops, and speed. It was unlike any other plan that had ever been created.

As a finishing touch, we added another surprise: We were flexible enough to attack ground first, air first, or simultaneously. (Each day had its own code: A-Day was air day, S-Day was SpecialOps day, G-Day was ground day.) This is something they could have never expected. In American military practice, control of the skies always comes first. And with good reason: It's risky not to control the skies. But Franks knew that nothing was more important to our Iraq campaign than the element of surprise, and his focus on this was a testament to his strategic brilliance. He has always been unconventional, and has never adhered to the concept of doing something one way simply because that was the way it had always been done.

The plan's strength raised another issue. Perhaps the biggest problem of all would come not if we were unsuccessful, but if we were *too* successful. The question we kept asking ourselves was: What if Iraq fell in thirty minutes? This, in fact, was our biggest fear. If the Iraqis surrendered before we had a chance to get our ground forces in, they would have no one to physically surrender to. You can't surrender to a satellite. Or, they could surrender, but if we had too few forces on the ground, they could surprise us and decide to fight. Or Saddam could surrender, but the Republican Guard could keep up the fight. Having forces in the air and at sea is crucial, but ultimately you need to have people on the ground to accept mass surrenders. If Iraq fell too soon, this would not be possible.

Over the weeks and months to come, as we fine-tuned the plan, Franks took multiple trips to the White House and Camp David to sit down with the president and others—including Vice President Cheney, Secretary of State Powell, National Security Advisor Rice, Secretary of Defense Rumsfeld, Deputy Secretary of Defense Wolfowitz, Chairman of the Joint Chiefs of Staff General Richard Myers (who had succeeded General Hugh Shelton in that post), and Director of Central Intelligence George Tenet—to go over the scenarios and details. This was a collaborative effort. As Franks said: "This was not a Tommy Franks plan. This was not a Don Rumsfeld plan. There was not friction between Franks and Rumsfeld on this plan. This was a national plan. It involved the service chiefs; it involved the service secretaries; it involved the president himself; it involved Don Rumsfeld; it involved me; it involved all of our staffs. I think we benefited from the fact that we had a long planning cycle, an opportunity to get ready." As the weeks approached, we came closer to a version acceptable to everyone.

That is, except the Joint Chiefs. Once again, they were unhappy with the plan. They didn't like the idea of possibly kicking off with a ground war first or even simultaneously with the air war. It was unprecedented. The Army always gave the Air Force several days of bombing before it went in, and the Joint Chiefs were concerned we were putting the ground troops at excessive risk. The Air Force, for matters of pride, wanted to be the first ones in.

Franks's answer: "Tough shit."

Franks had proved them wrong in Afghanistan, Rumsfeld was behind him, and they would grudgingly have to go along with his plan for Iraq, too.

Another big decision was to embed reporters. The idea originally arose in a discussion between myself, Franks, Rumsfeld, and Pentagon spokeswoman Tori Clarke. We studied the concept. We went back to Ernie Pyle days, and we saw that when reporters became part of the unit, they better understood what we were doing. But the U.S. military had not allowed embedded reporters since Vietnam, and the decision was controversial. Many of the senior generals in the armed forces were concerned that this would be a problem. Despite the flak, we decided to take our chances and go ahead with the idea. The only exception was Special Forces. Their missions were too sensitive to risk embedding reporters with them.

As time passed, it became obvious that Saddam was playing games with the United Nations. He was requiring the U.N. weapons inspectors to give a week's notice before their inspections. This gave him ample time to move whatever chemical or biological weapons he had, including, according to some intel reports, moving them to Syria or Lebanon. In November 2002, the United Nations backed us up with Resolution 1441. It reiterated and confirmed Iraq's many breaches of its obligations to cooperate with U.N. weapons inspectors. It also reaffirmed that the United Nations had authorized the use of "all necessary means to uphold and implement" Iraqi compliance. But it became clear over time that the U.N. Security Council would never explicitly authorize the United States to use force. I've yet to see any journalist provide an in-depth account of the vested interests that some members of the U.N. Security Council had in never going to war in Iraq. The permanent members of the U.N. Security Council are the United States, Great Britain, China, Russia, and France. The last three, as well as Germany, had substantial business interests in Iraq that helped determine their opposition to war:

- China had billions of dollars in building contracts in Iraq, including major infrastructure projects such as phone and underground electrical systems. From 1981 to 2001, China was the second largest supplier of weapons and arms to Iraq, supplying more than 18 percent of Iraq's weapons imports. The China National Oil Company had negotiated a twenty-two-year deal for future oil exploration in the Al Ahdab field in southern Iraq.

- The former Soviet Union was the premier supplier of Iraqi arms. From 1981 to 2001, Russia supplied Iraq with 50 percent of its arms, and a carryover of Soviet-era debt of between $7 and $8 billion was generated by unpaid arms sales to Iraq during the 1980 to 1988 Iran–Iraq War. In 2002, Russia and Iraq reportedly signed a $40 billion economic agreement to allow for extensive Russian oil exploration in western Iraq. Russia's LUKoil negotiated a $4 billion, twenty-three-year contract in 1997 to rehabilitate the fifteen-billion-barrel West Qurna oil field in southern Iraq. Three Russian firms are suspected of selling electronic jamming equipment, antitank missiles, and thousands of night-vision goggles to Iraq, in violation, of U.N. sanctions. France provided more than 20 percent of Iraq's imports.

- France's total trade with Iraq under the U.N. Oil-for-Food Program had totaled $3.1 billion since 1996, and in 2001, it became Iraq's largest European trading partner. France's largest oil company, Total Fina Elf, had negotiated extensive oil contracts to develop the Majnoon and Nahr Umar oil fields in southern Iraq, estimated to contain as much as 25 percent of the country's oil reserves—an estimated twenty-six billion barrels of oil. Based on the 2002 non-war price of $25 per barrel, the potential gross return from these fields was nearly $650 billion. Iraq owed France an estimated $6 billion in foreign debt accrued from arms sales in the 1970s and 1980s. And finally, French companies had signed contracts with Iraq worth more than $150 million that are suspected of being linked to its military operations. Some of the goods offered by French companies to Iraq, detailed by UN documents, included refrigerated trucks that could be used as storage facilities and mobile laboratories for biological weapons. From 1981 to 2001, France was responsible for more than 13 percent of Iraq's arms imports.

• Germany, whose government also opposed us on the Iraq War, had built a number of the underground tunnels in Iraq that were part of the defense infrastructure of the regime. Germany was owed billions by Iraq in foreign debt generated during the 1980s. Direct trade between Germany and Iraq amounted to about $350 million annually, and another $1 billion reportedly sold through third parties.

Based on all of these countries' vested interests in Iraq, it was clear they would use their UN votes to veto any authorization for war. And the way we saw it, it would be wiser to move forward without waiting for the United Nations' inevitable rejection.

There was much talk in the media that our attacking Iraq jeopardized our Coalition. As the one who personally put the Coalition together and presided over it, I can say with confidence that this was not the case. There were indeed countries in the Coalition that were uncomfortable with the war against Iraq—mostly for political reasons. For this reason, we simply made a second coalition, dedicated solely to countries who would be with us against Iraq. We requisitioned another parking lot at CentCom, filled it with additional trailers—wired with cables for secure phone lines and video teleconferences—and put the Iraqi Coalition in there. But the first Coalition—the one against terror—always remained intact. It did not suffer at all. Of the then fifty-five Coalition nations united against terror, only one of these withdrew—Yemen—and even Yemen rejoined the Coalition in late spring of 2003. Today, the Coalition against terror includes sixty-four nations, and is still growing.

On the contrary, as world opinion galvanized, more and more flags rose from the tops of the single- and double-wide trailers that served as offices for the Coalition members in Tampa. Stressed and sleep-deprived, I would often gaze through CentCom's windows and gain strength from the rows of flags dancing in the Florida breeze. I felt so strongly about the Coalition, I would never advocate anything that endangered it. During one of countless video teleconferences with administration and CentCom officials, I said, "In my mind, the Coalition is more important than the mission." This stopped the proceedings for a moment; nobody knew what to make of such a statement. Eventually, many of those wearing befuddled looks came to understand my point. To this day, I believe the unity of the world's countries in the fight against terror is more powerful than the fight itself.

In the midst of all of this, President Bush came down to visit CentCom. General Franks was gone, so I had the president for the day. Ten thousand people were there to see him, and I introduced him to the crowd.

As he finished his speech and was walking back to the car, I turned to him. "Mr. President, I've got fifty-five members of the Coalition nations here who, in my words, don't believe you like or trust the U.N.," I said. "I know it's not on your schedule, but if you could give them a short talk and answer questions, it would do a world of wonder for boosting their morale."

He looked at me. A smile slowly crossed his face.

"I'm the president," he said. "I'm a professional politician. You watch me. I'll go in there and knock their socks off. If I don't, hit me in the chest with your elbow when I come out."

I said I wasn't sure I'd hit him with my elbow (especially with his Secret Service officers hovering around him), but I was grateful that he'd talk to them.

He did talk to them, and they loved him—he got a standing ovation.

When he walked out, he came over to me, smiling, and elbowed *me* in the chest.

He said, "How did I do?"

I said, "You were magnificent."

And he was. Equally important, they got to talk to the president of the United States.

As war seemed imminent, we pressed our case with Turkey. A "yes" from them would mean we could open a whole northern front. It would have a significant impact either way, and we needed to plan.

The Turkish military was behind us. Historically, the Turkish military ran the government, and if this situation had occurred in the past, they probably would have approved our plan immediately. In recent times, however, the Turks, had elected a civilian government toward which the military was deferential. The decision was now up to the parliament and the people. They didn't want a war in their backyard. And they also claimed that we promised to pay them millions of dollars after the first Gulf War, money that they had not received. They were wary, to say the least.

To complicate matters, Turkey was within the territory of European Command (EUCOM), not CentCom. It was in their area of responsibility. The American unified commands are very territorial; each command not unlike a feudal fiefdom. The commands controls their AORs; if you cross the border into another AOR, it falls under another command's authority, and you no longer have any say. Thus, it was EUCOM's responsibility to deal with Turkey and get us a positive response.

For whatever reason, their efforts weren't working; they weren't able to deliver Turkey. And the closer we got to kickoff, the more we needed Turkey. Franks wasn't happy; Rumsfeld wasn't happy; and the president wasn't happy. It became obvious that we would not get Turkey (although EUCOM helped us a lot by providing senior liaison officers in Turkey and Israel). But we were prepared, and by then had alternate plans in place.

As war seemed imminent, we scrambled to make sure everything was in place. A year and a half of planning was coming to a close. We had already clandestinely shipped nearly one hundred thousand troops to the region, along with equipment, weaponry, and supplies. We had also upgraded the airports, ports, and bases that we expected we might need to use. As the final thirty days approached, there was less need to be clandestine. We started openly moving troops and carriers to the region. The buildup was accelerating at an incredible pace.

In January 2003, our deployable CentCom headquarters was finally ready. We had been constructing the deployable headquarters since January 2002, and working on the concept since the fall of 2000. Franks wanted something in place, in the AOR, that could be moved from country to country, depending on the event.

This was a massive operation, a warehouse outfitted to house fifteen hundred CentCom troops and staff to live and work while at war. We could have run the Iraq War out of Tampa, but it's just not the same. It's crucial to be in the same time zone, to be closer to the action, and for the troops, psychologically, to know that you are part of the action.

In February 2003, it was time to test it out. I took a trip to Qatar with a small staff to put it through its first dry run. By then, 150 of the eventual 1,500 CentCom staffers were on site; we'd been shipping them from Tampa, while at the same time bringing in more personnel to Tampa to make sure we weren't left empty handed. The headquarters was already filled with flat-screen monitors, computers, and operations and intel centers. I spent a week there going through all the systems, putting the command station through drills and mock battles that were tied back into Tampa. We made sure everything ran smoothly and worked out all the kinks. We didn't want any surprises. Incidentally, the Qatar base is now where the current commander of CentCom, General John Abizaid, spends most of his time.

When I returned to Tampa at the end of February, Franks was preparing to go to Qatar. If I'd had my preference, I would have been stationed in Qatar for the course of the war. Franks knew that. But he also knew that the Coalition needed me. I was the one who had built it, and I was the one who was holding the nations together. We were able to bring the active combat members of the Coalition to Qatar, but the vast majority remained in Tampa. If I had gone to Qatar, it would have jeopardized the Coalition, and we couldn't take that chance. With Franks gone and Abizaid gone, we'd also need someone to run the staff of more than two thousand in Tampa, and we'd need an afternoon answer man for Rumsfeld and the Department of Defense. Tampa was where I was needed, and I knew that. Again, I was the good soldier.

Before Franks left, he pulled me aside.

"I'm sorry you're not going there with me," he said, "because we've been in this together for two years."

"So am I," I said.

"If we get fired upon, we reserve the right to attack Iraq." That's what Israeli officials told us.

Israel had been hit by Scuds in the first Gulf War, and at U.S. insistence had not retaliated. This time, they told us, if Iraq fired on them they would hit back hard. This was the last thing we wanted. The Israelis are some of the best fighters in the world, but if they entered the war, it would be seen as a joint U.S. and Israel attack on Iraq. That would alienate all of our Arab allies, cost us bases throughout the region, and severely hamper our efforts. We could not allow this to happen. We sent a three-star general from EUCOM to Israeli headquarters, and kept him there. We wanted our lines of communication to be as open as possible. But at the end of the day, they said, "We still reserve the right to attack." It was one more concern, and one more reason we needed to take out the Scuds in western Iraq early.

To prepare for this, before the war began we sent SpecialOps teams through the huge, porous borders between Saudi Arabia, Jordan, and Iraq, where there was no clear perimeter. Our Special Forces once again would be the key. Under the command of then one-star Army general Gary Harrell— a twenty-five year SpecialOps veteran who had been badly wounded in Somalia—we sent about fifty teams into western Iraq. There were about three hundred of them, dressed as native Iraqis. We broke them up into small teams and spread them throughout the area so they would be impossible to spot as a single attacking force. We knew roughly where the Scuds were, and had half the SpecialOps teams get into position to take them when the time came. Once there, they had a lot of time on their hands to do nothing but wait—and remain undetected. When the signal came, they would have to take out the Scuds, either by capturing or destroying them. All of these Scuds were manned and could launch a missle within minutes of Hussein's command, so our troops would have to move quickly. It was hurry up and wait.

The other half of the SpecialOps forces took positions near the Iraqi border observation posts. There were more than a hundred of these towers, serving as Saddam's western eyes. When the time came, SpecialOps would have to blow them all up.

Up until the last minute, we were still trying to "what-if" everything. We had bases in Bahrain, UAE, Kuwait, Qatar, Oman, Saudi Arabia, and Jordan and were flying sorties through Egypt, and we wanted to make sure all of our troops were prepared in case Hussein fired a Scud at them. These countries were our partners in the Mideast, and we didn't want them getting hit either. So we started to make sure all the appropriate air defenses were in place, in case they had to shoot down Scuds.

We got decontamination units in place. We made sure our troops had at least two sets of nuclear-biochemical suits. We made sure we had enough of the right kinds of weapons at the right bases to match the airplanes we would use. We made sure we had all of our Tomahawk shooters in the right positions to launch their missiles.

We updated target lists. Unlike Afghanistan, Iraq had plenty of targets. At the top of the list were potential nuclear, chemical, and biological weapons sites. We didn't want to bomb these, because of the risk of dispersing toxic fallout, so the plan was to take them with ground forces. We targeted anything that provided power to any weapon system, for example, electrical power plants giving power to air defense systems. We couldn't bomb these, though; we would have to take them out with special types of weapons to make sure they were out only temporarily. We were already thinking of Iraq's future, and wanted to be able to reconstruct these speedily. This made it much more time consuming, but we wanted it done the right way. We targeted intel and military headquarters, the Republican Guard leadership, and other strategic locations. "Surgical" was the key word—we wanted to be able to put a bomb through a particular window of a particular building and leave the rest of it intact.

On February 27, 2003, UN weapons inspector Hans Blix reported, "Iraq still hasn't committed to disarming." The moments ticked heavily as the final days approached. Our Special Ops were already in Iraq, sitting in the desert, waiting. We had a massive buildup of troops in the region, and such a concentration of troops is always a target—especially in the Mideast. At this point, every day of waiting was dangerous.

On March 17, 2003, Bush delivered his forty-eight-hour ultimatum to Saddam to leave the country with his sons, and the world watched. What the world didn't see was that approximately eighteen hours after he'd delivered the ultimatum, Bush summoned all of his commanders of the ground, sea, air, and SpecialOps forces, and Franks and me, for a final video teleconference. The time had come.

One by one, the president asked each of us the same question: "Are you comfortable with what we're about to do?"

Each answered, "I am."

The president turned to me just before he turned to Franks. "I am," I said. "And what I am most comfortable about is that we have not lost our focus on

Afghanistan and not forgotten the War on Terror. We're ready to go in Iraq, but we're also ready to go in Afghanistan. If anybody asks, we are not doing anything to jeopardize the war on terrorism in Afghanistan."

That was the truth, and I said it because many in the media were arguing that we were diverting resources needed for the war on terrorism by preparing to attack Iraq. From where I was sitting, that was simply untrue. We didn't need to divert a single trooper from Afghanistan to Iraq. The Afghan War and the anti-terror Coalition did not suffer one bit. In fact, few people know that the very same day we launched our attack against Iraq, we also launched a massive operation in Afghanistan. The timing was coincidental, as we had no idea when the Iraq d-day would be. But we were able to handle both. The U.S. and the Coalition forces were that good. President Bush liked that. The reason I gave him that answer was because I wanted him to hear it from us and feel confident that was the case, so that when reporters should ask him that question, he could answer it confidently and comfortably. I was giving him a sound byte. Indeed, over the following days, I saw him use it.

As the video teleconference wound down, President Bush was in a somber mood. He was very presidential at that moment, and you could see that the decision to go to war was not one he had taken lightly. I am apolitical, and always have been. But I must say that in my interactions with President Bush he struck me as a man of strength and resolve; nothing could be further from the truth than the idea that he is dependent on his powerful Cabinet and on his advisors. I saw a man who handled proceedings with dignity and decisiveness, a man who made everyone feel comfortable while making one thing perfectly clear: He was in charge. Anyone who didn't know the participants could have told you within a minute, "That man's the president." If the public could see his National Security Council meetings and watch how he handled himself, I think they'd have a very positive opinion about him. He concluded the conference. "I believe the military forces of the country are in a position to do what must be done. You have the execution order. H-hour will be at the time specified."

All we could do was sit and wait. We watched, along with the rest of the country. We knew the time had come.

As it turned out, H-hour would be sooner than we thought.

On hour forty of the forty-eight-hour ultimatum, I received an urgent phone call from the chairman of the Joint Chiefs of Staff, General Richard Myers, calling from the Situation Room at the White House. Also on the line were Rumsfeld, Tenet, and Franks (who was already in our forward base in Qatar). Tenet had intel on where Saddam and his sons were sleeping. Tenet, Rumsfeld, and Myers had briefed the president, telling him he'd have to act fast.

"No," Bush had said. "I gave Saddam forty-eight hours, and I'm a man of my word. I said forty-eight hours and he'll get forty-eight hours."

The other men in the room were taken aback. Was Bush letting Saddam and his sons slip away, perhaps losing a chance to prevent the entire war, because he had given his word? It was a character-defining moment.

Now Tenet, Rumsfeld, and Myers wanted to know if we could still hit Saddam and his sons in that bunker after the forty-eight-hour mark, and if we could reach him in the deep cement-reinforced bunker he was in.

Franks conferred with his two-star operations general Gene Renuart and the Chief of Staff of the Air Force.

"It can't be a daylight strike," Franks said. "Too risky. And we can't use Tomahawks—they're already pre-positioned for other targets. Changing their positions at this late hour would screw up our air defense plan. We can do it, but we need to use F-117 Stealth Bombers. They're the only planes with bombs to reach deep enough."

"Would it screw up the war plan?" Rumsfeld asked.

"No," Franks said. "Before the war, we set aside several planes for a contingency like this. They're target-of-opportunity planes. It won't affect the plan at all."

"So can we do it?"

"There is a very small window between the expiration of the forty-eight hours and daylight. It's tight, but yes, they can do it. There's a full moon, and they'll be visible, and we haven't taken out Iraqi air defense yet—but we can clear the path for them as they go. We can do it."

"Let's do it," Rumsfeld said.

Franks ordered the two Stealth Bombers into the air. They were on their way to Iraq, hours before anyone else, two planes flying beneath a full moon, into a hostile country full of intact air defense systems. It was a brave mission and a bold choice. If successful, their strike could end the war before it began.

Chapter Five

IRAQ

"If we use a term from Soviet doctrine, it is 'inside the decision cycle.' Our forces were actually inside the ability of the enemy to react. The Iraqi forces were forty-eight to seventy-two hours behind our ability to see what they were doing."

—General Tommy Franks

THE TWO F-117 STEALTH BOMBERS began their three-hour flight to the Iraqi border, but were instructed not to cross Iraqi air space until given the command. They each carried two two-thousand-pound bombs, powerful enough to penetrate Saddam's deepest bunkers. If Saddam was there, he would, at the very least, have a bad headache.

In the CentCom base in Qatar, everyone around Franks was nervous. The CentCom Air Force generals, especially, were worried about the mission. Franks remained calm, though.

"Breathe through your nose," he said.

It was a trademark Franks phrase, and it calmed them—especially because it wasn't a request.

Finally, our jet pilots were given the command to enter Iraqi air space. They began the next two-hour leg of their flight, on their way to Saddam's bunker. As they went, we fired Tomahawk missiles from our naval carriers hundreds of miles away, targeting Iraqi air defense in the bombers' path. The Tomahawks landed on Iraqi air defense systems with absolutely perfect timing and precision. The coordination was incredible. Air defense systems blew up under the Stealth Bombers minutes before they flew over them. The jet pilots would have witnessed one explosion after the other, as if they were leaving a trail of devastation in their wake. So effective were the Tomahawks that not a single Iraqi missile was fired at our bombers that night.

Finally, the Stealth Bombers reached Saddam Hussein's preferred sleeping location for the night. It was a simple, anonymous, residential house, underneath which lay a German-built cement-reinforced bunker. The stealth jets dropped their bombs minutes after the forty-eight-hour ultimatum and minutes before daylight. They achieved their window. The explosion was tremendous.

The CIA's man on the scene witnessed the hit. But for whatever reason, he couldn't confirm or deny whether Saddam was dead. We knew we had to get somebody in there to go through the ruins and get a DNA sample, but that couldn't happen right away, and without that, we'd have to assume he was alive.

A lot of naysayers came out in the days that followed and said the decapitation strike screwed up the overall plan. But they were wrong. We were prepared for the unexpected, and using the Stealth Bombers did not alter anything. That flexibility was part of Franks's plan.

Bombing the bunker might, however, have instigated an Iraqi move towards the southern oil fields. We got intel that five divisions of the Iraqi regular army were mobilizing. We knew the fifteen hundred wellheads in the south were Iraqi targets. Even more troubling, our Predators showed us that three wellheads were already on fire. It didn't make any sense, because the Iraqi army hadn't reached those yet. We knew they'd been mined. Were they getting ready to blow them all? We had to move. If we waited twenty-four hours, we would lose our chance to save them.

The final plan had called for twenty-four hours of bombing first, to be followed by the ground forces. It would have given the ground forces some comfort and yet would still have caught the Iraqis by surprise, as bombing campaigns often last weeks before ground forces arrive. But if we wanted to save those oil wells—which we had to—the ground forces had to move now. The key to our plan was flexibility; if the ground forces had to go first, they were ready.

"Tell the Marines to accelerate their ground movement by twenty-four hours," Franks ordered our ground commander, Army Lieutenant General David McKiernan. With that, the ground war began.

In the south, taking the fifteen hundred oil fields was the responsibility of the 1st Marine Division, assisted by a British commando division. They raced toward Basra to capture the oil wells intact. It was a tall order; many things could go wrong. If we had a firefight at the wells, we could accidentally blow them. If we captured the wells intact, our boys still had to shut down the complex well system in the proper order; turning one wrong valve in the high-pressure system could blow them all. If the wells were destroyed, it would have been an environmental disaster and would have cost U.S. taxpayers additional billions of dollars to clean up the mess and rebuild the wells. At stake, though, was far more than money: if these wells blew, it could spread the pollution as far as India, and spark one of the greatest environmental disasters of all time.

Before they could even begin to roll, the ground forces first had to blow holes in thousands of massive sand barriers the Iraqis had constructed along the Kuwaiti border, stretching from one end of the desert to the other. The Iraqis had set up watch posts behind these barriers to target artillery on approaching forces. They thought the U.S. and Coalition tanks would have to drive over or through the barriers, which would make them easy targets for their artillery.

But we were prepared. Before the war kicked off, we had sent combat engineers (demolition experts) to rig the barriers with explosives. When the time came to kick off the ground war, we simply blew holes in them and rolled right through. Simultaneously, our pilots flew in and bombed all of the Iraqi watch posts and artillery positions.

The Marines made good time, reaching the oil wells in just a few hours. We had expected fierce resistance along the way, but there was little. We had expected the wells to be heavily guarded, but they were not. We had caught the Iraqis by surprise. They really thought we would never kick off a ground war without a prolonged air war first. Our boys did a fine job securing and shutting down the wells properly. By the end of day one, the wells were ours. It was a huge relief.

Using air power and SpecialOps, we launched attacks across Iraq on March 19. In the north, we began the air attack. We pounded their air defense, the eleven divisions of the regular Iraqi army, the two Republican Guard divisions, and other key targets. We had to, because without Turkey's permission to launch a ground invasion, the only way we could get our troops into the north was by air. We couldn't fly them in while the Iraqi air defense was still intact, and we needed to get them in there quickly to secure the north's one thousand oil wells and to keep the Kurds from engaging in aggressive actions that might bring Turkey into the war against them.

Our constant bombing in the north also helped add to the Iraqi regime's confusion. As we'd hoped, thirteen Iraqi divisions stayed frozen, expecting an invasion in the north. Our bombing, our ships off the coast of Turkey loaded with the U.S. Army's 4th Infantry Division, and our months of feeding the Iraqis misinformation had tricked Saddam. Up to the last minute he really thought we would use Turkey and invade from the north. Through deception alone, we had immobilized thirteen of his divisions.

Another relief was that the Kurds were behaving. They were not attacking the Iraqis, and the Iraqis were not attacking them either, which was also a relief. Additionally, the Turks were not invading the Kurdish territory. There was a lot of noise in the first few days that the Turks were sending troops into the Kurdish territory. This wasn't accurate. The Turks had always had a number of troops stationed in Northern Iraq; they did nothing unusual in those first few days or throughout the war—and neither did the Kurds. So far, things were going exactly as we had hoped.

In the west, our Special Forces, moving with speed and surprise, blew all the Iraqi observation posts and destroyed all the Scuds. They did a magnificent job. As a result of their efforts, Saddam wasn't able to fire a single missile at Israel or Jordan. As it turned out, Saddam had several Scuds hidden in southeastern Iraq, and he managed to fire about twenty of them at Kuwait. Our Patriot air defense missiles easily shot most of them down. The ones we chose not to hit landed harmlessly in the Kuwaiti desert or in the Gulf. Kuwait took no casualties.

Our Special Forces also managed to blow all of the Iraqi observation posts in the west. With the observation posts gone, Iraq no longer had any eyes in the west, and our troops could move freely. In the south, Saddam hadn't flooded the plains, another relief. He hadn't used any chemical or biological weapons yet either. Overall, there was a tremendous amount to be relieved about on that first day. Through great planning, speed, surprise, and excellent execution, our worst fears had been averted. There is so much Saddam could have done that he just did not do—and it's a mystery as to why. The Iraqi troops we captured and debriefed insisted that we had caught Saddam by surprise. Despite President Bush's forty-eight-hour ultimatum, Saddam had not believed the United States would attack—at worst, he had thought we might bomb Iraq for a few days. He didn't believe America had the stomach or the will for a full-scale invasion, especially if we didn't have a Turkish front. He was about to see how wrong he had been.

Within two days of kicking off Operation Iraqi Freedom, our forces had advanced more than 150 miles into Iraq, nearly halfway to Baghdad. To move an army that big that fast was unprecedented. Baghdad was our objective, and our troops took different routes to get there.

We sent the 1st Marine Expeditionary Force (MEF) and the Brits in a northeastern direction, toward Um Qasr and Basra. In addition to taking the oil fields, their job was to protect the right flank of the 3rd Army and defeat Iraqi divisions that could attack our rear, which would allow the 3rd Army to race straight up the middle toward Baghdad. We needed the 1st MEF and the Brits in the Um Qasr area for other reasons, too: Saddam had placed many divisions in the Basra area, and we had to confront them. If we didn't, we'd leave our rear wide open for attack. Additionally, Um Qasr was a port city; if we secured it, we could open the waters to ship supplies directly into Iraq, especially humanitarian supplies.

In the south central front, the 3rd Army raced due north for Baghdad. The first real resistance they hit was in the outskirts of the southern city of An Nasiriyah. We initially attempted to skirt the city, but the resistance from the Iraqi divisions there was too heavy. We diverted units to a fight that would rage for days while the bulk of the army continued to Baghdad.

We would find that the main points of resistance in our race to Baghdad would be on the outskirts of the major cities and at the river crossings. To get to Baghdad you have to cross bridges over the Euphrates and Tigris rivers, the two major rivers in Iraq. The bridges were tactical, as are bridges in every war. We were prepared. Days before the war kicked off, we sent in recon units to secure as many bridges as they could. They caught the Iraqis off guard, wiped them out, and secured many bridges. The Iraqis had mined and set most of their bridges for demolition before the war began, but we took so many so quickly that they were hardly able to blow any of them, and we captured most of them intact. This advance work by the recon units made many bridge crossings easier for the 3rd Army when the time came and allowed us to maintain our speed.

But some Iraqi bridges were heavily manned, and the recon units couldn't get to all of them. For these, we'd just have to wait for the regular forces to arrive and fight it out. That's one of the issues of waging a war with such a huge army: Everything comes on a grander scale. You can't capture one bridge—you have to capture a hundred. Sometimes we brought our own bridges. We had a corps of engineers that could place a bridge over a small river in a few hours. But that took time, manpower, and trucks. We didn't have that kind of time. Our preferred recourse was to save the ones we could.

In the first few days of the war, hundreds of small battles took place all over Iraq, and a lot of these were waged at river crossings. Our soldiers fought magnificently, with many medals handed out for bravery and hero-ism. We used airpower whenever possible to support the ground forces around the bridges, but we had to be careful not to bomb the bridges them-selves. We wanted most of them intact for us. We fought, but no matter what, we kept moving.

We were, in fact, criticized for moving so fast. We were advancing an unprecedented number of miles for an army that size. Critics said that we were moving too fast for our logistical units to catch up, that we would find ourselves outflanked and lacking supplies, fuel, and ammo. Embedded reporters complained that we had to abandon tanks that didn't have enough gas (not true). Our critics were wrong. The plan was to never pause, to never allow the enemy time to react, time to move into a better defensive position, or time to retreat to Baghdad or other major cities for urban combat. We had truck battalions in place to rush fuel and ammo up the line. We knew it wouldn't be easy, and it wasn't. We knew this would leave us with little secu-rity behind us, especially on the long roads between us and the supply units, and it did. But we also expected to keep the Iraqis too off-balance to take advantage of the risks we ran.

This is where the fedayeen came in. The fedayeen were paramilitary units of Saddam's secret police. We knew they existed, but we thought they would stay in Baghdad. This, for us, was one of the first surprises of the war. That said, the fedayeen were not the horribly menacing force the press made them out to be. They were sneaky. They attacked convoys in the rear, mainly hit-ting our gas trucks and logistical units on their shuttle runs. They were trained killers, ruthlessly murdering Iraqi civilians who fled the cities or sur-rendered to the Coalition. But what the press didn't understand was that the fedayeen were not good *military* fighters. They were not trained to fight an army, and were not effective as a military unit. They were great to terrorize civilians in the cities, but in the field they were less effective than even the regular Iraqi military. And they were cowardly and stupid. After they were done fighting for the day, they collapsed back into the cities—An Nasiriyah,

Najaf, Karbala—parking their trucks outside their headquarters. All we had to do was call in air strikes with choppers and fixed-wing aircraft. From then on, things did not go well for the fedayeen.

Early on, Army Lieutenant General David McKiernan came up with the idea of the "thunder run." It began in the smaller cities. The idea was that tanks and armored personnel carriers would batten down, close their latches, and race through the streets of a hostile city at full speed. They would inevitably get shot at with small arms fire and even RPGs. Anytime someone fired at them, they would fire back with their 120mm cannons, inflicting a devastating amount of damage upon the assailant. The Abrams tank is the best tank in the world, and could come out unscathed from even a direct hit from an RPG. The tanks never stopped, and never even slowed. As they went, they delivered messages over their loud speakers to surrender. After several runs, the Iraqis learned to stop firing back. By taking multiple thunder runs throughout a city, we could clear a city relatively quickly and safely.

By March 21, the second day of the ground assault, Iraq's 51st Army Division, consisting of approximately eight thousand men, surrendered in the south. We had been watching the 51st—we had been working on them for weeks before the war through our InformationOps, using our human intel contacts, targeting their highest leadership, dropping leaflets showing them how to surrender (as we did throughout Iraq). By day ten of the war, we had nine Iraqi generals surrender into our custody, which told us we were doing something right.

Our air campaign had begun on day two. We pounded key targets throughout the country, including leadership targets, military targets, air defense, and Iraqi regular army and Republican Guard divisions. If Iraqi divisions surrendered, we spared them from bombing; if they didn't, they paid the price. Ironically, it helped us that Saddam had been firing on our planes in the no-fly zones for twelve years—it had given us twelve years to target his air defenses. The level of precision achieved by our Navy, Air Force, and Marine bombers was spectacular. They were putting bombs through a particular window of a particular building from thousands of feet above, leaving the rest of the building intact. After a day or two, the Iraqi civilians realized this. They knew we wouldn't hit them, and they weren't scared. As our pilots flew missions, they saw Iraqi civilians walking out in the open, going to the market as usual, confident that they wouldn't be hit.

In the north, our SpecialOps, in conjunction with the Kurds, took control of the thousand northern oil fields. Our bombing continued around the clock there, hitting key targets in Mosul and Kirkuk, both major oil-producing cities, and clearing the way for an imminent landing of our airborne units that were waiting in Italy.

As the first few days of the war progressed, it became apparent that the embedded reporters were a great success. They were bringing great human-interest stories of the sons and daughters, husbands and wives of our forces into American living rooms in a way that can only be described as historic. They put a human face on the war, and this is what we needed. We needed America on our side.

During a video teleconference, the excitement started with the president and worked its way through everyone down the line. We were experiencing much fewer casualties than we'd expected. Thus far, everything was going to plan. We were not resting on our heels, but we were breathing easier. Baghdad was on the horizon, and things were looking up.

Then the weather changed.

On day three of the war, we got hit by raging sandstorms. They can hit at any time in Iraq, but they tend to hit most frequently in the summer, so we didn't expect it. When a sandstorm hits, it's very hard for our choppers to fly; they have GPS, but no visibility. Our troops can't be walking about; our tanks, like our choppers, have GPS but no visibility. Even our jets are affected: They drop laser-guided bombs, but lasers are guided by light, and sand refracts light, so when a storm hits, the laser splatters the marks all over the place and the accuracy drops dramatically. The storm lasted for days, and it slowed us to a crawl.

Of course, the talking heads immediately took to the airwaves. They claimed we were stopped by our logistics, not the weather. At every turn, Franks' war plan was questioned. There were constant complaints within the military that we were running to Baghdad too fast, that our boys were overextended and unprotected. As usual, they were wrong.

Even worse, armchair generals and retired-generals-(or even majors or colonels)-turned-commentators, such as future presidential candidate Wesley Clark and former drug czar Barry McCaffrey, offered opinions and predictions that were often wrong. They were out of the loop—in some cases had been for many years—and they succeeded only in misguiding American public opinion.

For example, when the term "shock and awe" was introduced, television commentators warned viewers to prepare for the most explosive and overwhelming display of military might ever seen. The American public was anticipating Genghis Khan with space-age technology, but that wasn't the intention. The intention was reliable, precision bombing meant to shock the regime into expecting a missile through the window. So when shock and awe started, people were disappointed. We told anyone who would listen that shock and awe signified focused firepower when we wanted it and where we wanted it. We could bomb a building and leave windows next door unbroken. It was "shocking" in its precision and "awesome" in its reliability. But you didn't get that from the retired generals. And if the public believed them, they were suddenly against us for no reason.

In some cases, networks wanted to get commentators on the cheap, or were so desperate for experts that they even put retired colonels and majors on the air—again, some were good and some were not. They were all disseminating mixed information (and sometimes dire predictions) to the American public, and this made our lives much harder. We often had to divert people to address or refute what had been said. And when they "guessed" correctly, that was even worse: They were giving away tactics to the enemy, potentially putting our troops in harm's way.

The media commentators weren't a petty nuisance for me—they were a constant pain. This was a touchy issue, because most of them were decorated and respected men who had served their country honorably. To come out and criticize them for not understanding the war wasn't always the best decision. They were also protected by the First Amendment (as they should be), and had a right to express their opinions. They weren't technically giving away state secrets, as they were just guessing. In reality, though, some of them were giving away secrets, and were being harmful. Rumsfeld and Myers were livid with these guys. During one news conference, Myers took them to task for a particularly ill-informed day of commentating. Afterwards I called him and said, "Thank you, General, I want you to know you made my day."

In fact, at our request, Myers went to all four service chiefs and told them to call their retired generals and ask them to be more responsible. It helped, some, but not enough. There is no simple solution, but I do know that things need to change. A standard needs to be put in place.

At this time we received word that the Iraqi police were deserting. They knew we were opposed to the Ba'ath Party, and in Iraq under Saddam, the Ba'ath Party had run everything, including the police. They didn't want to be held accountable after the war. It was another development we did not expect, and it did not bode well for the state of order and lawfulness in the wake of the war. But there wasn't anything we could do about it—we were in the midst of fighting the war, and all we could do was hope they would come back to their jobs after the hostilities were over. Otherwise, we'd have a big problem on our hands.

A more immediate problem for us, though, was Iraqi fighters dressing as civilians (sometimes even as women), or pretending to surrender, then firing on our troops. They also entrenched themselves at hospitals, mosques, schools, and other civilian, religious, and archeological buildings they knew we didn't want to hit. We realized very soon that we were up against a different kind of fighter.

We received intel that Saddam had authorized the use of prohibited weapons once the Coalition forces crossed a pre-set "red line." This was serious, especially because we also had intel that Saddam had equipped his Republican Guard with two new chemical/biological suits apiece, along with atropine (an antidote used to shield the attacker in chemical attacks). We were increasingly worried that we'd have to be prepared for the worst. We knew that Saddam could only use them once, but still, once was enough to do serious damage. One key to stopping Saddam from using "prohibited weapons" was proximity. If we were close to his own troops, Saddam couldn't gas us unless he wanted to kill them, too. That meant speed. Every hour we sat in that sandstorm was hurting us, because it kept us from closing with the enemy.

We were having early problems in Basra, too. After the first two days of fighting, the people of Basra had little fresh water or power, due both to collateral damage and to the sabotage of the fedayeen. United Nations secretary-general Kofi Annan said that "urgent measures" were needed; he was right. The key to helping the people of Basra was our taking the port of Um

Qasr, so that we could ship in humanitarian supplies in bulk. The problem was that Saddam had mined the ports. We couldn't get our ships in without blowing them. So we swept for mines and, in one of the little-known stories of the war, we used dolphins to help us. We had them trained to find the hidden mines, and they did a wonderful job, working around the clock. Until the ports were clear, we brought in hundreds of thousands of water bottles by driving them up the coast in trucks.

Also at this time we received a report that twelve of our soldiers had been captured or killed by Iraqi guerrilla forces outside of An Nasiriyah. They were a maintenance and logistics crew assigned to the 507th Maintenance Company, 3rd Infantry Division. Traveling in a truck convoy, they had gotten lost in the middle of the night and had driven into enemy territory. Among them was nineteen-year-old Private Jessica Lynch.

Shortly afterwards, the Arab television network Al Jazeera aired footage of captured American troops. We could see that they had been severely mistreated; there were dead bodies in the background, with bullets in their heads, wearing U.S. uniforms. We knew we had to move quickly if we wanted to save the rest. But we had no idea where they were. We had made it a priority to keep our emotions out of it, but this hit us hard. Franks put out a statement to all of the troops: "I want to execute a quick, well-thought-out plan to repatriate surviving U.S. military personnel. The plan will be executed on short order once we have a location."

If there was a low point to the war, this was it, with the POWs, the sandstorm, the renewed expectation of chemical warfare, the delays in taking and getting humanitarian aid to Basra, and the intel indicating that deserting Iraqi police might leave us with lawless cities. Then, as suddenly as it had begun, the storm lifted. Once again, we picked up the pace toward Baghdad. After several days of fierce fighting, we took most of Basra, the key point in southeast Iraq, though there remained significant pockets of resistance. Nearly one-third of the Iraqi army's strength lay in the Basra area. We also finally finished demining the port of Um Qasr, and got our ships in with their humanitarian supplies. We quickly distributed the supplies to the civilians of Basra and a crisis was averted. With the help of the Red Cross, we were also able to partially repair the Basra water facilities, so they could generate their own fresh water. By March 25, they were already back up to 40 percent of functional capacity.

The fedayeen weren't so kind, though. When the citizens of Basra had initially tried to flee, the fedayeen murdered their own countrymen. We would avenge them, first by hitting the fedayeen headquarters in Basra (filled with about two hundred assembled fedayeen) and then by targeting scores of Iraqi soldiers and fedayeen on the road south from Basra towards Um Qasr. We couldn't tell if they were fleeing Basra or trying to attack us in Um Qasr, but it didn't matter. We hit them on the way before they could even get close. British bombers took out a column of seventy Iraqi armored vehicles.

The British had a huge impact on the fight; they were doing an excellent job. We positioned them in Basra to keep the city under control (indeed, they would fight off major counterattacks), and free up our Marine divisions to move toward An Nasiriyah and back up our other troops.

An Nasiriyah was the site of probably some of the fiercest and most prolonged fighting of the war. This was partly because Saddam had positioned many of his divisions in the South, hoping to stop us before we began, and partly because the city was home to key Euphrates River bridges on the route to Baghdad. We couldn't skirt it. Battles raged with machine gun fire, mortars, tanks, and helicopter units involved. Marines and Iraqi fighters squared off on either side of the Euphrates. After nearly nine days of hard fighting, we took the city. To make it safe, we still had to go block by block, eliminating paramilitary units loyal to Saddam.

Meanwhile, the 101st Airborne was moving up towards Najaf, a city about a hundred miles directly south of Baghdad, and the 3rd Army was moving with lightning speed to Fallujah, a strategic city about thirty miles directly west of Baghdad. The 1st Marine Division, fresh from its victories in the south, joined in the race for Fallujah to support the rear of the 3rd Army. We were on the move everywhere.

Between Najaf and Baghdad lay the strategic city of Karbala. About fifty miles south of Baghdad, Karbala was home to two Republican Guard divisions—Medina and Baghdad—which was not unusual, given its proximity to the capital. From day one, we pounded these divisions with relentless bombing campaigns. It was imperative to us that there be no "Battle of Baghdad," and that meant we couldn't give Saddam a chance to bring his divisions in and circle his wagons. The Republican Guard divisions were the best Iraq had to offer. If we took them out, it would demoralize the rest of the Iraqi army. They tried to retreat to Baghdad, but it was too late. Unless they surrendered, we pounded them constantly, using our jets and Apache attack helicopters to interdict the space between the Iraqi divisions and Baghdad, denying them the ability to move back to the capital city. They were stuck, weakened, and with no chance of retreat, forced to fight our approaching fighters from the south.

In the north, our constant bombing had taken out enough Iraqi air defense for us to fly in our airborne troops. We deployed more than one thousand paratroopers from the 173rd Airborne, stationed in Italy, and flew them in over eastern Jordan, bypassing Turkish air space. We flew troops and equipment into airstrips in northeastern Iraq, which we had secured in advance with U.S. Special Forces and Kurdish troops. They landed safely, and their landing meant we could open a northern front. With them there, we could have a ground presence for the Iraqis to surrender to, keep the Kurds from attacking, keep control of the oil fields, and work our way south to Tikrit and Baghdad. Among their missions was destroying a major Iraq-sponsored terrorist camp in the north, one of the links between Saddam's regime and al-Qaeda.

On March 30, we got a fix on the whereabouts of Army private Jessica Lynch. As it turned out, an Iraqi from a local hospital told a nearby U.S. unit that he thought there was a female American soldier in one of the hospital's rooms. The POWs had been on the forefront of our minds since their capture seven days before, and as soon as we got word, Franks issued an order: "Put an op together and get her out of there. Use all the assets you need."

One of the hardest operations to execute well is the rescue of POWs. The chances are high that the guards will kill the POWs if they see you coming—especially in a scenario like Iraq, where we knew that they had executed some POWs and had badly beaten others. In such a case, you can put POWs at greater risk by trying to rescue them. Successfully rescuing a POW is an enormously intricate operation. There are textbook procedures you must follow. First, you must secure and cordon off the area so nobody can get in or out. You must sever communications, so no one can tip off the people on the inside. You must enter the target site from multiple directions and in multiple ways, to optimize your chances of a guard not getting back to the POW in time. You have to monitor the compound in advance, listen in on their communications, figure out how they operate. In this case, our intel was shaky: Some said the captors had left, others said they were still there. We just didn't know, and we had to prepare for the worst. In such a situation, you always assume the enemy is there.

With such an intricate operation, it's easiest to use a set of forces from one branch of the military. That way, you know everybody, you know how everybody works, and the synchronization is easy. But we didn't have time for that in the case of Private Lynch. It had to be a joint operation if we wanted to get her in time. That meant putting together a rescue squad consisting of Special Forces troops, Marines, Marine helicopters, Air Force fixed-wing aircraft, and Army helicopters. Additionally, we had to get this joint op together within twelve hours. Joint forces don't always work together as smoothly as one would like—especially with such little time to plan. But in the case of the rescue of Jessica Lynch, they came together as one.

The Marines cordoned off the area. The SpecialOps came in the middle of the night. We had a hand-drawn map of where she was, and they used it and broke into the hospital. The place was empty aside from her. Private Lynch looked up, dazed, and said, "I'm a soldier, too."

Getting word of Lynch's rescue—and the subsequent rescue of other POWs two weeks later—was the high point of the war for us. It was the only time since September 11 that we'd felt an outpouring of emotion, the only time since then that we'd allowed ourselves to really feel good about something. From my perspective, as one of the few people on the inside who witnessed the entire rescue op from beginning to end, it was one of the most spectacularly executed rescue operations I'd ever seen. There would be much talk in the media in the months to come (and with the publication of Lynch's own book) that the rescue operation was played up, that we used it for publicity, that Lynch was a product of the military PR machine. But that is not even remotely true; our hearts were pure. No one was in this operation for the publicity—we were in it to save one of our own. We got word where she was and we moved on it. We had no idea what sort of enemy forces we might encounter guarding her, or what other hostile forces were in the area. The troops who executed the operation decided to film it at their own behest (the order didn't come from us), and it was probably a good thing they did, as it turned out to be a textbook example of a rescue and the film can be used to train other soldiers.

The rescue of Jessica Lynch was probably most significant—aside from the rescue itself—in that it was one more indication of how the military is successfully transforming itself from being service-based to being joint-based. More than anything, this was a credit to General Franks: He never allowed service favoritism to determine who or what would do the mission. From day one at CentCom, he set the atmosphere for a joint military. That atmosphere trickled down and influenced every soldier in every branch. They knew they were expected to work together.

An event that was never reported was an internal push to award Private Lynch a medal. The pressure came from politicians in her home state. She was a young, attractive girl from West Virginia, and perhaps the politicians saw in it an opportunity. The first reports that came in stated that she had emptied her weapons into all of the bad guys, that she went down fighting, that she was a hero. Based on this, the politicians wanted to award her the Medal of Honor.

The politicians' request climbed up the ladder until it reached me, and I told them the answer was no. First reports are nearly always wrong. We would have to wait until the final reports had come in, until we knew exactly what she had or had not done. The politicians and I had a heated discussion through a congressional liaison. They called many times, pressuring him to push it through. He would call me, and I would consistently tell him, "Got to wait."

"This is a big deal," they told him. "It would be good for females in the military."

"This has nothing to do with females in the military," I replied. "This has to do with what really happened."

If it turned out she was indeed a hero, we would go through the system. Our early indications, though, were that the reports were wrong. Rumsfeld knew this, and he backed me up. The politicians were overruled.

As it turned out, the initial reports were indeed wrong. Ballistic tests on her weapon showed she never fired a shot. She was merely a passenger in a vehicle that got lost on the road, encountered enemy fire, and crashed. It was a bad crash—some of the troopers aboard died, and Jessica was badly hurt. She didn't fight back—in her condition, she couldn't. There was nothing wrong with her actions, but there was nothing inherently heroic either. I bet that she would agree that she shouldn't be singled out for her actions any more than her fellow captives.

The rest of the war in Iraq was going well. By March 26, we had moved more than 220 miles into Iraq, despite the weather. By March 27, more than one-third of our 290,000 Coalition troops in the Persian Gulf region had entered Iraq, and we'd deployed another 30,000 troops from the Army's 3rd Corps in Fort Hood, Texas. We were preparing for the final stretch. With Lynch's rescue behind us (and soon the rescue of five other POWs), a front established in the north, Nasiriyah and Najaf in our hands, the sandstorms behind us, we could finally home in on the primary goal of our campaign: Baghdad.

In many ways, April 1 marked the turning point of the war. From then on, our momentum built rapidly. Whereas before that date nothing was certain, after April 1 the noose tightened on an already crumbling regime.

That is not to say there was no longer heavy resistance. There was. In Karbala and in the "Karbala Gap" (a twenty- to twenty-five-mile-wide stretch about fifty miles south of Baghdad, between the Euphrates River and Lake Razzaza), there remained significant Republican Guard resistance. We turned more attention to the area. On April 1, after a fierce battle, the Army's 3rd Infantry Division took Karbala, and the 1st Marine Expeditionary Force attacked the Republican Guard's Baghdad division. On April 2, the Marines took a key bridge and crossed the Tigris, and by the end of that day, the Marines had left the Medina and Baghdad Republican Guard divisions badly beaten.

On April 3, the Army's 3rd Infantry, in the face of constant fire, pushed its way through the Karbala Gap. On that same day, the Marines secured a Republican Guard base and an Iraqi air base outside of Kut, a strategic city on the Tigris River forty miles south of Baghdad. The 101st Airborne division came in and took control of Najaf, proving very effective at maintaining order in the captured city. SpecialOps seized one of Saddam's palaces in Tharthar, sixty miles north of Baghdad. Also on April 3, after many days of intense bombing, we launched a ground assault on Saddam International Airport, southwest of Baghdad. It was a key objective, and that put our forces only ten miles from the city.

By April 4, the airport was ours; the Iraqis counterattacked, but we held it. This was key, as it gave us a base and airfield close to the capital. In the southeast, the Marines, with Kut safely in their possession, pushed on toward Baghdad. On the way they accepted the surrender of twenty-five thousand Republican Guard troops. We also turned up the heat on our Baghdad bombing campaign. After fourteen days of bombing, Baghdad's Republican Guard troops were down to minimum capacity, numerous key leadership targets were taken out, and Iraqi military communications were in disarray. On the 4th, with our soldiers on the outskirts, we bombed even more, softening the way for our first forays into the city itself.

Hundreds of civilians fled the city. As we found out later, many of these "civilians" were really Iraqi soldiers, slipping into civilian clothes and trying to make a run for it to Jordan or Syria. Most of the real civilians stayed. In fact, Jordan had set up refugee camps before the war, expecting thousands to cross the border, but they had to shut the camps down after no one showed up. The Iraqi people were so confident in our precision strikes that few of them fled. Incredibly, despite thousands of dropped bombs, the lights never permanently went out in Baghdad. Our laser- and GPS-guided bombs were that accurate. It was unlike any campaign waged in the history of war.

On April 5, we made our first forays into Baghdad. The Army's V Corps moved into the capital from the south, while the 1st MEF moved in from the southeast. The 1st Battalion, 7th Marines approached the suburbs from the east. There was resistance; the fighting was close and tough, with some fights delving into hand-to-hand combat. We were feeling our way, testing the city from different positions. We conducted multiple "thunder runs," putting to use what we'd learned from fighting in the other cities. As a result, we became emboldened that Baghdad could be ours quickly, without the prolonged fight everyone feared. Within hours we were able to determine that chemical weapons would not be used, that the invisible "red line" was truly invisible. A protracted urban battle for Baghdad was not in the offing.

On April 6, we tightened the noose, completely encircling Baghdad and cutting off all highways leading into and out of the city. Any Iraqi forces stuck in the city were on their own. We flew our first plane—a C-130 Hercules transport plane filled with troops and equipment— into the Baghdad airport under cover of darkness. Baghdad's fall was just days away.

Iraq's Information Minister Mohammed Saeed al-Sahaf (or "Baghdad Bob," as we called him) didn't see it that way. With our troops in the background, firing behind him, he took to the airwaves (as he had throughout the war), and proclaimed that the United States had no troops within five miles of Baghdad, that Iraq still controlled the airport, and that Baghdad would soon be the "graveyard" for Coalition troops. He said, "American troops are beginning to commit suicide on the walls of Baghdad. The soldiers of Saddam Hussein have given them a lesson they will never forget. We will in fact encourage them to commit more suicides. We have given them death and poison. These mercenaries, I swear by God, those who are still in Washington, they have sent their troops to be burned."

Reporters asked him what the firing was behind him, and he said it was the Iraqis killing some of the U.S. forces. We had to hand it to this guy: He had balls big enough for a wheelbarrow. He was the definition of chutzpah. A minister of lies, he was indicative of Saddam's regime. He was so ridiculous, all we could do was laugh. He provided much comic relief in the dark days at CentCom, especially as we knew we were on Baghdad's doorstep.

Indeed we were. On April 7, our tanks raced into Baghdad on yet another thunder run, this time seizing two of Saddam's palaces. By April 9, we had secured so much of Baghdad that the Iraqi civilians, realizing the war was over (at least here), took to the streets in massive numbers, joyously celebrating. They tore down government posters, and the Marines helped them topple a massive statue of Saddam in a scene captured by television cameras and broadcast around the world.

Baghdad was in our hands.

When the statue fell, it felt like the right thing at the right time, a great Kodak moment, and the culmination of a lot of hard work. It was a great thing for the Iraqi people, the ones who had suffered through Saddam's regime. When the U.S. flag was briefly draped over the statue, a little uneasiness rose up from Washington to Tampa to General Franks's office in Qatar. It was understandable, in the excitement of the moment, but the ROE were clear: We're not conquering Iraq. The American flag was not to be displayed after the occupation of any Iraqi cities. We were pleased it didn't stay up there very long.

As one problem ended, another began. We expected some looting, as occurs in the wake of any war, but the damage Iraqi civilians committed against their own capital surprised us. They looted Saddam's palaces, government buildings, hospitals, banks, museums. They took everything from paintings to cash to couches to hospital beds. We took a lot of heat for not stopping them.

What most people didn't understand was that there was not a lot we could do. The relatively small number of troops we had in Baghdad had to be reserved for fighting, patrolling, and maybe guarding a few of the major facilities. Baghdad was ours, but it was still unstable, and we would need all our resources to hold it peacefully and fight the remaining Saddam loyalists and terrorists in the city. We would also need all of our resources to continue the fighting in Tikrit, Mosul, Kirkuk, Hillah, and Al Quim. Contrary to the images seen on TV, Operation Iraqi Freedom was not yet over.

Additionally, we had been afforded only a small front in Kuwait through which to bring in our ground forces. Given how small that front was, we could move in only so many troops at a time. We had to prioritize. Only the most crucial fighting forces could be sent in first—that meant infantry and logistics. The forces allocated for peacekeeping—the military police (MPs)—would come in when they could. We had to fight a war first; we couldn't have all of our MPs on the front lines. That meant that after we took Baghdad it would take time for most of the MPs to catch up.

We never expected looting would happen on such massive scale. There were three key reasons for this. Any one of them could have hurt our efforts to restore order, and all three of them combined to make for a level of lawlessness we could never have anticipated. They were:

> 1. Saddam's decision in late March to open the doors of Iraq's prisons and let the incarcered run free. These, we discovered, were not political prisoners; most who expressed public dissent were not in prison—they were already dead, killed by Saddam's secret police. Somewhere between thirty and fifty thousand prisoners were released. They were bad people, the worst of the worst. Shortly after the release of the prisoners, anecdotal evidence from the Iraqi streets began to filter back to Washington and Tampa. The U.S. soldiers on the streets were arresting and killing a number of the looters, murderers, and armed robbers. In many cases, these violent offenders, were free to make their way through streets with uncertain authority and were responsible

for creating the first tears in the Iraqi social fabric.

2. The "resignation" of the Iraqi police force. This was probably the most unexpected factor and the most detrimental to our cause. We needed order in the city, and when the police disappeared into the population, all semblance of order disappeared with them. And as much as it might hurt to admit, we couldn't be entirely sure we didn't cause it. Our information campaign worked well, maybe too well. We asked Iraqi soldiers to lay down their arms, but the police took it a step further and stepped out of their uniforms.

3. The Iraqi army's decision to also walk out of their uniforms and blend into the general population. If they had remained in uniform, some of them could have stepped up to fill the void left by the police force; they could have been transformed into a peacekeeping force to help restore order to their country. But again, they apparently were afraid of being associated with Saddam and the old regime. So not only were they not there to help us, but we now had thousands of armed, unemployed young men on the streets to add to the confusion. Making matters worse was the political decision to disband the Iraqi army, which made it impossible for them to return and help us restore order.

Ahmad Chalabi's several-hundred-man battalion of "freedom fighters"—favored by some in the administration—didn't end up being the helpful force they were advertised to be. We got them in early, since Chalabi had promised they would be hugely beneficial in acting as a police force and helping maintain order. They did help, in some local skirmishes, but like the current Iraqi police force, some melted back into the population and some turned out to be common looters.

There was some good news—good news that contradicted many media reports that were never corrected. For instance, we were blamed for the loss of innumerable, irreplaceable Iraqi treasures from Baghdad's museums. But most people don't realize that the museum workers, seeing what was coming, had the foresight to hide most of the treasures in advance of our arrival in Baghdad, so that at the end of the day, much of it was saved. They were the archaeological heroes of the war.

Our troops were also finding massive stashes of cash, gold, and other presidential treasures. In one operation, Operation Desert Scorpion, our troops detained one thousand Saddam loyalists and confiscated $9,463,000 in American dollars, 1,557,000,000 Iraqi dinars, and 1,071 bars of gold—along with hundreds of AK-47s, hand grenades, RPGs, machine guns, pistols, rifles, and almost ten thousand rounds of ammunition. It is a credit to the integrity of U.S. and Coalition soldiers that of the two hundred ninety thousand troops we had deployed in the region, there were only a couple of instances of our soldiers trying to keep loot for themselves. These soldiers were caught and dealt with. It became very clear to the Iraqis that we were not there to plunder their country.

The fighting continued outside of Baghdad and in many parts of the country. In Hillah, a city fifty miles south of Baghdad, we ended up in a fierce battle with holdout Saddam loyalists involving tanks, attack helicopters, and air support from F/A-18 Hornets and A-10 Thunderbolts. In the north, our SpecialOps units fought for control of a strategic highway linking Mosul and Kirkuk. We wanted to cut off these cities before taking them. In the southern city of Basra, British troops fought for control for the remaining 20 percent of the city held by the enemy. In the west, our forces fought for control of Al Qaim, a small city on the Syrian border that was the site for the largest number of surface-to-surface missiles fired during the first Gulf War (and that might once have been a nuclear weapons program site). Most important, there was Tikrit, a small city north of Baghdad. Tikrit was Saddam's birthplace, home to many Saddam loyalists, and perhaps where Saddam himself was hiding.

We reinforced our defenses around Tikrit, and turned up the heat on the bombing, pounding the city night and day. By April 12 we felt confident enough about our having softened Tikrit to roll our 1st Marine Expeditionary Unit out of Baghdad and towards Tikrit. On the 13th, the fighting began and twenty-five hundred Saddam loyalists inside the city made their last stand.

In the north, the 173rd Airborne moved into Kirkuk, which had surrendered to the Kurds. The looting was as bad as in Baghdad, with civilians smashing windows and loading up their cars and trucks with everything they could get their hands on, from furniture to appliances. (Incidentally, they destroyed a soda factory owned by Saddam Hussein's son Uday.) The liberation of Kurdish Iraq made the Turks nervous, and our presence in Kirkuk helped pacify them.

On April 13, Mosul fell. The 101st took Hillah in the south, defeating the last of the resistance. In the southeast, civic leaders of Kut worked out a deal, and the Marines peacefully took the city. We recovered seven more POWs in the vicinity of Tikrit. Five of them had been in the crash with Jessica Lynch and the other two were downed helicopter gunship pilots. And after a day of our jets crisscrossing Baghdad, we could fly with impunity through the Iraqi skies.

On April 14, the final significant combat action occurred in Tikrit, Saddam's hometown and the last Iraqi holdout. It fell faster than we had expected. By the day's end, we switched gears, to patrolling the city and setting up checkpoints.

The major fighting was over. There was still no sign of Saddam, but we did receive a report that his son Uday was, incredibly, seen partying in a nightclub in Baghdad. We put together a quick operation, but cancelled it at the last second after receiving conflicting reports about its credibility. We didn't want to take the chance of harming innocent civilians.

In the south, near Kut, Marines took control of another terrorist camp, run by al-Quds, a radical anti-U.S. and anti-Israel organization. The British found the first of the many mass graves we would find, coming across a warehouse filled with bodies in boxes. Torture chambers were also found. The Iraqi intelligence service's records and archives building yielded a notebook related to the UN Oil-for-Food Program that tracked an obvious profit-skimming operation. Saddam had been stealing the money Iraq received from the United Nations. in its Oil-for-Food Program and had been using it to build more palaces and lavishing it on his sons and inner circle. When Franks visited Saddam's palaces and saw his gold-plated plumbing, he joked that the program had been corrupted by Saddam into an "oil-for-palaces program."

In a raid on a house in Al Qaim, we discovered a stash of Russian-made

GPS jammers, one of our main concerns leading up to the war. The address labels on the gear showed it had been delivered to the Iraqi embassy in Moscow in January 2003. In other words, Russia had been providing Iraq with military assistance in the months leading up to the war. Russia received a diplomatic cable expressing our displeasure, and the Russian government responded by saying that it knew nothing about it; it must have been the action of an independent company. Around this time, we also discovered that Syria had been shipping military supplies, including night vision goggles, to Iraq. Rumsfeld said to the press, "We consider such trafficking as hostile acts." In either case, it was increasingly surprising and disconcerting to see the extent of support Iraq was secretly receiving from other countries in waging a war against us.

On April 14, Franks made a surprise visit to the troops in Baghdad. He didn't let anyone know he was coming, and the press didn't know he was there until after he had left. He wasn't there for PR—he was there to thank and encourage the troops. And it meant the world to them.

On May 1, 2003, forty-three days after announcing the beginning of the Iraq War, President Bush addressed the nation, declaring that "major combat operations in Iraq had ended." He delivered this address from the deck of the USS *Abraham Lincoln*. Surprisingly, this turned out to be a controversial incident; the press accused President Bush of declaring major operations over prematurely and of grandstanding by making such a declaration from aboard an aircraft carrier.

In all fairness, if anyone was to blame for his declaration, it was us at CentCom. Franks and I were the ones who asked him to do it. And there was good reason: We had many countries who wanted to join peacekeeping operations in Iraq, but their governments wouldn't allow that until "major combat operations" had ceased, as "peacekeeping" is technically defined by the end of major combat operations. By making such a declaration, it would allow many more countries into the Coalition and give us a huge, immediate amount of support in postwar Iraq. It was a legal issue, and we urged Rumsfeld to urge Bush to make the declaration. Saying that "major combat operations in Iraq had ended," did not mean the fighting was over; it meant literally that major combat operations had ended. It was the truth then and is the truth now, regardless of the number of casualties we have had as a result of suicide bombings.

As far as his landing on the carrier, that was not our idea, but we were pleased he did it. For our soldiers and sailors—the ones fighting the war—it was a tremendous boost. There were five thousand sailors on board the *Lincoln*, all of whom had just returned from Iraq, and President Bush took the time to shake hands with each and every one of them.

The Iraqi regime was fractured, our mission accomplished. The Iraqi people were free of the shackles of one of the most unjust dictatorships in world history. The war, in essence, was completed. It was now time to turn our attention to the next major obstacle: winning the peace.

Chapter Six

IRAQ: THE AFTERMATH

"Well, I'd like to do it all over again. The whole thing. And more than that—more than anything—I'd like to see once again the face of every Marine I've ever served with."

—General Lewis "Chesty" Puller, June 26, 1960,
when asked what he would like to do after his retirement

I WAS ON A CONFERENCE CALL WITH FRANKS, Rumsfeld, Myers, Wolfowitz, Marine Corps General Peter Pace (vice chairman of the Joint Chiefs), and several of Rumsfeld's deputies. The topic of discussion was the Ba'ath Party. Major combat operations in Iraq had just ended, and they wanted our recommendation on how to handle the party that dominated every aspect of Iraqi life. Ambassador L. Paul Bremer, Chalabi, the Iraqi National Council, and Wolfowitz wanted to abolish it.

Franks and I wanted to discuss this. We knew from our intel that Saddam's Ba'ath Party was not unlike the Communist Party: It ran everything from the dams to the power plants, from the local electricity to the waterworks, from the policemen to the trash collectors—every worker was a member. If you wanted a government job in Iraq, you had to join, whether you believed in the party or not. By outlawing it, we'd not just outlaw the fedayeen and Saddam's cabinet—we'd outlaw half the country. In our view, any hope for a seamless transition of power depended on the participation of certain segments of the Ba'ath Party.

We recommended that we "fire" only the senior-level membership, politicians, and other Saddam loyalists, but offer selective amnesty for lower-level party members, especially the "blue collar" power workers, so that we could keep the country running. Our intel indicated that most of the low-level members didn't believe in the party anyway, and so our recommendation was nothing if not practical. We needed skilled workers to keep the lights on and the water flowing in Iraq. And that was the plan. But the execution of the plan inside Iraq did not go well. As a result, the Ba'ath Party members either quit or were fired.

On May 12, 2003, we announced the end of the Ba'ath Party in Iraq. As we predicted, it had a ripple effect throughout the country. Everything stopped. Iraqi workers walked away from oil wells, electricity plants, and gas stations. We immediately brought in military people, but it wasn't working. Now they were afraid; the police didn't want to come back once we declared an end to the Ba'ath Party. We had to start from scratch, building a new Iraqi civil infrastructure—from an Iraqi police force to an Iraqi workforce capable of running the electricity, gas, water, and other industries and necessary services—and building it rapidly. In a time of chaos and confusion, this set back our efforts in Iraq. Not only did we have to find and hire new Iraqi employees quickly, but hiring them was difficult because they were afraid of retribution from the Ba'athists.

The other recommendation Franks made (before major combat operations were over) was that we needed to have a provisional government ready for a new Iraq, headed by a prominent American diplomat. It needed to be someone recognized as acceptable by the United Nations, the State Department, and the Department of Defense; someone who'd done substantially similar work in the past. Running an interim Iraq required someone who could help calm the fears on all sides, be respected throughout the world, and at the same time be a political gorilla able to cut hard deals and make tough decisions.

The administration chose Jay Garner. Garner was a retired Army three-star general and a very good and talented person, but he was not a professional diplomat, and certainly not the gorilla that Iraq needed at the time. On May 7, Garner was replaced by L. Paul Bremer III. Bremer was a former ambassador and was well respected by the State Department, by the administration, and in the Middle East. Bremer was the right man for the job.

Militarily, we were still occupied with rooting out the remaining militants and rounding up the most important members of Saddam's regime who were in hiding throughout the country. We had a list of about fifty high-priority, high-ranking Saddam loyalists who had to be found right away. Franks and I were on a conference phone call with CIA staff and Department of Defense staff when someone suggested we turn our list into a deck of cards Everyone thought the idea was fine—none of us gave it much thought. The feeling was, go ahead, whatever works. None of us had any idea it would become the incredibly beneficial public relations tool that it did.

The deck was released two days after the toppling of Saddam's statue.

We hadn't given the deck much thought, but it was one of the best decisions made from a public relations standpoint, and tactically it was extremely useful to help our troops in the field to spot and prioritize the bad guys we needed to arrest. And as the bad guys were captured and their cards marked off one by one, it gave the troops a feeling of accomplishment and progress. (Incidentally, CentCom also approved a deck of the "good guys," which few people know about. Bush was the Ace of Spades and Franks was the Ace of Diamonds. I was the Queen of Clubs.)

As we used the deck, the hunt continued, and on July 22, 2003, we got word that we had a fix on the whereabouts of two top cards: Saddam's sons, Uday and Qusay Hussein. Our soldiers stormed a villa in the northern city of Mosul, but took heavy fire and had to retreat. We sent them back in, buttressed by tank rounds and antitank rounds, making sure that this time none of our men would be in danger. They stormed again and finished the job, overtaking the hostile forces.

When word reached us that the men on the ground believed they had killed both of Saddam's sons, we were guarded (because of our experiences with bin Laden and Saddam) but optimistic. We had a pretty good idea we were in the right place at the right time with the right firepower. Then verified word came back that it was true: Uday and Qusay Hussein, two of the world's truly loathsome human beings, were dead. After months of hard searching, finding these two was a major triumph for our Coalition forces Following the identification of the bodies, we decided to make the photos of their corpses public. We were later criticized for this, but our purpose was to convince the Iraqi people that these monsters were truly dead—and the photos did indeed serve that necessary and useful purpose of providing proof.

General Abizaid and I had a running joke in which he called me Qusay and I called him Uday. We were both deputy commanders of CentCom at the time (General Abizaid is now commander of CentCom), so the joke seemed to fit. When word reached me that the real Qusay and Uday might be dead, I called General Abizaid.

"Uday," I said, "it looks like we're both dead."

"Qusay," he said, "I sure hope so."

Franks returned from our forward base in Qatar to the CentCom base in

Tampa shortly after major combat operations had ended. It had been just over three months since he had left. In that time, the world had changed.

We had been talking every day during that period, sometimes for hours at a time, and had also seen each other daily on video teleconferences. Still, it was good to have him back on American soil. There was a big military procession waiting to greet him.

When Franks got off the plane, he came over to me and, without a word, gave me a hug. It had been a long three months for both of us. No words needed to be said.

Franks's term at CentCom was due to end shortly after the Iraq War, on July 1, 2003. He was asked to stay on as commander for another year, and was also offered the position of Chief of Staff of the Army. He chose neither. He was tired. We had worked as hard as two people could possibly work over those last three years at CentCom. It was seven days a week, twenty-two hours a day, and by God, he had been successful: after Afghanistan and Iraq, Franks was at the height of his success and popularity. He had guided our militarily magnificently. The time was right for him to retire, and to go out on top.

"I've done everything I can possibly do," Franks said to me. "It's time for me to do something else."

"I understand," I said. "Those are my sentiments exactly."

Franks officially retired on July 1, 2003, our last working day together. There was a large change of command ceremony, with more than ten thousand people attending, to celebrate his departure and to celebrate General Abizaid taking command of CentCom. Among the many illustrious people in attendance were Donald Rumsfeld and the heads of all the services. I ran the ceremony.

Rumsfeld, Franks, and Abizaid gave speeches. Though it was Franks's day, he said, "And to my friend, General Michael 'Rifle' DeLong, commander of troops, thanks a lot for not only what you have done, Mike; thanks for what you're doing standing there and honoring us today. You are, in fact, quite special." Abizaid said, "Mike DeLong, thank you for leading this great formation and thank you, Mike, for being my wingman during the war. I can't think of a finer Marine or a finer person that serves anywhere in this armed forces." I was honored by those comments, and it was an honor for me to work with those two men and to serve my country.

On my last day with Franks, he came into my office and said his goodbye. It was quite a journey we'd had over the previous three years. We'd been through the bombing of the USS *Cole*, September 11, the war in Afghanistan, and the war in Iraq. If that won't forge a relationship, nothing will. Franks remained a tough man, but over time we'd grown fond of each other, and I would miss working with him. We had some difficult times, but we never lost our mutual admiration and respect for one another.

At CentCom, it's customary for the deputy commander to stay on for a few months after the commander retires, to ensure a smooth transition. Thus, while Franks retired July 1, I was scheduled to retire September 1. That meant that in my last two months at CentCom I'd be General Abizaid's deputy commander. I was happy to work for him, too. Abizaid and I had worked together for so many years that the transition was seamless. At the end, he asked me to stay on and serve as his deputy commander for another year. But I was done. The protocol is that deputy commanders at CentCom serve a two-year term. I was already the only deputy commander in the history of CentCom to serve three years. I thought four was pushing it.

There was talk of a four-star job for me if I stayed on. But after thirty-six years, I'd had enough. I'd been shot down three times during my career, had multiple back, knee, and shoulder operations, and six broken ankles. I'd been promising my wife I'd retire when the time was right. The time had come.

In the days leading up to my departure, I received letters from ministers of defense from forty countries congratulating me. Building the Coalition had been a great honor, and I would be sad not to spend time with them anymore. On September 1, 2003, I walked out the doors of CentCom for the last time. My active duty at CentCom, and my active duty in the military, were over.

A few days before my retirement, I received a cold call from an employee at a company named the Shaw Group, based in Baton Rouge, Louisiana. He explained that it was a large manufacturing, engineering, construction, and environmental corporation, and wanted, among other things, to help rebuild Iraq. He asked if I'd be interested in hearing them out for a potential job offer. I said I would.

This young man, Dan Shapiro, flew down from Baton Rouge to see me, bringing the CEO of the company, Jim Bernhard, Jr. Jim and I hit it off. He was a great salesman and, more important, a great person. He had a strong philanthropic streak, and I could tell from talking to him that he was truly interested in building a better Iraq and in helping the Iraqi people. He offered me a job. I said I'd think it over. A week later, he flew my wife and me to Baton Rouge to meet all of Shaw's leadership. The Shaw Group had sixteen thousand employees and did $3.4 billion a year in gross revenue. It was an impressive group of people, and an impressive company. I decided to take the job.

Thus it happened that, after a three-day break, I walked right back into a full-time job. I received a congratulatory phone call from Dick Greco, the four-time mayor of Tampa. "What's the nicest thing about working for Shaw?" he asked.

"If I make a mistake now," I replied, "nobody will die."

When I left the military, I thought that to a large extent my journey into harm's way had ended, and that I would finally put Iraq behind me. Nothing could have been further from the truth. Ironically, my job with the Shaw Group would have me traveling to Iraq constantly.

The biggest misconception in America and around the world was that the reconstruction needed in Iraq was due to the damage we did during the war. Most people don't understand that we did very little physical damage to Iraq during the war; it was, in fact, one of the most surgical and precise bombing and ground campaigns in the history of warfare. In our bombing of military, Republican Guard, and Ba'ath Party targets, the peripheral damage we did to oil, water, and electric plants was minimal. We were able to fix these within weeks. In fact, fewer than 20 percent of the current reconstruction efforts in Iraq are aimed at fixing the damage we did during the war.

The bulk of reconstruction Iraq needed was due to the damage that Saddam Hussein had done to his own country. Iraq had been deteriorating since the early 1980s, and the electricity, oil and, waterworks systems were in serious disrepair. Old damage from the first Gulf War (1991) and from the 1980 to 1988 Iraq–Iran war was still pervasive.

The rest of our reconstruction efforts were aimed at fixing the damage done by Iraqi looters. The Iraqi people stole everything, from pieces of machinery off of oil well heads to copper wires from transmission lines. In fact, so much copper was stolen in Iraq that the worldwide price of copper dropped. They were flooding the market with stolen copper.

Such thievery only highlighted Iraq's urgent need for a new police force and a new army, two gaping holes left because of the decision to abolish the Ba'ath Party. Franks and I had expected that the existing Iraqi army and police, purged of their committed Ba'athist elements, would be the building block for the new Iraqi defense forces. A democratic Iraq will face a powerful enemy in Iran, a hostile Syria, and, like every other country, threats from radical Islamic terrorists. Iraq needs a strong professional army and police force to maintain peace and security and to protect its commercial lifeline: its oil industry.

Probably the most important reconstruction task in Iraq was getting the oil wells pumping to their full capacity, which was the key to quickly reviving Iraq's economy. Saddam had left them in such a state of disrepair that they were pumping far below their potential. As of June 2004, Iraq was pumping just shy of three million barrels a day. It has the potential to pump seven million barrels a day, which would put it on par with Saudi Arabia as the largest oil producer in the world.

The Iraqi dams and locks also needed to be fixed so we could irrigate Iraq's agricultural fields and get fresh drinking water to Iraqis. Electrically, all the transmission wires and underground cables (which the Iraqis had looted) needed to be put back in. Iraq also needed new telecommunication systems. Over the last twelve years they had tried to put in more advance telecommunications, but every time they shot at our planes we took out something of theirs—and usually that was a telecommunication system. We had purposely wanted to keep Iraq in a telecommunication ice age so we could monitor their phones. It had worked. But with Saddam gone, it was time to rebuild and bring them up to date.

Iraq needed a new police force, too, along with a new army. It was in our interests to help build and assist these, as we needed Iraq to be powerful enough to defend itself from its neighbors, especially Syria and Iran. Without an army, Iraq was vulnerable to attack.

This is where the Shaw Group came in. My work with the Shaw Group has me, among other things, overseeing the building of the first new Iraqi army base. It is a massive base with 183 buildings, situated in northern Iraq near Mosul. We are providing all the electrical power, wiring the base inside and out, and providing fresh water and waste facilities. When done, it will have a dining facility, a workout facility, a rifle and pistol range, and will be enclosed by a massive fence. It could house up to a division's worth of soldiers (approximately seven thousand troops). They will live and train there.

A big myth is that America is making itself rich on reconstruction contracts, and that this was an ulterior motive for our attacking Iraq. This new army base—and the work of the Shaw Group in general—prove this to be a fallacy. More than 80 percent of the money we receive for this job is being put back into Iraq, and we have employed approximately five thousand Iraqi workers on this job alone. We are taking the money and putting it back into the hands of the Iraqis. And we are putting Iraqis to work, something which they desperately want and for which they are grateful. The Shaw Group is devoted to hiring mostly Iraqi workers.

Security is the first and foremost concern of the Shaw Group. Our CEO, Jim Bernhard, won't accept a job if it puts his workers at risk. That's also where I come in. I've been able to help round up an excellent security force with a solid intel system. In June 2004, my intel sources dissuaded me, at the last minute, from staying at the hotel we'd selected. The next morning, its windows were blown out.

Working with the Shaw Group has given me the opportunity to spend extended time on the ground in Iraq, traveling extensively throughout the country to sit down and talk with some of the Iraqi tribal chiefs. I have had more face time with Iraqi leaders than just about any other American not in the Coalition Provisional Authority. Not unlike Afghanistan, Iraq is made up of numerous local and national tribes, each run with an iron fist by its tribal chief. If you're part of the tribe, anyone who tries to kill you or your family will be killed by the tribe. Some of these tribes have memberships in the millions. The Shammar tribe, probably the most powerful tribe in Iraq, has a membership of nearly eleven million Iraqis. They took a liking to me, and made me an unofficial member of their tribe. It was a great honor for me—and great for my security in Iraq. In 2003, I had an opportunity to have a sit-down with their leader, Dari Mash'an al-Faisal al-Jarba, at a dinner in Amman, Jordan.

Al-Jarba and I had a long discussion about the future of Iraq. He told me that fewer than 1 percent of the Iraqis approved of the then "Iraqi governing council," and that no Iraqi took Chalabi seriously. (This corresponded with my own impressions.)

He also said, "I think I can make the Coalition soldiers more acceptable in

Iraq."

"Tell me," I said.

"When your soldiers inadvertently kill someone—civilian or military—they need to publicly apologize to the family," he said. "If you don't acknowledge that it was an accidental killing, show some sort of remorse, and pay a fixed 'accidental killing' fee, then we are required by our tribal law to hunt you down and kill you. That member's family must take an oath to kill the people who killed him."

"That's easier said than done," I said. "There are a large number of people we have passing through here. We can't always be sure who we killed, captured, or wounded."

"Then you need to create some sort of an organization that keeps track of that," he said. "It will make life for the U.S.—and the Coalition—much easier."

I met many times with Ambassador Paul Bremer's staff, with his deputy ambassador, Dick Jones, with Iraq's minister of electricity, the minister of oil, and of course with General Abizaid and General Ricardo Sanchez. Based on my personal experience in Iraq and my time talking to many of the leaders of its reconstruction, I feel I have a fairly informed opinion about the country and its future. I'd like to share it here.

To begin with, anybody who says we have to bring the troops home now simply does not understand what's going on. In Iraq, security is the most pressing need. Today, the U.S. and Coalition troops are the only forces capable of providing security in Iraq. We have 130,000 troops there. They need to stay there until the Iraqis can reliably provide their own security, and that will be a matter of years rather than months. My own gauging of Iraqi public opinion is that the majority of the Iraqis approve of our forces being there. The Iraqi people can see, as I do, that for every terrorist outrage that happens, at least fifty good things happen across the country thanks to the security the Coalition troops provide. Moreover, the Iraqis do like Americans. What they don't like is being occupied. They are proud people. That is why when we are able to transfer more and more authority to the Iraqis—including finally removing our troops—our relationship with them will get stronger.

It's not the average Iraqi citizen who is causing problems right now. The problems today are coming from six sources:

1. Saddam Hussein released between thirty and fifty thousand hardened criminals from the nation's prisons. Many have yet to be rounded up and are on a crime spree.

2. A full-strength Iraqi police force is needed to curtail the crime, and it is slow to build back up again.

3. Terrorists and al-Qaeda members are pouring into the country from other Arab states; al-Qaeda sees Iraq as a major front for its global war and is offering terrorists ten thousand dollars in family stipends for suicide bombings and other killings of Americans.

4. Radical clerics are inciting their followers. Fortunately, these radicals (like Muqtada al-Sadr, for example) are the minority. The more important and respected clerics, such as Grand Ayatollah Ali al-Sistani, while not pro-American, have publicly repudiated al-Sadr.

5. Remnants of the Ba'ath Party leadership remain a major problem in the country.

6. There are many unemployed males who can easily be convinced to join local riots.

The general dissatisfaction needs to find a target, and unfortunately, the American and Coalition forces often end up as targets. None of these problems appear to stem from ordinary Iraqis, and the majority of the current problems are regional, in areas such as Fallujah, Najaf, Mosul and today, Bagdad. The religious leaders know we need to stay. Radicals like al-Sadr are in the minority, and the important leaders, like Sistani, come out against them on our behalf. Terrorists and al-Qaeda want to cause havoc and destabilize the country so that they can turn world opinion against us and force us to abandon Iraq. They want to make Iraq a terrorist-controlled state (as they did with the Taliban in Afghanistan). But for the good of the Iraqi people and the good of the world, we cannot buckle to this minority and let them have their way.

In the immediate wake of the war, when Franks and I were active, there weren't as many suicide bombings and other problems as there are today. It has grown worse, partly because al-Qaeda discovered that they could go after the United States more easily in the chaos of Iraq. General Abizaid is a great commander, and has done a fantastic job of running CentCom since we left. He has been handed an impossible mission in Iraq, and has made it better.

I also believe the precise and surgical nature of our bombing campaign may have had unintended consequences. Maybe we were too precise. Maybe we didn't scare the right people. There are times in war when you have to grab hold of the people's will. Did that happen? I'm not sure. I do know that Iraqi people were shopping on the same block as buildings that were being bombed. They weren't worried. They saw that we could put a missile into a particular room in a particular building, even through a particular window in that particular room. The precision of our weapons is astounding, but maybe we have to consider these unintended consequences.

The good news is that there is a lot more good news than is reported on the press. Things are getting better. Jobs are filled every week; hospitals are now fully operational; schools are open again; mosques are being rebuilt at no charge; farmers are getting free seeds for crops. We've fixed many of the oil pipelines. And tens of billions of dollars in reconstruction funds are going into the country. In the long run, Iraq will be okay—in fact, better than okay. Iraq has the potential to be a very prosperous nation.

Our hunting down of Saddam's loyalists has worked, and will continue to work. Our capture of Saddam himself was a huge accomplishment. We are making tremendous progress, and it bodes well for our worldwide hunt for al-Qaeda. I am confident that we will catch bin Laden. We will catch him the same way we caught Saddam—using a combination of human and technical intel, and showing the locals that we're there to help them. Eventually, somebody will give him up. He can't live on the run forever.

On another matter of controversy, let me say categorically that we will eventually find Iraqi WMD. The intelligence evidence we had before the war was too overwhelming to be wrong. Iraq is a country the size of

California, and not only is it easy to hide such weapons—chemical weapons can be hidden on a single truck; biological weapons can be hidden in a brief-case—but the Iraqis were masters at hiding these weapons after more than a decade of playing shell games with UN weapons inspectors. Part of the problem is that the members of Saddam's inner circle we have captured are experts at lying—they had to be in order to survive under Saddam's reign. The people who managed to survive in his inner circle did so by either being non-threatening yes-men (and are still too terrified of Saddam to talk), or by hiding information. They know. They're just not talking.

There is a lot of reason for hope regarding the future of CentCom's AOR. What's not mentioned in the press is that we've built tremendous goodwill among many Arab countries, and continue to do so every day. We have great relations with Egypt, Bahrain, the United Arab Emirates, Qatar, Afghanistan, Omar, Kuwait, Jordan, Pakistan, Saudi Arabia, , and many more. These nations know that the War on Terror is a global fight, and that we are all fighting the fight together.

At the same time, there is also reason for worry in the AOR. Back in 2004, when the first edition of this book published, I stated that Iran, Syria, and Lebanon were of particular concern and that they were problems that had to be dealt with. I continue to state as much. We know that Iran and Syria were making chemical and biological weapons at an unprecedented rate before the Iraq War, and continue to do so today. We know that Syria was a hiding place for Iraqi WMD. We know that Syria provided haven for Saddam sympathizers and both Syria and Iran are harboring al-Qaeda and other terrorist organizations. In fact, on May 7, 2003, in the immediate aftermath of the war, a leading Syrian official acknowledged that some senior Iraq officials had escaped to Syria. And we know they are sponsoring terrorists and sending suicide bombers across their borders into Iraq. Most troubling of all is Iran's rapid pursuit of developing nuclear weapons.

During the war, we told Iran, Syria, and Lebanon that we thought they were hiding WMD from Iraq. They claimed to know nothing. They still do. Are there grounds to take action? I think so. Should we? I don't know the answer. This could be worked out diplomatically. Over time, what action we should (or should not) take will become more clear.

In either case, Syria and Iran are problems that have to be dealt with.
In reflecting on the Afghan and Iraq wars, I ask myself what was most

extraordinary about them, the people, the wars themselves. What was accomplished?

Politically, there are many unsung heroes of these wars, including Pakistani president Pervez Musharraf and Jordanian King Abdullah. As Franks said, "What Musharraf has done is like jumping off a cliff without a parachute and hoping that someone will give it to you before you hit the bottom." He supported the United States in the face of tremendous internal political opposition. He walked a political tightrope because he was farsighted enough to know that Pakistan's long-term interests do not lie with the Taliban, al-Qaeda, and radical Islam. The same holds true for King Abdullah, who knows that the long-term security interests of his country are not the interests of al-Qaeda, radical Islam, or the Ba'ath Party of Saddam Hussein. He's making decisions for the security of his country fifty years from now. That's not always easy when you have people who want bread on their tables now. It was especially hard for King Abdullah to support the United States, given that 60 percent of his country is Palestinian. He and President Musharraf must be applauded.

Militarily, both campaigns were an unqualified success. The use of the Northern Alliance was a bold act of genius. The speed of the march to Baghdad was executed with precision and professionalism. And I have no doubt that the United States is more secure today than it was before we won these wars.

In addition to the victories in Afghanistan and Iraq, we achieved another victory that few people realize, one that will have long-lasting repercussions on our military for time to come: true joint operations. Technology, necessity, and discipline forced the different services to work together and to trust each other during the Afghan and Iraq wars. "Simultaneity" became the all-important term. And this was thanks to the atmosphere set by Franks. He had a vision for the future of the military, and he enforced it.

The most famed incident of the war—the rescue of Private Jessica Lynch—was a perfect example of "jointness": Marines, Air Force, Army, Navy, and Special Forces troops all worked seamlessly together with less than twenty-four hours' notice in a complex operation—and pulled it off miraculously. "Jointness" made it possible.

The focus on Special Operations helped jumpstart this new attitude. One of its proponents was the CentCom SpecialOps Commander, now Major General Gary Harrell. I asked him for his thoughts on this topic:

The Afghan and Iraq wars exhibited the best examples of joint operations I had ever seen. We broke the parochialism. For example, I never had to worry if I needed planes—all I had to do was pick up the phone and call [CentCom Air Force chief] Buzz Mosley. There they were.

Never before had we been able to have Special Forces and conventional forces working together in that proximity. The best way I could explain it is this: in the past, we had coordination. This time, the different services were fighting together and watching each other's backs. That's a huge distinction.

Before these wars, if I had been on a video teleconference and made a mistake, it was pretty much a sure thing that somebody from one of the services would swoop down and call me on it, give me a hard time. During Operation Iraqi Freedom, if I made a mistake, the other commanders, instead of trying to ambush me, would look for a way to help me out, to extend me a stick to pull me out of the mud. That was due in large part to the mood that Franks set. This is a good thing. If we achieved anything in these wars, we achieved this. We have to really make sure that we try to keep it for the future.

Of course, when people hear about this, they might say, well, why not just combine all the services into one service? In fact, there are some politicians today who make that argument and are trying to do that very thing. That would be a bad thing. A guy who joins the Air Force does not want to join the Navy; a guy who joins the Army does not want to join the Marines. Having separate services brings in more overall people to the armed services, as each attracts a different type of person. Each offers its own ethos and pride, which is helpful in the recruiting process. Some people choose a service because their father was in that service, or because they like the idea of being at sea, or even because they like the color of their uniforms.

In reality, what that recruit will learn is that the services are much more complex than he thinks. The Army is famed for being a ground force, and yet the Army has more planes than the Air Force and more ships than the Navy. The Air Force has ships. Marines now have units assigned to Special Forces. There's a lot of crossover. Again, some people argue that's a bad thing, but I think it's important. Redundancy is good. Would you want to fly on a plane that didn't have a backup system?

Different services are good. What's important is that they continue to work so closely together.

In 2003, in my last official trip before I retired, I visited Iraq and inspected an Iraqi prison. It was not just any prison—it was a prison housing the most notorious of the Iraqi prisoners. I wanted to see how the special prisoners were being taken care of, and to make sure that our guys were treating them well. I had no reason to think otherwise. Up until my retirement in September 2003, I had never seen any reports of prison abuse in Iraq. The few reports we'd received had to do with Afghanistan. We'd had two cases there of prisoner deaths under suspicious circumstances. In both instances the cases were reported immediately and investigations were conducted. Franks and I had a saying, the lesson of which we strictly adhered to: "Bad news doesn't get better with time." Whenever something bad happened, we never tried to hide it—on the contrary, the first people we spoke to were our public affairs people to make sure we aired our problems immediately. In any war—or indeed any gathering of three hundred thousand people—there are going to be some people who do stupid, unfortunate things. You can't prevent that. All you can do is stop it, investigate it, find out why it happened, punish the people who did it, and take precautions to keep it from happening again.

Thus, my trip to the Iraqi prison was a formality, a routine function. I didn't expect to find any surprises.

And I didn't. The prison was in immaculate shape. The prisoners all looked healthy and well taken care of. They were served high-quality Iraqi food, and their cells were very clean. Many of them were high-profile and I recognized their faces from television. Oddly enough, the first thing I noticed was that most of them now had gray hair, whereas on TV their hair had been black. Of course, they were without hair dye in prison.

I put a regular jacket on over my uniform so that no prisoner could see my name and insignia of rank. I went from cell to cell, asking each prisoner (through an interpreter) about their welfare and if they wanted to talk. None of them wanted to talk. A female prisoner was there, too—the notorious "Dr. Germ"—who was especially uncommunicative.

There was an exception to the bunch. The last prisoner on the row: Chemical Ali. Unlike the others, he started talking right away. Hardly had I crossed his cell when he started peppering me with questions.

"Who are you?" he asked. There was a big smile on his face. "Why are you here?"

I looked at him.

"I'm just a person who's interested in your welfare," I said.

He looked at the entourage accompanying me.

"Are you a senior person?" he asked. "Why are you dressed differently than the other men? Are you important?"

I didn't respond.

He rattled on about how good the prison officials were to him, how courteous the guards were, how well he was being kept.

"I would like to cooperate however I can," he said.

"Then where are the chemicals?" I asked.

A huge smile crossed his face. "I have no idea," he said.

"If you want to help us, then you'll tell us where they are."

He simply shrugged.

My life has been filled with remarkable events. I have been in combat. I have made life-changing decisions as a leader of thousands of fine U.S. military men and women. Still, my time in this prison, assessing the conditions and welfare of the incarcerated, was nothing short of a life-changing moment. Here was Chemical Ali, the man in charge of Saddam's chemical and biological weapons. In a cell before me was one of the worst human beings on the face of the planet, a man responsible for killing thousands of Kurds with mustard gas and other chemical weapons. He had killed more people than you or I will ever meet in a lifetime, and to look directly into his eyes—into the face of evil—was a startling moment. Imprisoned, his run of inhumanity finished, he was still attempting to work an angle. This man, perhaps more than any other, embodied the evil of Saddam's rule. Here was the justification for all of our hard work, sitting before me, still trying to run a con.

I was staring at the very reason we went to war.

Appendix A

Statement by General Tommy Franks

United States Army, Former Commander, Central Command
Before the House Armed Services Committee
United States House of Representatives

Operation Iraqi Freedom, July 10, 2003

Mr. Chairman and members of the Committee, I am honored to appear before you today. Since we last met here together, much has taken place in the Central Command area of responsibility. We have removed a brutal regime in Iraq and have begun to help Iraq build its new future. Our forces have continued to help Afghanistan make strides towards independence, and have continued to help the Afghan people develop their nation while continuing to seek and destroy terrorists and their networks all across the Central region. I look forward to discussing these important subjects with you and to your questions.

Let me begin by bringing you a message from the more than 281,000 US and Coalition troops that I have been privileged to command. That message is thank you. Throughout both Operation Iraqi Freedom and Operation Enduring Freedom, our forces in the field have been blessed to serve civilian leaders who set clear military objectives and then provide our men and women in uniform the tools they need to win. On their behalf, let me thank you for all that you continue to do for the troops.

As you know, earlier this week General John Abizaid took the reins of command at CENTCOM. He is a principled leader and soldier who has been tested under fire, and I am confident about the future of CENTCOM under his leadership.

I would like to begin today by recognizing the Coalition nations whose contributions of forces, equipment, and economic support have signaled a worldwide commitment to eradicate terrorism. Over the past twelve months, the Coalition has been steadfast. Today there are 63 nations represented at Central Command's Tampa headquarters.

We have built a force in the CENTCOM Area of Responsibility (AOR) to help achieve our objectives in Operation Iraqi Freedom and Operation Enduring Freedom—to deny terrorists the use of weapons of mass destruction (WMD), and to bring terrorists to justice and dismantle their terrorist networks. We have also established a more visible and viable presence in the Horn of Africa (HOA) in order to combat terrorism and promote stability. Work in the Central Region is underway, but as I will discuss in the sections ahead, the environment within the region remains challenging. Securing US interests and ensuring regional stability will involve risks and will require continuing commitment of resources.

USCENTCOM Area of Responsibility (AOR)

Our AOR encompasses 6.4 million square miles, from Egypt and Jordan to the Horn of Africa, the Arabian Peninsula, Pakistan in South Asia, and the Central Asian states as far north as Kazakhstan. It includes the waters of the Red Sea, the Northern Indian Ocean, the Persian Gulf, and the key maritime choke points of the Suez Canal, the Bab el Mandeb, and the Strait of Hormuz. The area is home to more than 500 million people, representatives of all the world's major religions and at least 18 major ethnic groups. National economies produce annual per capita incomes varying from a few hundred dollars to tens of thousands of dollars. CENTCOM's AOR includes dictatorships, absolute monarchies, failed states, democracies and governments in transition toward democracy. Humanitarian crises, resource depletion and overuse, religious and ethnic conflicts, demographic challenges and military power imbalances that generate social, economic, and military volatility characterize this area. These factors are particularly significant given the geographical and economic importance of the region where natural resources provide extraordinary economic opportunities. However, they also give rise to a range of socioeconomic problems and rivalries. Some states have compensated for their lack of mineral wealth through the industry of their people. However, other nations have not generated the will, resources or organization to move ahead. These factors will not be easily or quickly overcome and signal additional challenges in the future.

In the past two years, USCENTCOM has been at the leading edge of the Global War on Terrorism (GWOT). The Command is engaged with

U.S. and coalition forces both in Afghanistan and Iraq. Our commitment remains strong as our leaders and troopers work to bring security throughout the region.

On the ground in Iraq today, our troops are conducting ongoing operations, combining Civil Military Operations with direct military action to seek out and bring to justice leaders of the fallen regime. Our priorities include forming and training police, security forces, and the New Iraqi Army; improving the infrastructure; supporting the establishment of local government and providing emergency medical care and other humanitarian assistance. Much dangerous work remains to be done, but millions of Iraqis have freedoms today which four months ago were only a dream.

Our troops are working closely with Ambassador Jerry Bremer and his civilian team to provide the tools he needs to be successful. Progress is being made, and our country is justifiably proud of all that has been accomplished.

Operation Iraqi Freedom—Lessons Learned

Decisive combat in Iraq saw a maturing of joint force operations in many ways. Some capabilities reached new performance levels. From a Joint Integration perspective, our experience in Operations Southern and Northern Watch, and Enduring Freedom helped to develop a joint culture in our headquarters and in our components. These operations helped to improve joint interoperability and improve our joint C4I networks as joint force synergy was taken to new levels of sophistication. Our forces were able to achieve their operational objectives by integrating ground maneuver, special operations, precision lethal fires and non-lethal effects. We saw for the first time integration of forces rather than deconfliction of forces. This integration enabled conventional (air, ground, and sea) forces to leverage SOF capabilities to deal effectively with asymmetric threats and enable precision targeting simultaneously in the same battle space. Likewise, Special Operators were able to use conventional forces to enhance and enable special missions. Operational fires spearheaded our ground maneuver, as our forces sustained the momentum of the offense while defeating enemy formations in open, complex, and urban terrain.

We saw jointness, precision munitions, C2, equipment readiness, state of training of the troops, and Coalition support as clear "winners" during OIF.

That said, we also identified a number of areas which require additional work. Fratricide prevention suffered from a lack of standardized combat identification. Units in theater arrived with seven different combat ID systems, and our commanders were forced to overcome these shortcomings "on the fly". Deployment planning and execution were cumbersome, and need to be improved to meet the operational demands of the 21st Century. And, Coalition information sharing must be improved at all levels. Finally, human intelligence and communications bandwidth are also areas which will require continuing focus.

Operation Enduring Freedom—Lessons Learned

In Afghanistan, Coalition forces continue to deny anti-coalition elements sanctuary while disrupting their ability to plan, target, rehearse and execute operations. This is accomplished through active combat patrolling from secure fire bases and forward operating bases (FOB) in order to promote stability, enhance the legitimacy of the Interim Transitional Government of Afghanistan (ITGA), and prevent the re-emergence of terrorism.

During OEF, we saw a number of functional areas and capabilities that reached new levels of performance. In some areas, improvements were made prior to Operation Iraqi Freedom. For example the DoD/CIA synergy which worked well during OEF was built upon the integration of liaison officers in each of our headquarters which facilitated teamwork and paid great dividends in Iraq.

Also, we continued to leverage coalition strengths as new Coalition members were added. "The mission determines the Coalition; the Coalition does not determine the mission."

Advanced technologies employed during OEF were also critical. The command and control of air, ground, naval, and SOF from 7,000 miles away was a unique experience in warfare as our forces achieved unprecedented real time situational awareness and C2 connectivity. We learned that precision-guided munitions represent a force multiplier. Low collateral damage during both OEF and OIF was a fundamental factor in achieving our objectives. Early in OEF we saw the need for an unmanned sensor-to-shooter capability to support time-sensitive targeting (TST). The armed Predator demonstrates great potential and will be a high payoff system in the future. Blue Force Tracking and enhanced C4I systems increase lethality and decrease response time, and also represent transformational technologies. We will continue with development of Global Hawk as an unmanned, high-altitude, long loiter time, beyond line-of-sight multi-sensor UAV, and will work to incorporate laser designation and delivery of precision weaponry from that platform.

The integrated common operating picture (COP) was a very powerful tool. Tracking systems were previously Service unique. Workarounds were developed for OIF, but there is a need to develop one integrated, user-friendly, C4I architecture that captures blue and red air, ground and maritime forces.

Strategic lift and tanker aircraft availability were stretched during OEF and OIF. These forces are critical to rapid future force projection and we must enhance this vital capability in the years ahead.

Combined and joint training of our forces was also a key factor during OEF and was carried over into OIF. Our military forces are the best-prepared forces in the world and I thank the members of Congress for providing assets and funding to train these wonderful fighting men and women to give them every possible advantage.

Finally, our ability to take action in OEF was predicated on "Strategic Anchors," one of which was "Cooperative Security" relationships, which paid high dividends in basing, staging and over flight rights during recent crisis.

Regional Concerns
Iraq

Although security continues to improve, portions of Iraq are now, and will remain for some time, dangerous. The term "stability operations" does not infer that combat actions have ended. Military forces are still required to set conditions that enable progress. As we move forward, the composition and size of our forces will change to match emerging requirements. Factors that influence our force mix will include Coalition force contributions, threat, and success in fielding Iraqi police forces, security, and the New Iraqi Army.

Integration of Coalition forces is a major near-term effort. The United Kingdom and Poland are committed to leading Divisions in Southern Iraq, and many partner nations have offered forces to fill those units. Deployment of those forces has already begun. We continue discussions with India and Pakistan. At this moment, 19 Coalition partners are on the ground in support of military operations in Iraq, with deployment pending for 19 additional countries. An additional 11 nations are conducting military to military discussions with respect to possibly deploying forces to Iraq in support of stability and security operations.

At this point some 35,000 police have been hired. This fills about half of the requirement nationwide. Throughout the country, many of these law enforcement officers are conducting joint patrols with U.S. military forces, and we will ultimately transition responsibility for security and stability to the Iraqis. In the near-term, we must build upon the momentum we have generated in this area.

Creation of the New Iraqi Army is moving forward. The plan envisions three divisions located near Mosul, Baghdad, and Basrah to provide territorial defense and conduct stability operations. In the first year, the goal is to field approximately nine battalions. Initially, Iraqi forces will focus on performing security functions at fixed sites, convoy security, and border control. As it develops, this force will work with Coalition forces to contribute to stability and security throughout Iraq.

Underlying all security functions is the need to continue humanitarian assistance and the conduct of civil-military operations to improve the quality of life for the Iraqi people. In this regard, our regional allies have been invaluable. Neighboring nations have provided hospitals, medical supplies, water, food, and expertise in beginning the rebuilding process. The fact that there has been no humanitarian disaster in Iraq; no widespread outbreak of disease, hunger, refugees or displaced persons; or any of the other predicted consequences of war is due, in large part, to the generosity of our allies. The CPA and Coalition forces will continue to work in concert with international and non-governmental agencies to reverse the result of years of neglect by a brutal regime.

Afghanistan

Our efforts in Afghanistan have given the Afghan people a chance to break the chain of violence, civil war, and poverty that many have endured their entire lives. Our Coalition has made considerable progress over the last 18 months, but much remains to be done. The average Afghan now enjoys basic freedoms, a higher quality of life, and prospects for a better future. A Loya Jirga to ratify a new Constitution will be held this fall and national elections are scheduled for next summer. President Karzai's transitional government continues to develop as he works to expand its authority beyond Kabul. Security and stability are the keys to President Karzai's success. Since 1 May, our primary focus has shifted to stability operations. A stable and secure environment enables reconstruction. U.S. Civil-Military Operations forces have completed more than 150 projects and nearly 300 more are underway. To date, these projects have improved drinking water, medical care, transportation, communications, irrigation, and agriculture throughout the country. To further our reconstruction efforts and to help foster stability, Provincial Reconstruction Teams (PRT) are working in Bamian, Konduz, and Gardez. A fourth U.K. led team will soon deploy to Mazar-e-Sharif, and other PRTs are being planned for future deployments to additional provinces.

A critical step toward stability in Afghanistan is building the Afghanistan National Army (ANA). The U.S. is leading this effort, supported by five Coalition partners. To date, three brigades of professional Afghan soldiers have been fielded; we project ANA strength of approximately 8,500 soldiers by Dec 03.

Horn of Africa

Several countries in the Horn of Africa responded positively to President Bush's call for support against worldwide terrorism. However, these states are challenged to conduct successful anti-terrorism campaigns. Over 21 million people remain at risk of starvation in the region. Long-term conflicts have intensified the debilitating effects of natural disasters, especially drought. This forces the dislocation of affected populations seeking food, medical care, and safety. Existing governments find difficulty meeting the needs of their populations, creating an environment hospitable to terrorist cells and trans-national threats.

USCENTCOM has addressed these issues by standing up a Combined Joint Task Force in Djibouti. This Task Force provides a forward presence; trains counter-terrorism forces; and supervises a number of humanitarian assistance efforts to enhance security, improve public health and combat famine. These initiatives are key elements of our Security Cooperation strategy. Close cooperation with interagency and international aid organizations facilitates a regional approach to the humanitarian effort and maximizes the effects of our efforts.

The Horn will require a long-term commitment of resources to achieve stability, thereby setting conditions that will make it less hospitable to terrorists.

Iran

Iran has long pursued a goal of regional hegemony through modernization of a regionally capable military force, the development of weapons of mass destruction (WMD), and the use and promotion of terrorism as an instrument of foreign policy.

Tehran perceives itself encircled by the U.S. The enmity and abiding mistrust of the U.S. government is implacable among Iran's ruling hard-liners furthering security concerns. Iran's principal security objectives remain unaltered with the fall of Baghdad, namely the survival of the Islamic state and the preservation of Iranian independence, with the secondary goal of expanding Iranian influence in the Persian Gulf, Central Asia, and the broader Islamic world. Iran's national security policies appear focused on maintaining political stability and internal security, expanding diplomatic and economic relations, establishing WMD and long-range missile forces backed up by unconventional warfare capabilities and maintaining a robust terrorism apparatus.

Shifts in regional security relationships are expected as a result of the formation of a stable and productive post-war Iraq. Of course, those realignments and perturbations extend beyond Iraq's borders and will be of concern to Iran. Following the ouster of the Saddam regime in Iraq, Iran has mounted an increasingly sophisticated and multi-faceted influence campaign that will prove persistent in its focus to create an anti-Coalition, predominantly anti- U.S., sentiment among Iraqis.

Just as complex is deciphering Iran's dual-track foreign policy and often contradictory public statements. Iran's efforts to promote itself as a responsible member nation of the international community are in direct contrast with its long-standing covert and public support to radical resistance groups and terrorists as well as its failure to meet its Nuclear Nonproliferation Treaty (NPT) and International Atomic Energy Agency (IAEA) obligations.

The Iranian regime's proclivity for violence through terrorism, in concert with its past support of terrorism and an established pattern of developing nuclear and other WMD and missile programs, will continue to be of concern.

Gulf States

Transnational terrorists remain throughout the Gulf region. Violent, anti-Western ideology appeals to some segments of the populace, due in part to the increasing failure of regional governments to meet the basic needs of the people. As populations increase, regional governments struggle to provide adequate education, housing, infrastructure, and jobs. Closed political systems are only just beginning to reform. Regional politics and long-standing, hard-line stances concerning the Palestinian-Israeli situation exacerbate regional instability.

However, there are also hopeful signs. Many of the Gulf countries are moving toward a more representational government. Bahrain and Qatar have begun municipal elections; Oman continues working toward opening its economy and political system; and Saudi Arabia has begun efforts to change the educational system, privatize state industries, and open a domestic dialogue on other needed social reforms. Substantive improvements will require a long-term, determined effort.

The Gulf States have stepped up their antiterrorism efforts in response to 9/11 and the May attacks in Saudi Arabia. On-going efforts include increasing law enforcement, stemming the flow of illegal financial support, tracking personnel movements, and monitoring terrorist activities. While their cooperation is extensive, these governments continue to prefer working behind the scenes.

Militarily, the Gulf States continue to perceive a long-term threat from Iran. In a show of support for Operation Iraqi Freedom (OIF), the Gulf States, for the first time, deployed the Peninsula Shield force in defense of Kuwait. Outstanding OIF basing and access support from the Gulf States demonstrates tangible results of our active security cooperation programs. They understand that our "footprint" in the region is likely to change, and each state continues to advocate security cooperation with the U.S.

While most citizens are relieved that the Iraqi regime has been removed, opinions differ on Coalition activities and what type of Iraqi society will eventually emerge. Regional governments are looking to the CPA to ensure

Iraq does not become segmented. Gulf leaders look forward to lucrative trade and economic relations with a rebuilt Iraq.

South and Central Asia

Pakistan's support has been fundamental to our success in Operation Enduring Freedom. President Musharraf has committed substantial national resources against terrorism to include arresting a number of Al Qaida leaders, freezing the financial accounts of known terrorists and banning fundraising to support Kashmiri militancy. He has pursued these actions despite ongoing tensions with India and significant domestic pressure, and he continues on a path toward democracy and sustained economic development. The US has expressed gratitude and solidified his political position by lifting sanctions and granting economic assistance. CENTCOM will continue to support our mil-to-mil relationship and build closer security cooperation with Pakistan.

The Central Asian States remain dedicated partners in the Global War on Terrorism. Each country declared its support for the US immediately after the attacks of 9/11. All offered to host U.S. personnel and equipment. Bases established in the Central Asian States have been critical to the success of our operations in Afghanistan. The defeat of the Taliban and the removal of Al Qaida from Afghanistan have enabled the Central Asian States to refocus their attention on internal development. We will continue working with our Central Asian partners to prevent the resurgence of terrorism, and the Department of State and the Bureau of Customs and Border Protection will continue to improve their capacity to secure their borders against the flow of illegal narcotics.

WMD Proliferation

The proliferation of technologies related to weapons of mass destruction (WMD) and long-range delivery systems continues to be a significant concern in the Central Region. As some nations and international extremist groups pursue chemical, biological, radiological, and nuclear capabilities, some regional allies will seek to offset such threats by pursuing strategic weapons of their own, thus perpetuating the proliferation cycle. Security cooperation is our best hedge against this possibility.

Iran continues to pursue WMD. Its nuclear programs are under the continuing scrutiny of the International Atomic Energy Agency, and its chemical weapons stockpile and probable biological weapons program are of concern.

In South Asia, the missile and nuclear race between Pakistan and India is also troubling. Both states continue to develop advanced missiles and the risk of miscalculation leading to escalation remains of concern.

We face a severe threat in the potential for chemical, biological, radiological or, less likely, nuclear attacks by terrorists. Documents found (during the exploitation of suspect WMD sites in Afghanistan) indicated the al-Qaida terrorist network had explored methods for producing toxins and was seeking to establish a biological warfare capability. Terrorists will continue to seek WMD capabilities as their need for more sensational attacks intensifies. The extensive press coverage of the October 2001 anthrax mail attacks highlighted U.S. vulnerabilities and exacerbated an already dangerous situation in the Central Region, where many extremists are based and exploring such capabilities.

Terrorism and Counterterrorism

Over the past year, the Global War on Terrorism has been marked by major achievements. Multiple terrorist operations sponsored by al-Qaida and affiliated extremists have been disrupted; and many terrorists, including high-ranking operational planners, have been captured. Al-Qaida has proven unable to reestablish the extensive training infrastructure it had earlier instituted in Afghanistan. The dispersal of its leaders and cadre from Afghanistan continues to impede al-Qaida's ability to accomplish timely and secure communications exchanges.

Nevertheless, al-Qaida has responded to our counter-terrorism initiatives; in this context, several lesser-known personalities have emerged and this has translated into strikes such as the May 2003 bombings of multiple housing complexes in Riyadh. So far, these attacks have focused on "soft" targets; however, al-Qaida retains an interest in striking larger, more spectacular targets.

Counterterrorism operations against al-Qaida, U.S. victories in Iraq and Afghanistan, and the persistent conflict between Israel and the Palestinians have generated pressure throughout the USCENTCOM AOR. Jihadist groups and disgruntled individuals constitute another important source of potential terrorist threats. Given this setting, we are constantly working to identify vulnerabilities and refine our force protection measures.

Security Cooperation Overview

Our success in gaining basing, staging and over-flight rights for Enduring Freedom and Iraqi Freedom and our influence in the region are directly related to an active security cooperation program. USCENTCOM's program builds relationships that promote U.S. interests, build allied and friendly nations' military capabilities, and provide U.S. forces with access and en route infrastructure. Prosecution of the GWOT requires continued fiscal and political investment in these vital programs. I would like to highlight a few dividends of our approach.

The FY03 supplemental appropriation of $908M in FMF is currently enabling the training of a professional Afghan National Army and allowing Pakistan to restore its military forces. Additionally, long-standing partners such as Jordan are increasing their interoperability through FMF-funded purchases. Continued investment in security assistance allows USCENT-COM to improve the capabilities of friendly nations by enabling them to provide for their own security.

International Military Education and Training (IMET) remains a low-cost, high-pay off investment that helps shape the security environment. Courses offered under IMET provide military members of regional states an opportunity to attend courses in U.S. military institutions such as Command and Staff Colleges and Senior Service Schools. IMET participation by students from the Central Region supports Congressionally-mandated initiatives: providing exposure to the U.S. concepts of military professionalism, respect for human rights, and subordination to civilian authority. The Counter Terrorism Fellowship, a new DoD appropriation, enables us to provide flexible course offerings to several nations who are key partners in the GWOT.

Conclusion

The Global War on Terrorism is underway. The precision, determination, and expertise of our military forces and our Coalition partners brought about the liberation of Afghanistan and Iraq in lightning speed with minimum bloodshed. However, these two nations have only taken only the first steps toward freedom, and United States and our Coalition partners must be there to support the whole journey.

While we have accomplished much, the potential for terrorist acts and other setbacks remains very real. Afghanistan has a new government, a new army, and with Coalition support the nation is making great strides towards long term stability. In Iraq, Saddam Hussein's regime was destroyed and regime supporters are being rooted out. Our focus has changed from military destruction of a regime to providing security and humanitarian assistance to the Iraqi people, while helping to establish a representative form of Government. Decisive combat operations have been completed, but much work remains.

I am very proud of each and every one of the men and women who continue to serve selflessly and tirelessly in the execution of our mission from Egypt to Kazakhstan, from the Suez to Pakistan, regardless of the uniform of service they wear or the nation from which they come. I thank the Congress and the American people for the tremendous support you have given them.

Appendix B

Maps

On the following pages are maps used by CentCom during the Afghan and Iraq wars. They detail CentCom's AOR and the surrounding area, and how some of the major campaigns were waged. They also provide data about the region prior to and after U.S. military action, demonstrating the great progress that has been made. (Map and data slides from author's unclassified late-2003 presentation.)

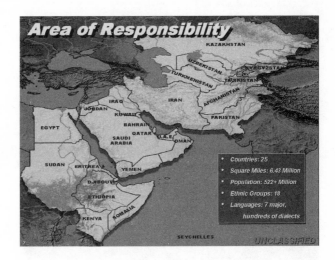

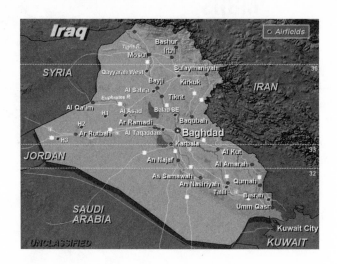

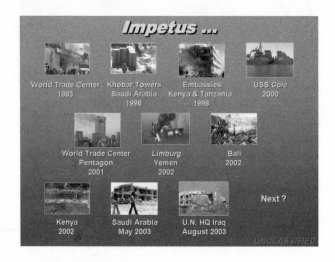

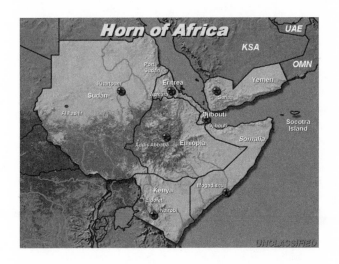

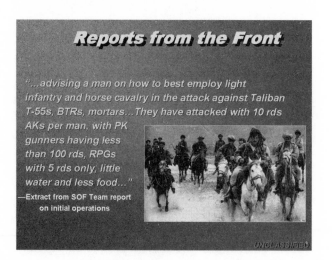

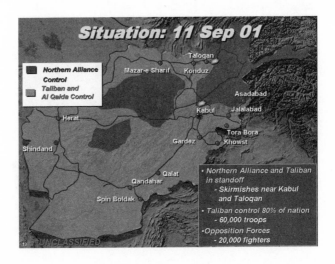

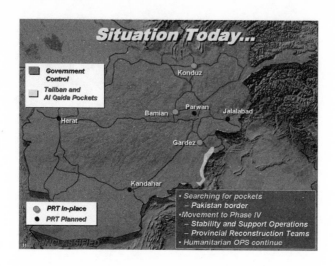

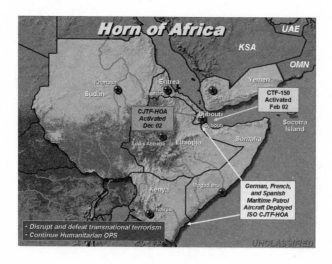

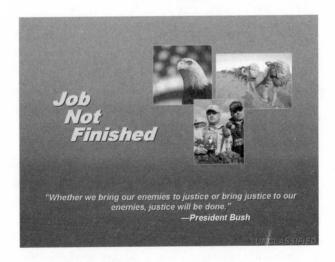

The National Security Strategy of the United States of America
September 2002

THE WHITE HOUSE
WASHINGTON

The great struggles of the twentieth century between liberty and totalitarianism ended with a decisive victory for the forces of freedom—and a single sustainable model for national success: freedom, democracy, and free enterprise. In the twenty-first century, only nations that share a commitment to protecting basic human rights and guaranteeing political and economic freedom will be able to unleash the potential of their people and assure their future prosperity. People everywhere want to be able to speak freely; choose who will govern them; worship as they please; educate their children—male and female; own property; and enjoy the benefits of their labor. These values of freedom are right and true for every person, in every society—and the duty of protecting these values against their enemies is the common calling of freedom-loving people across the globe and across the ages.

Today, the United States enjoys a position of unparalleled military strength and great economic and political influence. In keeping with our heritage and principles, we do not use our strength to press for unilateral advantage. We seek instead to create a balance of power that favors human freedom: conditions in which all nations and all societies can choose for themselves the rewards and challenges of political and economic liberty. In a world that is safe, people will be able to make their own lives better. We will defend the peace by fighting terrorists and tyrants. We will preserve the peace by building good relations among the great powers. We will extend the peace by encouraging free and open societies on every continent.

Defending our Nation against its enemies is the first and fundamental commitment of the Federal Government. Today, that task has changed dramatically. Enemies in the past needed great armies and great industrial capabilities to endanger America. Now, shadowy networks of individuals can bring great chaos and suffering to our shores for less than it costs to purchase a single tank. Terrorists are organized to penetrate open societies and to turn the power of modern technologies against us.

To defeat this threat we must make use of every tool in our arsenal—military power, better homeland defenses, law enforcement, intelligence, and vigorous efforts to cut off terrorist financing. The war against terrorists of global reach is a global enterprise of uncertain duration. America will help nations that need our assistance in combating terror. And America will hold to account nations that are compromised by terror, including those who harbor terrorists— because the allies of terror are the enemies of civilization. The United States and countries cooperating with us must not allow the terrorists to develop new home bases. Together, we will seek to deny them sanctuary at every turn.

The gravest danger our Nation faces lies at the crossroads of radicalism and technology. Our enemies have openly declared that they are seeking weapons of mass destruction, and evidence indicates that they are doing so with determination. The United States will not allow these efforts to succeed. We will build defenses against ballistic missiles and other means of delivery. We will cooperate with other nations to deny, contain, and curtail our enemies' efforts to acquire dangerous technologies. And, as a matter of common sense and self-defense, America will act against such emerging threats before they are fully formed. We cannot defend America and our friends by hoping for the best. So we must be prepared to defeat our enemies' plans, using the best intelligence and proceeding with deliberation. History will judge harshly those who saw this coming danger but failed to act. In the new world we have entered, the only path to peace and security is the path of action.

As we defend the peace, we will also take advantage of an historic opportunity to preserve the peace. Today, the international community has the best chance since the rise of the nation-state in the seventeenth century to build a world where great powers compete in peace instead of continually prepare for war. Today, the world's great powers find ourselves on the same side—united by common dangers of terrorist violence and chaos. The United States will build on these common interests to promote global security. We are also increasingly united by common values. Russia is in the midst of a hopeful transition, reaching for its democratic future and a partner in the war on terror. Chinese leaders are discovering that economic freedom is the only source of national wealth. In time, they will find that social and political freedom is the only source of national greatness. America will encourage the advancement of democracy and economic openness in both nations, because these are the best foundations for domestic stability and international order. We will strongly resist aggression from other great powers—even as we welcome their peaceful pursuit of prosperity, trade, and cultural advancement.

Finally, the United States will use this moment of opportunity to extend the benefits of freedom across the globe. We will actively work to bring the hope of democracy, development, free markets, and free trade to every corner of the world. The events of September 11, 2001, taught us that weak states, like Afghanistan, can pose as great a danger to our national interests as strong states. Poverty does not make poor people into terrorists and murderers. Yet poverty, weak institutions, and corruption can make weak states vulnerable to terrorist networks and drug cartels within their borders. The United States will stand beside any nation determined to build a better future by seeking the rewards of liberty for its people. Free trade and free markets have proven their ability to lift whole societies out of poverty—so the United States will work with individual nations, entire regions, and the entire global trading community to build a world that trades in freedom and therefore grows in prosperity. The United States will deliver greater development assistance through the New Millennium Challenge Account to nations that govern justly, invest in their people, and encourage economic freedom. We will also continue to lead the world in efforts to reduce the terrible toll of HIV/AIDS and other infectious diseases.

In building a balance of power that favors freedom, the United States is guided by the conviction that all nations have important responsibilities. Nations that enjoy freedom must actively fight terror. Nations that depend on international stability must help prevent the spread of weapons of mass destruction. Nations that seek international aid must govern themselves wisely, so that aid is well spent. For freedom to thrive, accountability must be expected and required.

We are also guided by the conviction that no nation can build a safer, better world alone. Alliances and multilateral institutions can multiply the strength of freedom-loving nations. The United States is committed to lasting institutions like the United Nations, the World Trade Organization, the Organization of American States, and NATO as well as other long-standing alliances. Coalitions of the willing can augment these permanent institutions. In all cases, international obligations are to be taken seriously. They are not to be undertaken symbolically to rally support for an ideal without furthering its attainment.

Freedom is the non-negotiable demand of human dignity; the birthright of every person—in every civilization. Throughout history, freedom has been threatened by war and terror; it has been challenged by the clashing wills of powerful states and the evil designs of tyrants; and it has been tested by widespread poverty and disease. Today, humanity holds in its hands the opportunity to further freedom's triumph over all these foes. The United States welcomes our responsibility to lead in this great mission.

THE WHITE HOUSE,
September 17, 2002

Table of Contents

I. Overview of America's International Strategy

II. Champion Aspirations for Human Dignity

III. Strengthen Alliances to Defeat Global Terrorism and Work to Prevent Attacks Against Us and Our Friends

IV. Work with others to Defuse Regional Conflicts

V. Prevent Our Enemies from Threatening Us, Our Allies, and Our Friends with Weapons of Mass Destruction

VI. Ignite a New Era of Global Economic Growth through Free Markets and Free Trade

VII. Expand the Circle of Development by Opening Societies and Building the Infrastructure of Democracy

VIII. Develop Agendas for Cooperative Action with the Other Main Centers of Global Power

IX. Transform America's National Security Institutions to Meet the Challenges and Opportunities of the Twenty-First Century

I. Overview of America's International Strategy

"Our Nation's cause has always been larger than our Nation's defense. We fight, as we always fight, for a just peace—a peace that favors liberty. We will defend the peace against the threats from terrorists and tyrants. We will preserve the peace by building good relations among the great powers. And we will extend the peace by encouraging free and open societies on every continent."

President Bush
West Point, New York
June 1, 2002

The United States possesses unprecedented— and unequaled—strength and influence in the world. Sustained by faith in the principles of liberty, and the value of a free society, this position comes with unparalleled responsibilities, obligations, and opportunity. The great strength of this nation must be used to promote a balance of power that favors freedom.

For most of the twentieth century, the world was divided by a great struggle over ideas: destructive totalitarian visions versus freedom and equality.

That great struggle is over. The militant visions of class, nation, and race which promised utopia and delivered misery have been defeated and discredited. America is now threatened less by conquering states than we are by failing ones. We are menaced less by fleets and armies than by catastrophic technologies in the hands of the embittered few. We must defeat these threats to our Nation, allies, and friends.

This is also a time of opportunity for America. We will work to translate this moment of influence into decades of peace, prosperity, and liberty. The U.S. national security strategy will be based on a distinctly American internationalism that reflects the union of our values and our national interests. The aim of this strategy is to help make the world not just safer but better. Our goals on the path to progress are clear: political and economic freedom, peaceful relations with other states, and respect for human dignity.

And this path is not America's alone. It is open to all.

To achieve these goals, the United States will:

• champion aspirations for human dignity;

• strengthen alliances to defeat global terrorism and work to prevent attacks against us and our friends;

• work with others to defuse regional conflicts;

• prevent our enemies from threatening us, our allies, and our friends, with weapons of mass destruction;

• ignite a new era of global economic growth through free markets and free trade;

• expand the circle of development by opening societies and building the infrastructure of democracy;

- develop agendas for cooperative action with other main centers of global power; and

- transform America's national securi-

ty institutions to meet the challenges and opportunities of the twenty-first century.

II. Champion Aspirations for Human Dignity

"Some worry that it is somehow undiplomatic or impolite to speak the language of right and wrong. I disagree. Different circumstances require different methods, but not different moralities."

President Bush
West Point, New York
June 1, 2002

In pursuit of our goals, our first imperative is to clarify what we stand for: the United States must defend liberty and justice because these principles are right and true for all people everywhere. No nation owns these aspirations, and no nation is exempt from them. Fathers and mothers in all societies want their children to be educated and to live free from poverty and violence. No people on earth yearn to be oppressed, aspire to servitude, or eagerly await the midnight knock of the secret police.

America must stand firmly for the nonnegotiable demands of human dignity: the rule of law; limits on the absolute power of the state; free speech; freedom of worship; equal justice; respect for women; religious and ethnic tolerance; and respect for private property.

These demands can be met in many ways. America's constitution has served us well. Many other nations, with different histories and cultures, facing different circumstances, have successfully incorporated these core principles into their own systems of governance. History has not been kind to those nations which ignored or flouted the rights and aspirations of their people.

America's experience as a great multiethnic democracy affirms our conviction that people of many heritages and faiths can live and prosper in peace. Our own history is a long struggle to live up to our ideals. But even in our worst moments, the principles enshrined in the Declaration of Independence were there to guide us. As a result, America is not just a stronger, but is a freer and more just society.

Today, these ideals are a lifeline to lonely defenders of liberty. And when openings arrive, we can encourage change—as we did in central and eastern Europe between 1989 and 1991, or in Belgrade in 2000. When we see democratic processes take hold among our friends in Taiwan or in the Republic of Korea, and see elected leaders replace generals in Latin America and Africa, we see examples of how authoritarian systems can evolve, marrying local history and traditions with the principles we all cherish.

Embodying lessons from our past and using the opportunity we have today, the national security strategy of the United States must start from these core beliefs and look outward for possibilities to expand liberty.

Our principles will guide our government's decisions about international cooperation, the character of our foreign assistance, and the allocation of resources. They will guide our actions and our words in international bodies.

We will:

• speak out honestly about violations of the nonnegotiable demands of human dignity using our voice and vote in international institutions to advance freedom;

• use our foreign aid to promote freedom and support those who struggle non-violently for it, ensuring that nations moving toward democracy are rewarded for the steps they take;

• make freedom and the development of democratic institutions key themes in our bilateral relations, seeking solidarity and cooperation from other democracies while we press governments that deny human rights to move toward a better future; and

• take special efforts to promote freedom of religion and conscience and defend it from encroachment by repressive governments.

We will champion the cause of human dignity and oppose those who resist it.

III. Strengthen Alliances to Defeat Global Terrorism and Work to Prevent Attacks Against Us and Our Friends

"Just three days removed from these events, Americans do not yet have the distance of history. But our responsibility to history is already clear: to answer these attacks and rid the world of evil. War has been waged against us by stealth and deceit and murder. This nation is peaceful, but fierce when stirred to anger. The conflict was begun on the timing and terms of others. It will end in a way, and at an hour, of our choosing."

President Bush
Washington, D.C. (The National Cathedral)
September 14, 2001

The United States of America is fighting a war against terrorists of global reach. The enemy is not a single political regime or person or religion or ideology. The enemy is terrorism— premeditated, politically motivated violence perpetrated against innocents.

In many regions, legitimate grievances prevent the emergence of a lasting peace. Such grievances deserve to be, and must be, addressed within a political process. But no cause justifies terror. The United States will make no concessions to terrorist demands and strike no deals with them. We make no distinction between terrorists and those who knowingly harbor or provide aid to them.

The struggle against global terrorism is different from any other war in our history. It will be fought on many fronts against a particularly elusive enemy over an extended period of time. Progress will come through the persistent accumulation of successes—some seen, some unseen.

Today our enemies have seen the results of what civilized nations can, and will, do against regimes that harbor, support, and use terrorism to achieve their political goals. Afghanistan has been liberated; coalition forces continue to hunt down the Taliban and al-Qaida. But it is not only this battlefield on which we will engage terrorists. Thousands of trained terrorists remain at large with cells in North America, South America, Europe, Africa, the Middle East, and across Asia.

Our priority will be first to disrupt and destroy terrorist organizations of global reach and attack their leadership; command, control, and communications; material support; and finances. This will have a disabling effect upon the terrorists' ability to plan and operate.

We will continue to encourage our regional partners to take up a coordinated effort that isolates the terrorists. Once the regional campaign localizes the threat to a particular state, we will help ensure the state has the military, law enforcement, political, and financial tools necessary to finish the task.

The United States will continue to work with our allies to disrupt the financing of terrorism. We will identify and block the sources of funding for terrorism, freeze the assets of terrorists and those who support them, deny terrorists access to the international financial system, protect legitimate charities from being abused by terrorists, and prevent the movement of terrorists' assets through alternative financial networks.

However, this campaign need not be sequential to be effective, the cumulative effect across all regions will help achieve the results we seek. We will disrupt and destroy terrorist organizations by:

direct and continuous action using all the elements of national and international power. Our immediate focus will be those terrorist organizations of global reach and any terrorist or state sponsor of terrorism which attempts to gain or use weapons of mass destruction (WMD) or their precursors;

• defending the United States, the American people, and our interests at home and abroad by identifying and destroying the threat before it reaches our borders. While the United States will constantly strive to enlist the support of the international community, we will not hesitate to act alone, if necessary, to exercise our right of self-defense by acting preemptively against such terrorists, to prevent them from doing harm against our people and our country; and

• denying further sponsorship, support, and sanctuary to terrorists by convincing or compelling states to accept their sovereign responsibilities. We will also wage a war of ideas to win the battle against international terrorism. This includes:

• using the full influence of the United States, and working closely with allies and friends, to make clear that all acts of terrorism are illegitimate so that terrorism will be viewed in the same light as slavery, piracy, or genocide: behavior that no respectable government can condone or support and all must oppose;

• supporting moderate and modern government, especially in the

Muslim world, to ensure that the conditions and ideologies that promote terrorism do not find fertile ground in any nation;

- diminishing the underlying conditions that spawn terrorism by enlisting the international community to focus its efforts and resources on areas most at risk; and

- using effective public diplomacy to promote the free flow of information and ideas to kindle the hopes and aspirations of freedom of those in societies ruled by the sponsors of global terrorism.

While we recognize that our best defense is a good offense, we are also strengthening America's homeland security to protect against and deter attack. This Administration has proposed the largest government reorganization since the Truman Administration created the National Security Council and the Department of Defense. Centered on a new Department of Homeland Security and including a new unified military command and a fundamental reordering of the FBI, our comprehensive plan to secure the homeland encompasses every level of government and the cooperation of the public and the private sector.

This strategy will turn adversity into opportunity. For example, emergency management systems will be better able to cope not just with terrorism but with all hazards. Our medical system will be strengthened to manage not just bioterror, but all infectious diseases and mass-casualty dangers. Our border controls will not just stop terrorists, but improve the efficient movement of legitimate traffic.

While our focus is protecting America, we know that to defeat terrorism in today's globalized world we need support from our allies and friends. Wherever possible, the United States will rely on regional organizations and state powers to meet their obligations to fight terrorism. Where governments find the fight against terrorism beyond their capacities, we will match their willpower and their resources with whatever help we and our allies can provide.

As we pursue the terrorists in Afghanistan, we will continue to work with international organizations such as the United Nations, as well as non-governmental organizations, and other countries to provide the humanitarian, political, economic, and security assistance necessary to rebuild Afghanistan so that it will never again abuse its people, threaten its neighbors, and provide a haven for terrorists.

In the war against global terrorism, we will never forget that we are ultimately fighting for our democratic values and way of life. Freedom and fear are at war, and there will be no quick or easy end to this conflict. In leading the campaign against terrorism, we are forging new, productive international relationships and redefining existing ones in ways that meet the challenges of the twenty-first century.

IV. Work with others to Defuse Regional Conflicts

"We build a world of justice, or we will live in a world of coercion. The magnitude of our shared responsibilities makes our disagreements look so small."

President Bush
Berlin, Germany
May 23, 2002

Concerned nations must remain actively engaged in critical regional disputes to avoid explosive escalation and minimize human suffering. In an increasingly interconnected world, regional crisis can strain our alliances, rekindle rivalries among the major powers, and create horrifying affronts to human dignity. When violence erupts and states falter, the United States will work with friends and partners to alleviate suffering and restore stability.

No doctrine can anticipate every circumstance in which U.S. action—direct or indirect—is warranted. We have finite political, economic, and military resources to meet our global priorities. The United States will approach each case with these strategic principles in mind:

- The United States should invest time and resources into building international relationships and institutions that can help manage local crises when they emerge.

- The United States should be realistic about its ability to help those who are unwilling or unready to help themselves. Where and when people are ready to do their part, we will be willing to move decisively.

The Israeli-Palestinian conflict is critical because of the toll of human suffering, because of America's close relationship with the state of Israel and key Arab states, and because of that region's importance to other global priorities of the United States.

There can be no peace for either side without freedom for both sides. America stands committed to an independent and democratic Palestine, living beside Israel in peace and security. Like all other people, Palestinians deserve a government that serves their interests and listens to their voices. The United States will continue to encourage all parties to step up to their responsibilities as we seek a just and comprehensive settlement to the conflict.

The United States, the international donor community, and the World Bank stand ready to work with a reformed Palestinian government on economic development, increased humanitarian assistance, and a program to establish, finance, and monitor a truly independent judiciary. If Palestinians embrace democracy, and the rule of law, confront corruption, and firmly reject terror, they can count on American support for the creation of a Palestinian state.

Israel also has a large stake in the success of a democratic Palestine. Permanent occupation threatens Israel's identity and democracy. So the United States continues to challenge Israeli leaders to take concrete steps to support the emergence of a viable, credible Palestinian state. As there is progress towards security, Israel forces need to withdraw fully to positions they held prior to September 28, 2000. And consistent with the recommendations of the Mitchell Committee, Israeli settlement activity in the occupied territories must stop. As violence subsides, freedom of movement should be restored, permitting innocent Palestinians to resume work and normal life. The United States can play a crucial role but, ultimately, lasting peace can only come when Israelis and Palestinians resolve the issues and end the conflict between them.

In South Asia, the United States has also emphasized the need for India and Pakistan to resolve their disputes. This Administration invested time and resources building strong bilateral relations with India and Pakistan. These strong relations then gave us leverage to play a constructive role when tensions in the region became acute. With Pakistan, our bilateral relations have been bolstered by Pakistan's choice to join the war against terror and move toward building a more open and tolerant society. The Administration sees India's potential to become one of the great democratic powers of the twenty-first century and has worked hard to transform our relationship accordingly. Our involvement in this regional dispute, building on earlier investments in bilateral relations, looks first to concrete steps by India and Pakistan that can help defuse military confrontation.

Indonesia took courageous steps to create a working democracy and respect for the rule of law. By tolerating ethnic minorities, respecting the rule of law, and accepting open markets, Indonesia may be able to employ the engine of opportunity that has helped lift some of its neighbors out of poverty and desperation. It is the initiative by Indonesia that allows U.S. assistance to make a difference.

In the Western Hemisphere we have formed flexible coalitions with countries that share our priorities, particularly Mexico, Brazil, Canada, Chile, and Colombia. Together we will promote a truly democratic hemisphere where our integration advances security, prosperity, opportunity, and hope. We will work with regional institutions, such as the Summit

of the Americas process, the Organization of American States (OAS), and the Defense Ministerial of the Americas for the benefit of the entire hemisphere.

Parts of Latin America confront regional conflict, especially arising from the violence of drug cartels and their accomplices. This conflict and unrestrained narcotics trafficking could imperil the health and security of the United States. Therefore we have developed an active strategy to help the Andean nations adjust their economies, enforce their laws, defeat terrorist organizations, and cut off the supply of drugs, while—as important—we work to reduce the demand for drugs in our own country.

In Colombia, we recognize the link between terrorist and extremist groups that challenge the security of the state and drug trafficking activities that help finance the operations of such groups. We are working to help Colombia defend its democratic institutions and defeat illegal armed groups of both the left and right by extending effective sovereignty over the entire national territory and provide basic security to the Colombian people.

In Africa, promise and opportunity sit side by side with disease, war, and desperate poverty. This threatens both a core value of the United States— preserving human dignity—and our strategic priority—combating global terror. American interests and American principles, therefore, lead in the same direction: we will work with others for an African continent that lives in liberty, peace, and growing prosperity. Together with our European allies, we must help strengthen Africa's fragile states, help build indigenous capability to secure porous borders, and help build up the law enforcement and intelligence infrastructure to deny havens for terrorists.

An ever more lethal environment exists in Africa as local civil wars spread beyond borders to create regional war zones.

Forming coalitions of the willing and cooperative security arrangements are key to confronting these emerging transnational threats.

Africa's great size and diversity requires a security strategy that focuses on bilateral engagement and builds coalitions of the willing. This Administration will focus on three interlocking strategies for the region:

- countries with major impact on their neighborhood such as South Africa, Nigeria, Kenya, and Ethiopia are anchors for regional engagement and require focused attention;

- coordination with European allies and international institutions is essential for constructive conflict mediation and successful peace operations; and

- Africa's capable reforming states and sub-regional organizations must be strengthened as the primary means to address transnational threats on a sustained basis.

Ultimately the path of political and economic freedom presents the surest route to progress in sub-Saharan Africa, where most wars are conflicts over material resources and political access often tragically waged on the basis of ethnic and religious difference. The transition to the African Union with its stated commitment to good governance and a common responsibility for democratic political systems offers opportunities to strengthen democracy on the continent.

V. Prevent Our Enemies from Threatening Us, Our Allies, and Our Friends with Weapons of Mass Destruction

"The gravest danger to freedom lies at the crossroads of radicalism and technology. When the spread of chemical and biological and nuclear weapons, along with ballistic missile technology—when that occurs, even weak states and small groups could attain a catastrophic power to strike great nations. Our enemies have declared this very intention, and have been caught seeking these terrible weapons. They want the capability to blackmail us, or to harm us, or to harm our friends—and we will oppose them with all our power."

President Bush
West Point, New York
June 1, 2002

The nature of the Cold War threat required the United States—with our allies and friends—to emphasize deterrence of the enemy's use of force, producing a grim strategy of mutual assured destruction. With the collapse of the Soviet Union and the end of the Cold War, our security environment has undergone profound transformation.

Having moved from confrontation to cooperation as the hallmark of our relationship with Russia, the dividends are evident: an end to the balance of terror that divided us; an historic reduction in the nuclear arsenals on both sides; and cooperation in areas such as counterterrorism and missile defense that until recently were inconceivable.

But new deadly challenges have emerged from rogue states and terrorists. None of these contemporary threats rival the sheer destructive power that was arrayed against us by the Soviet Union. However, the nature and motivations of these new adversaries, their determination to obtain destructive powers hitherto available only to the world's strongest states, and the greater likelihood that they will use weapons of mass destruction against us, make today's security environment more complex and dangerous.

In the 1990s we witnessed the emergence of a small number of rogue states that, while different in important ways, share a number of attributes. These states:

- brutalize their own people and squander their national resources for the personal gain of the rulers;

- display no regard for international law, threaten their neighbors, and callously violate international treaties to which they are party;

- are determined to acquire weapons of mass destruction, along with other advanced military technology, to be used as threats or offensively to achieve the aggressive designs of these regimes;

- sponsor terrorism around the globe; and

- reject basic human values and hate the United States and everything for which it stands.

At the time of the Gulf War, we acquired irrefutable proof that Iraq's designs were not limited to the chemical weapons it had used against Iran and its own people, but also extended to the acquisition of nuclear weapons and biological agents. In the past decade North Korea has become the world's principal purveyor of ballistic missiles, and has tested increasingly capable missiles while developing its own WMD arsenal. Other rogue regimes seek nuclear, biological, and chemical weapons as well. These states' pursuit of, and global trade in, such weapons has become a looming threat to all nations.

We must be prepared to stop rogue states and their terrorist clients before they are able to threaten or use weapons of mass destruction against the United States and our allies and friends. Our response must take full advantage of strengthened alliances, the establishment of new partnerships with former adversaries, innovation in the use of military forces, modern technologies, including the development of an effective missile defense system, and increased emphasis on intelligence collection and analysis.

Our comprehensive strategy to combat WMD includes:

- *Proactive counterproliferation efforts.* We must deter and defend against the threat before it is unleashed. We must ensure that key capabilities—detection, active and passive defenses, and counterforce capabilities—are integrated into our defense transformation and our homeland security systems. Counterproliferation must also be integrated into the doctrine, training, and equipping of our forces and those of our allies to ensure that we can prevail in any conflict with WMD-armed adversaries.

- *Strengthened nonproliferation efforts to prevent rogue states and terrorists from acquiring the materials, technolo-*

gies, and expertise necessary for weapons of mass destruction. We will enhance diplomacy, arms control, multilateral export controls, and threat reduction assistance that impede states and terrorists seeking WMD, and when necessary, interdict enabling technologies and materials. We will continue to build coalitions to support these efforts, encouraging their increased political and financial support for nonproliferation and threat reduction programs. The recent G-8 agreement to commit up to $20 billion to a global partnership against proliferation marks a major step forward.

• *Effective consequence management to respond to the effects of WMD use, whether by terrorists or hostile states.* Minimizing the effects of WMD use against our people will help deter those who possess such weapons and dissuade those who seek to acquire them by persuading enemies that they cannot attain their desired ends. The United States must also be prepared to respond to the effects of WMD use against our forces abroad, and to help friends and allies if they are attacked.

It has taken almost a decade for us tocomprehend the true nature of this new threat. Given the goals of rogue states and terrorists, the United States can no longer solely rely on a reactive posture as we have in the past. The inability to deter a potential attacker, the immediacy of today's threats, and the magnitude of potential harm that could be caused by our adversaries' choice of weapons, do not permit that option. We cannot let our enemies strike first.

• In the Cold War, especially following the Cuban missile crisis, we faced a generally status quo, risk-averse adversary. Deterrence was an effective defense. But deterrence based only upon the threat of retaliation is less likely to work against leaders of rogue states more willing to take risks, gambling with the lives of their people, and the wealth of their nations.

• In the Cold War, weapons of mass destruction were considered weapons of last resort whose use risked the destruction of those who used them. Today, our enemies see weapons of mass destruction as weapons of choice. For rogue states these weapons are tools of intimidation and military aggression against their neighbors. These weapons may also allow these states to attempt to blackmail the United States and our allies to prevent us from deterring or repelling the aggressive behavior of rogue states. Such states also see these weapons as their best means of overcoming the conventional superiority of the United States.

• Traditional concepts of deterrence will not work against a terrorist enemy whose avowed tactics are wanton destruction and the targeting of innocents; whose so-called soldiers seek martyrdom in death and whose most potent protection is statelessness. The overlap between states that sponsor terror and those that pursue WMD compels us to action.

For centuries, international law recognized that nations need not suffer an attack before they can lawfully take action to defend themselves against forces that present an imminent danger of attack. Legal scholars and international jurists often conditioned the legitimacy of preemption on the existence of an imminent threat—most often a visible mobilization of armies, navies, and air forces preparing to attack.

We must adapt the concept of imminent threat to the capabilities and objectives of today's adversaries. Rogue states and terrorists do not seek to attack us using conventional means. They know such attacks would fail. Instead, they rely on acts of terror and, potentially, the use of weapons of mass destruction—weapons that can be easily concealed, delivered covertly, and used without warning.

The targets of these attacks are our military forces and our civilian population, in direct violation of one of the principal norms of the law of warfare. As was demonstrated by the losses on September 11, 2001, mass civilian casualties is the specific objective of terrorists and these losses would be exponentially more severe if terrorists acquired and used weapons of mass destruction.

The United States has long maintained the option of preemptive actions to counter a sufficient threat to our national security. The greater the threat, the greater is the risk of inaction— and the more compelling the case for taking anticipatory action to defend ourselves, even if uncertainty remains as to the time and place of the enemy's attack. To forestall or prevent such hostile acts by our adversaries, the United States will, if necessary, act preemptively.

The United States will not use force in all cases to preempt emerging threats, nor should nations use preemption as a pretext for aggression. Yet in an age where the enemies of civilization openly and actively seek the world's most destructive technologies, the United States cannot remain idle while dangers gather. We will always proceed deliberately, weighing the consequences of our actions. To support preemptive options, we will:

• build better, more integrated intelligence capabilities to provide timely, accurate information on threats, wherever they may emerge;

• coordinate closely with allies to form a common assessment of the most dangerous threats; and

• continue to transform our military forces to ensure our ability to conduct rapid and precise operations to achieve decisive results.

The purpose of our actions will always be to eliminate a specific threat to the United States or our allies and friends. The reasons for our actions will be clear, the force measured, and the cause just.

VI. Ignite a New Era of Global Economic Growth through Free Markets and Free Trade

"When nations close their markets and opportunity is hoarded by a privileged few, no amount-no amount-of development aid is ever enough. When nations respect their people, open markets, invest in better health and education, every dollar of aid, every dollar of trade revenue and domestic capital is used more effectively."

President Bush
Monterrey, Mexico
March 22, 2002

A strong world economy enhances our national security by advancing prosperity and freedom in the rest of the world. Economic growth supported by free trade and free markets creates new jobs and higher incomes. It allows people to lift their lives out of poverty, spurs economic and legal reform, and the fight against corruption, and it reinforces the habits of liberty.

We will promote economic growth and economic freedom beyond America's shores. All governments are responsible for creating their own economic policies and responding to their own economic challenges. We will use our economic engagement with other countries to underscore the benefits of policies that generate higher productivity and sustained economic growth, including:

• pro-growth legal and regulatory policies to encourage business investment, innovation, and entrepreneurial activity;

• tax policies—particularly lower marginal tax rates—that improve incentives for work and investment;

• rule of law and intolerance of corrup-

tion so that people are confident that they will be able to enjoy the fruits of their economic endeavors;

• strong financial systems that allow capital to be put to its most efficient use;

• sound fiscal policies to support business activity;

• investments in health and education that improve the well-being and skills of the labor force and population as a whole; and

• free trade that provides new avenues for growth and fosters the diffusion of technologies and ideas that increase productivity and opportunity.

The lessons of history are clear: market economies, not command-and-control economies with the heavy hand of government, are the best way to promote prosperity and reduce poverty. Policies that further strengthen market incentives and market institutions are relevant for all economies—industrialized countries, emerging markets, and the developing world.

A return to strong economic growth in

Europe and Japan is vital to U.S. national security interests. We want our allies to have strong economies for their own sake, for the sake of the global economy, and for the sake of global security. European efforts to remove structural barriers in their economies are particularly important in this regard, as are Japan's efforts to end deflation and address the problems of non-performing loans in the Japanese banking system. We will continue to use our regular consultations with Japan and our European partners—including through the Group of Seven (G-7)—to discuss policies they are adopting to promote growth in their economies and support higher global economic growth.

Improving stability in emerging markets is also key to global economic growth. International flows of investment capital are needed to expand the productive potential of these economies. These flows allow emerging markets and developing countries to make the investments that raise living standards and reduce poverty. Our long-term objective should be a world in which all countries have investment-grade credit ratings that allow them access to international capital markets and to invest in their future.

We are committed to policies that will help emerging markets achieve access to larger capital flows at lower cost. To this end, we will continue to pursue reforms aimed at reducing uncertainty in financial markets. We will work actively with other countries, the International Monetary Fund (IMF), and the private sector to implement the G-7 Action Plan negotiated earlier this year for preventing financial crises and more effectively resolving them when they occur.

The best way to deal with financial crises is to prevent them from occurring, and we have encouraged the IMF to improve its efforts doing so. We will continue to work with the IMF to streamline the policy conditions for its lending and to focus its lend-

ing strategy on achieving economic growth through sound fiscal and monetary policy, exchange rate policy, and financial sector policy.

The concept of "free trade" arose as a moral principle even before it became a pillar of economics. If you can make something that others value, you should be able to sell it to them. If others make something that you value, you should be able to buy it. This is real freedom, the freedom for a person—or a nation—to make a living. To promote free trade, the Unites States has developed a comprehensive strategy:

- *Seize the global initiative.* The new global trade negotiations we helped launch at Doha in November 2001 will have an ambitious agenda, especially in agriculture, manufacturing, and services, targeted for completion in 2005. The United States has led the way in completing the accession of China and a democratic Taiwan to the World Trade Organization. We will assist Russia's preparations to join the WTO.

- *Press regional initiatives.* The United States and other democracies in the Western Hemisphere have agreed to create the Free Trade Area of the Americas, targeted for completion in 2005. This year the United States will advocate market-access negotiations with its partners, targeted on agriculture, industrial goods, services, investment, and government procurement. We will also offer more opportunity to the poorest continent, Africa, starting with full use of the preferences allowed in the African Growth and Opportunity Act, and leading to free trade.

- *Move ahead with bilateral free trade agreements.* Building on the free trade agreement with Jordan enacted in 2001, the Administration will work this year to complete free trade agreements with Chile and Singapore. Our aim is to achieve free trade agreements with a mix of developed and developing countries in all regions of the world. Initially, Central America, Southern Africa, Morocco, and Australia will be our principal focal points.

• *Renew the executive-congressional partnership.* Every administration's trade strategy depends on a productive partnership with Congress. After a gap of 8 years, the Administration reestablished majority support in the Congress for trade liberalization by passing Trade Promotion Authority and the other market opening measures for developing countries in the Trade Act of 2002. This Administration will work with Congress to enact new bilateral, regional, and global trade agreements that will be concluded under the recently passed Trade Promotion Authority.

• *Promote the connection between trade and development.* Trade policies can help developing countries strengthen property rights, competition, the rule of law, investment, the spread of knowledge, open societies, the efficient allocation of resources, and regional integration—all leading to growth, opportunity, and confidence in developing countries. The United States is implementing The Africa Growth and Opportunity Act to provide market-access for nearly all goods produced in the 35 countries of sub- Saharan Africa. We will make more use of this act and its equivalent for the Caribbean Basin and continue to work with multilateral and regional institutions to help poorer countries take advantage of these opportunities. Beyond market access, the most important area where trade intersects with poverty is in public health. We will ensure that the WTO

intellectual property rules are flexible enough to allow developing nations to gain access to critical medicines for extraordinary dangers like HIV/AIDS, tuberculosis, and malaria.

• *Enforce trade agreements and laws against unfair practices.* Commerce depends on the rule of law; international trade depends on enforceable agreements. Our top priorities are to resolve ongoing disputes with the European Union, Canada, and Mexico and to make a global effort to address new technology, science, and health regulations that needlessly impede farm exports and improved agriculture. Laws against unfair trade practices are often abused, but the international community must be able to address genuine concerns about government subsidies and dumping. International industrial espionage which undermines fair competition must be detected and deterred.

• *Help domestic industries and workers adjust.* There is a sound statutory framework for these transitional safeguards which we have used in the agricultural sector and which we are using this year to help the American steel industry. The benefits of free trade depend upon the enforcement of fair trading practices. These safeguards help ensure that the benefits of free trade do not come at the expense of American workers. Trade adjustment assistance will help workers adapt to the change and dynamism of open markets.

• *Protect the environment and workers.* The United States must foster economic growth in ways that will provide a better life along with widening prosperity. We will incorporate labor and environmental concerns into U.S. trade negotiations, creating a healthy "network" between multilateral environmental agreements with the WTO, and use the International Labor Organization, trade preference programs, and trade talks to improve working conditions in conjunction with freer trade.

- *Enhance energy security.* We will strengthen our own energy security and the shared prosperity of the global economy by working with our allies, trading partners, and energy producers to expand the sources and types of global energy supplied, especially in the Western Hemisphere, Africa, Central Asia, and the Caspian region. We will also continue to work with our partners to develop cleaner and more energy efficient technologies.

- Economic growth should be accompanied by global efforts to stabilize greenhouse gas concentrations associated with this growth, containing them at a level that prevents dangerous human interference with the global climate. Our overall objective is to reduce America's greenhouse gas emissions relative to the size of our economy, cutting such emissions per unit of economic activity by 18 percent over the next 10 years, by the year 2012. Our strategies for attaining this goal will be to:

- remain committed to the basic U.N. Framework Convention for international cooperation;

- obtain agreements with key industries to cut emissions of some of the most potent greenhouse gases and give transferable credits to companies that can show real cuts;

- develop improved standards for measuring and registering emission reductions;

- promote renewable energy production and clean coal technology, as well as nuclear power—which produces no greenhouse gas emissions, while also improving fuel economy for U.S. cars and trucks;

- increase spending on research and new conservation technologies, to a total of $4.5 billion—the largest sum being spent on climate change by any country in the world and a $700 million increase over last year's budget; and

- assist developing countries, especially the major greenhouse gas emitters such as China and India, so that they will have the tools and resources to join this effort and be able to grow along a cleaner and better path.

VII. Expand the Circle of Development by Opening Societies and Building the Infrastructure of Democracy

"In World War II we fought to make the world safer, then worked to rebuild it. As we wage war today to keep the world safe from terror, we must also work to make the world a better place for all its citizens."

President Bush
Washington, D.C. (Inter-American Development Bank)
March 14, 2002

A world where some live in comfort and plenty, while half of the human race lives on less than $2 a day, is neither just nor stable. Including all of the world's poor in an expanding circle of development—and opportunity—is a moral imperative and one of the top priorities of U.S. international policy.

Decades of massive development assistance have failed to spur economic growth in the poorest countries. Worse, development aid has often served to prop up failed policies, relieving the pressure for reform and perpetuating misery. Results of aid are typically measured in dollars spent by donors, not in the rates of growth and poverty reduction achieved by recipients. These are the indicators of a failed strategy.

Working with other nations, the United States is confronting this failure. We forged a new consensus at the U.N. Conference on Financing for Development in Monterrey that the objectives of assistance—and the strategies to achieve those objectives—must change.

This Administration's goal is to help unleash the productive potential of individuals in all nations. Sustained growth and poverty reduction is impossible without the right national policies. Where governments have implemented real policy changes, we will provide significant new levels of assistance. The United States and other developed countries should set an ambitious and specific target: to double the size of the world's poorest economies within a decade.

The United States Government will pursue these major strategies to achieve this goal:

• Provide resources to aid countries that have met the challenge of national reform. We propose a 50 percent increase in the core development assistance given by the United States. While continuing our present programs, including humanitarian assistance based on need alone, these billions of new dollars will form a new Millennium Challenge Account for projects in countries whose governments rule justly, invest in their people, and encourage economic freedom. Governments must fight corruption, respect basic human rights, embrace the rule of law, invest in health care and education, follow responsible economic policies, and enable entrepreneurship. The Millennium Challenge Account will reward countries that have demonstrated real policy change and challenge those that have not to implement reforms.

- Improve the effectiveness of the World Bank and other development banks in raising living standards. The United States is committed to a comprehensive reform agenda for making the World Bank and the other multilateral development banks more effective in improving the lives of the world's poor. We have reversed the downward trend in U.S. contributions and proposed an 18 percent increase in the U.S. contributions to the International Development Association (IDA)—the World Bank's fund for the poorest countries—and the African Development Fund. The key to raising living standards and reducing poverty around the world is increasing productivity growth, especially in the poorest countries. We will continue to press the multilateral development banks to focus on activities that increase economic productivity, such as improvements in education, health, rule of law, and private sector development. Every project, every loan, every grant must be judged by how much it will increase productivity growth in developing countries.

- Insist upon measurable results to ensure that development assistance is actually making a difference in the lives of the world's poor. When it comes to economic development, what really matters is that more children are getting a better education, more people have access to health care and clean water, or more workers can find jobs to make a better future for their families. We have a moral obligation to measure the success of our development assistance by whether it is delivering results. For this reason, we will continue to demand that our own development assistance as well as assistance from the multilateral development banks has measurable goals and concrete benchmarks for achieving those

goals. Thanks to U.S. leadership, the recent IDA replenishment agreement will establish a monitoring and evaluation system that measures recipient countries' progress. For the first time, donors can link a portion of their contributions to IDA to the achievement of actual development results, and part of the U.S. contribution is linked in this way. We will strive to make sure that the World Bank and other multilateral development banks build on this progress so that a focus on results is an integral part of everything that these institutions do.

- Increase the amount of development assistance that is provided in the form of grants instead of loans. Greater use of results-based grants is the best way to help poor countries make productive investments, particularly in the social sectors, without saddling them with ever-larger debt burdens. As a result of U.S. leadership, the recent IDA agreement provided for significant increases in grant funding for the poorest countries for education, HIV/AIDS, health, nutrition, water, sanitation, and other human needs. Our goal is to build on that progress by increasing the use of grants at the other multilateral development banks. We will also challenge universities, nonprofits, and the private sector to match government efforts by using grants to support development projects that show results.

- Open societies to commerce and investment. Trade and investment are the real engines of economic growth. Even if government aid increases, most money for development must come from trade, domestic capital, and foreign investment. An effective strategy must try to expand these flows as well. Free markets and free trade are key priorities of our national security strategy.

• Secure public health. The scale of the public health crisis in poor countries is enormous. In countries afflicted by epidemics and pandemics like HIV/AIDS, malaria, and tuberculosis, growth and development will be threatened until these scourges can be contained. Resources from the developed world are necessary but will be effective only with honest governance, which supports prevention programs and provides effective local infrastructure. The United States has strongly backed the new global fund for HIV/AIDS organized by U.N. Secretary General Kofi Annan and its focus on combining prevention with a broad strategy for treatment and care. The United States already contributes more than twice as much money to such efforts as the next largest donor. If the global fund demonstrates its promise, we will be ready to give even more.

• Emphasize education. Literacy and learning are the foundation of democracy and development. Only about 7 percent of World Bank resources are devoted to education. This proportion should grow. The United States will increase its own funding for education assistance by at least 20 percent with an emphasis on improving basic education and teacher training in Africa. The United States can also bring information technology to these societies, many of whose education systems have been devastated by HIV/AIDS.

• Continue to aid agricultural development. New technologies, including biotechnology, have enormous potential to improve crop yields in developing countries while using fewer pesticides and less water. Using sound science, the United States should help bring these benefits to the 800 million people, including 300 million children, who still suffer from hunger and malnutrition.

VIII. Develop Agendas for Cooperative Action with the Other Main Centers of Global Power

"We have our best chance since the rise of the nation-state in the 17th century to build a world where the great powers compete in peace instead of prepare for war."

President Bush
West Point, New York
June 1, 2002

America will implement its strategies by organizing coalitions—as broad as practicable— of states able and willing to promote a balance of power that favors freedom. Effective coalition leadership requires clear priorities, an appreciation of others' interests, and consistent consultations among partners with a spirit of humility.

There is little of lasting consequence that the United States can accomplish in the world without the sustained cooperation of its allies and friends in Canada and Europe. Europe is also the seat of two of the strongest and most able international institutions in the world: the North Atlantic Treaty Organization (NATO), which has, since its inception, been the fulcrum of transatlantic and inter-European security, and the European Union (EU), our partner in opening world trade.

The attacks of September 11 were also an attack on NATO, as NATO itself recognized when it invoked its Article V self-defense clause for the first time. NATO's core mission—collective defense of the transatlantic alliance of democracies — remains, but NATO must develop new structures and capabilities to carry out that mission under new circumstances. NATO must build a capability to field, at short notice, highly mobile, specially trained

forces whenever they are needed to respond to a threat against any member of the alliance.

The alliance must be able to act wherever our interests are threatened, creating coalitions under NATO's own mandate, as well as contributing to mission-based coalitions. To achieve this, we must:

• expand NATO's membership to those democratic nations willing and able to share the burden of defending and advancing our common interests;

• ensure that the military forces of NATO nations have appropriate combat contributions to make in coalition warfare;

• develop planning processes to enable those contributions to become effective multinational fighting forces;

• take advantage of the technological opportunities and economies of scale in our defense spending to transform NATO military forces so that they dominate potential aggressors and diminish our vulnerabilities;

• streamline and increase the flexibility of command structures to meet new operational demands and the associated requirements of training, integrating, and experimenting with new force configurations; and

- maintain the ability to work and fight together as allies even as we take the necessary steps to transform and modernize our forces.

If NATO succeeds in enacting these changes, the rewards will be a partnership as central to the security and interests of its member states as was the case during the Cold War. We will sustain a common perspective on the threats to our societies and improve our ability to take common action in defense of our nations and their interests. At the same time, we welcome our European allies' efforts to forge a greater foreign policy and defense identity with the EU, and commit ourselves to close consultations to ensure that these developments work with NATO. We cannot afford to lose this opportunity to better prepare the family of transatlantic democracies for the challenges to come.

The attacks of September 11 energized America's Asian alliances. Australia invoked the ANZUS Treaty to declare the September 11 was an attack on Australia itself, following that historic decision with the dispatch of some of the world's finest combat forces for Operation Enduring Freedom. Japan and the Republic of Korea provided unprecedented levels of military logistical support within weeks of the terrorist attack. We have deepened cooperation on counterterrorism with our alliance partners in Thailand and the Philippines and received invaluable assistance from close friends like Singapore and New Zealand.

The war against terrorism has proven that America's alliances in Asia not only underpin regional peace and stability, but are flexible and ready to deal with new challenges. To enhance our Asian alliances and friendships, we will:

- look to Japan to continue forging a leading role in regional and global affairs based on our common interests, our common values, and our close defense and diplomatic cooperation;

- work with South Korea to maintain vigilance towards the North while preparing our alliance to make contributions to the broader stability of the region over the longer term;

- build on 50 years of U.S.-Australian alliance cooperation as we continue working together to resolve regional and global problems—as we have so many times from the Battle of the Coral Sea to Tora Bora;

- maintain forces in the region that reflect our commitments to our allies, our requirements, our technological advances, and the strategic environment; and

- build on stability provided by these alliances, as well as with institutions such as ASEAN and the Asia-Pacific Economic Cooperation forum, to develop a mix of regional and bilateral strategies to manage change in this dynamic region.

We are attentive to the possible renewal of old patterns of great power competition. Several potential great powers are now in the midst of internal transition—most importantly Russia, India, and China. In all three cases, recent developments have encouraged our hope that a truly global consensus about basic principles is slowly taking shape.

With Russia, we are already building a new strategic relationship based on a central reality of the twenty-first century: the United States and Russia are no longer strategic adversaries. The Moscow Treaty on Strategic Reductions is emblematic of this new reality and reflects a critical change in Russian thinking that promises to lead to productive, long-term relations with the Euro-Atlantic community and the United States. Russia's top leaders have a realistic assessment of their country's current weakness and the policies—internal and external—needed to reverse those weaknesses. They understand, increasingly, that Cold War approaches do not serve their national interests and that Russian and American strategic interests overlap in many areas.

United States policy seeks to use this turn in Russian thinking to refocus our relationship on emerging and potential common interests and challenges. We are broadening our already extensive cooperation in the global war on terrorism. We are facilitating Russia's entry into the World Trade Organization, without lowering standards for accession, to promote beneficial bilateral trade and investment relations. We have created the NATO-Russia Council with the goal of deepening security cooperation among Russia, our European allies, and ourselves. We will continue to bolster the independence and stability of the states of the former Soviet Union in the belief that a prosperous and stable neighborhood will reinforce Russia's growing commitment to integration into the Euro-Atlantic community.

At the same time, we are realistic about the differences that still divide us from Russia and about the time and effort it will take to build an enduring strategic partnership. Lingering distrust of our motives and policies by key Russian elites slows improvement in our relations. Russia's uneven commitment to the basic values of free-market democracy and dubious record in combating the proliferation of weapons of mass destruction remain matters of great concern. Russia's very weakness limits the opportunities for cooperation. Nevertheless, those opportunities are vastly greater now than in recent years—or even decades.

The United States has undertaken a transformation in its bilateral relationship with India based on a conviction that U.S. interests require a strong relationship with India. We are the two largest democracies, committed to political freedom protected by representative government. India is moving toward greater economic freedom as well. We have a common interest in the free flow of commerce, including through the vital sea lanes of the Indian Ocean. Finally, we share an interest in fighting terrorism and in creating a strategically stable Asia.

Differences remain, including over the development of India's nuclear and missile programs, and the pace of India's economic reforms. But while in the past these concerns may have dominated our thinking about India, today we start with a view of India as a growing world power with which we have common strategic interests. Through a strong partnership with India, we can best address any differences and shape a dynamic future.

The United States relationship with China is an important part of our strategy to promote a stable, peaceful, and prosperous Asia-Pacific region. We welcome the emergence of a strong, peaceful, and prosperous China. The democratic development of China is crucial to that future. Yet, a quarter century after beginning the process of shedding the worst features of the Communist legacy, China's leaders have not yet made the next series of fundamental choices about the character of their state. In pursuing advanced military capabilities that can threaten its neighbors in the Asia-Pacific region, China is following an outdated path that, in the end, will hamper its own pursuit of national greatness. In time, China will find that social and political freedom is the only source of that greatness.

The United States seeks a constructive relationship with a changing China. We already cooperate well where our interests overlap, including the current war on terrorism and in promoting stability on the Korean peninsula. Likewise, we have coordinated on the future of Afghanistan and have initiated a comprehensive dialogue on counterterrorism and similar transitional concerns. Shared health and environmental threats, such as the spread of HIV/AIDS, challenge us to promote jointly the welfare of our citizens.

Addressing these transnational threats will challenge China to become more open with information, promote the development of civil society, and enhance individual human rights. China has begun to take the road to political openness, permitting many personal freedoms and conducting village-level elections, yet remains strongly committed to national one-party rule by the Communist Party. To make that nation truly accountable to its citizen's needs and aspirations, however, much work remains to be done. Only by allowing the Chinese people to think, assemble, and worship freely can China reach its full potential.

Our important trade relationship will benefit from China's entry into the World Trade Organization, which will create more export opportunities and ultimately more jobs for American farmers, workers, and companies. China is our fourth largest trading partner, with over $100 billion in annual two-way trade. The power of mar-

ket principles and the WTO's requirements for transparency and accountability will advance openness and the rule of law in China to help establish basic protections for commerce and for citizens. There are, however, other areas in which we have profound disagreements. Our commitment to the self-defense of Taiwan under the Taiwan Relations Act is one. Human rights is another. We expect China to adhere to its nonproliferation commitments. We will work to narrow differences where they exist, but not allow them to preclude cooperation where we agree.

The events of September 11, 2001, fundamentally changed the context for relations between the United States and other main centers of global power, and opened vast, new opportunities. With our long-standing allies in Europe and Asia, and with leaders in Russia, India, and China, we must develop active agendas of cooperation lest these relationships become routine and unproductive.

Every agency of the United States Government shares the challenge. We can build fruitful habits of consultation, quiet argument, sober analysis, and common action. In the long-term, these are the practices that will sustain the supremacy of our common principles and keep open the path of progress.

IX. Transform America's National Security Institutions to Meet the Challenges and Opportunities of the Twenty-First Century

"Terrorists attacked a symbol of American prosperity. They did not touch its source. America is successful because of the hard work, creativity, and enterprise of our people."

President Bush
Washington, D.C. (Joint Session of Congress)
September 20, 2001

The major institutions of American national security were designed in a different era to meet different requirements. All of them must be transformed.

It is time to reaffirm the essential role of American military strength. We must build and maintain our defenses beyond challenge. Our military's highest priority is to defend the United States. To do so effectively, our military must:

• assure our allies and friends;

• dissuade future military competition;

• deter threats against U.S. interests, allies, and friends; and

• decisively defeat any adversary if deterrence fails.

The unparalleled strength of the United States armed forces, and their forward presence, have maintained the peace in some of the world's most strategically vital regions. However, the threats and enemies we must confront have changed, and so must our forces. A military structured to deter massive Cold War-era armies must be transformed to focus more on how an adversary might fight rather than where and when a war might occur. We will channel our energies to overcome a host of operational challenges.

The presence of American forces overseas is one of the most profound symbols of the U.S. commitments to allies and friends. Through our willingness to use force in our own defense and in defense of others, the United States demonstrates its resolve to maintain a balance of power that favors freedom. To contend with uncertainty and to meet the many security challenges we face, the United States will require bases and stations within and beyond Western Europe and Northeast Asia, as well as temporary access arrangements for the long-distance deployment of U.S. forces.

Before the war in Afghanistan, that area was low on the list of major planning contingencies. Yet, in a very short time, we had to operate across the length and breadth of that remote nation, using every branch of the armed forces. We must prepare for more such deployments by developing assets such as advanced remote sensing, long-range precision strike capabilities, and transformed maneuver and expeditionary forces. This broad portfolio of military capabilities must also include the ability to defend the homeland, conduct information operations, ensure U.S. access to distant theaters, and protect critical U.S. infrastructure and assets in outer space.

Innovation within the armed forces will rest on experimentation with new approaches to warfare, strengthening joint operations, exploiting U.S. intelligence advantages, and taking full advantage of science and technology. We must also transform the way the Department of Defense is run, especially in financial management and recruitment and retention. Finally, while maintaining near-term readiness and the ability to fight the war on terrorism, the goal must be to provide the President with a wider range of military options to discourage aggression or any form of coercion against the United States, our allies, and our friends.

We know from history that deterrence can fail; and we know from experience that some enemies cannot be deterred. The United States must and will maintain the capability to defeat any attempt by an enemy—whether a state or non-state actor—to impose its will on the United States, our allies, or our friends. We will maintain the forces sufficient to support our obligations, and to defend freedom. Our forces will be strong enough to dissuade potential adversaries from pursuing a military build-up in hopes of surpassing, or equaling, the power of the United States.

Intelligence—and how we use it—is our first line of defense against terrorists and the threat posed by hostile states. Designed around the priority of gathering enormous information about a massive, fixed object—the Soviet bloc—the intelligence community is coping with the challenge of following a far more complex and elusive set of targets.

We must transform our intelligence capabilities and build new ones to keep pace with the nature of these threats. Intelligence must be appropriately integrated with our defense and law enforcement systems and coordinated with our allies and friends. We need to protect the capabilities we have so that we do not arm our enemies with the knowledge of how best to surprise us. Those who would harm us also seek the benefit of surprise to limit our prevention

and response options and to maximize injury.

We must strengthen intelligence warning and analysis to provide integrated threat assessments for national and homeland security. Since the threats inspired by foreign governments and groups may be conducted inside the United States, we must also ensure the proper fusion of information between intelligence and law enforcement.

Initiatives in this area will include:

- strengthening the authority of the Director of Central Intelligence to lead the development and actions of the Nation's foreign intelligence capabilities;

- establishing a new framework for intelligence warning that provides seamless and integrated warning across the spectrum of threats facing the nation and our allies;

- continuing to develop new methods of collecting information to sustain our intelligence advantage;

- investing in future capabilities while working to protect them through a more vigorous effort to prevent the compromise of intelligence capabilities; and

- collecting intelligence against the terrorist danger across the government with all-source analysis.

As the United States Government relies on the armed forces to defend America's interests, it must rely on diplomacy to interact with other nations. We will ensure that the Department of State receives funding sufficient to ensure the success of American diplomacy. The State Department takes the lead in managing our bilateral relationships with other governments. And in this new era, its people and institutions must be able to interact equally adroitly with non-governmental organizations and international institutions. Officials trained mainly in international politics must also extend their reach to understand complex issues of domestic governance around the world, including public health, education, law enforcement, the judiciary, and public diplomacy.

Our diplomats serve at the front line of complex negotiations, civil wars, and other humanitarian catastrophes. As humanitarian relief requirements are better understood, we must also be able to help build police forces, court systems, and legal codes, local and provincial government institutions, and electoral systems. Effective international cooperation is needed to accomplish these goals, backed by American readiness to play our part.

Just as our diplomatic institutions must adapt so that we can reach out to others, we also need a different and more comprehensive approach to public information efforts that can help people around the world learn about and understand America. The war on terrorism is not a clash of civilizations. It does, however, reveal the clash inside a civilization, a battle for the future of the Muslim world. This is a struggle of ideas and this is an area where America must excel.

We will take the actions necessary to ensure that our efforts to meet our global security commitments and protect Americans are not impaired by the potential for investigations, inquiry, or prosecution by the International Criminal Court (ICC), whose jurisdiction does not extend to Americans and which we do not accept. We will work together with other nations to avoid complications in our military operations and cooperation, through such mechanisms as multilateral and bilateral agreements that will protect U.S. nationals from the ICC. We will implement fully the American Servicemembers Protection Act, whose provisions are intended to ensure and enhance the protection of U.S. personnel and officials.

We will make hard choices in the coming year and beyond to ensure the right level and allocation of government spending on national security. The United States Government must strengthen its defenses to win this war. At home, our most important priority is to protect the homeland for the American people.

Today, the distinction between domestic and foreign affairs is diminishing. In a globalized world, events beyond America's borders have a greater impact inside them. Our society must be open to people, ideas, and goods from across the globe. The characteristics we most cherish—our freedom, our cities, our systems of movement, and modern life—are vulnerable to terrorism. This vulnerability will persist long after we bring to justice those responsible for the September 11 attacks. As time passes, individuals may gain access to means of destruction that until now could be wielded only by armies, fleets, and squadrons. This is a new condition of life. We will adjust to it and thrive—in spite of it.

In exercising our leadership, we will respect the values, judgment, and interests of our friends and partners. Still, we will be prepared to act apart when our interests and unique responsibilities require. When we disagree on particulars, we will explain forthrightly the grounds for our concerns and strive to forge viable alternatives. We will not allow such disagreements to obscure our determination to secure together, with our allies and our friends, our shared fundamental interests and values.

Ultimately, the foundation of American strength is at home. It is in the skills of our people, the dynamism of our economy, and the resilience of our institutions. A diverse, modern society has inherent, ambitious, entrepreneurial energy. Our strength comes from what we do with that energy. That is where our national security begins.

National Strategy to Combat Weapons of Mass Destruction December 2002

"The gravest danger our Nation faces lies at the crossroads of radicalism and technology. Our enemies have openly declared that they are seeking weapons of mass destruction, and evidence indicates that they are doing so with determination. The United States will not allow these efforts to succeed. ... History will judge harshly those who saw this coming danger but failed to act. In the new world we have entered, the only path to peace and security is the path of action."

President Bush
The National Security Strategy of the United States of America
September 17, 2002

INTRODUCTION

Weapons of mass destruction (WMD)—nuclear, biological, and chemical—in the possession of hostile states and terrorists represent one of the greatest security challenges facing the United States. We must pursue a comprehensive strategy to counter this threat in all of its dimensions.

An effective strategy for countering WMD, including their use and further proliferation, is an integral component of the National Security Strategy of the United States of America. As with the war on terrorism, our strategy for homeland security, and our new concept of deterrence, the U.S. approach to combat WMD represents a fundamental change from the past. To succeed, we must take full advantage of today's opportunities, including the application of new technologies, increased emphasis on intelligence collection and analysis, the strengthening of alliance relationships, and the establishment of new partnerships with former adversaries.

Weapons of mass destruction could enable adversaries to inflict massive harm on the United States, our military forces at home and abroad, and our friends and allies. Some states, including several that have supported and continue to support terrorism, already possess WMD and are seeking even greater capabilities, as tools of coercion and intimidation. For them, these are not weapons of last resort, but militarily useful weapons of choice intended to overcome our nation's advantages in conventional forces and to deter us from responding to aggression against our friends and allies in regions of vital interest. In addition, terrorist groups are seeking to acquire WMD with the stated purpose of killing large numbers of our people and those of friends and allies—without compunction and without warning.

We will not permit the world's most dangerous regimes and terrorists to threaten us with the world's most destructive weapons. We must accord the highest priority to the protection of the United States, our forces, and our friends and allies from the existing and growing WMD threat.

PILLARS OF OUR NATIONAL STRATEGY

Our National Strategy to Combat Weapons of Mass Destruction has three principal pillars:

Counterproliferation to Combat WMD Use

The possession and increased likelihood of use of WMD by hostile states and terrorists are realities of the contemporary security environment. It is therefore critical that the U. S. military and appropriate civilian agencies be prepared to deter and defend against the full range of possible WMD employment scenarios. We will ensure that all needed capabilities to combat WMD are fully integrated into the emerging defense transformation plan and into our homeland security posture. Counterproliferation will also be fully integrated into the basic doctrine, training, and equipping of all forces, in order to ensure that they can sustain operations to decisively defeat WMD-armed adversaries.

Strengthened Nonproliferation to Combat WMD Proliferation

The United States, our friends and allies, and the broader international community must undertake every effort to prevent states and terrorists from acquiring WMD and missiles. We must enhance traditional measures—diplomacy, arms control, multilateral agreements, threat reduction assistance, and export controls—that seek to dissuade or impede proliferant states and terrorist networks, as well as to slow and make more costly their access to sensitive technologies, material, and expertise. We must ensure compliance with relevant international agreements, including the Nuclear Nonproliferation Treaty (NPT), the Chemical Weapons Convention (CWC), and the Biological Weapons Convention (BWC). The United States will continue to work with other states to improve their capability to prevent unauthorized transfers of WMD and missile technology, expertise, and material. We will identify and pursue new methods of prevention, such as national criminalization of proliferation activities and expanded safety and security measures.

Consequence Management to Respond to WMD Use

Finally, the United States must be prepared to respond to the use of WMD against our citizens, our military forces, and those of friends and allies. We will develop and maintain the capability to reduce to the extent possible the potentially horrific consequences of WMD attacks at home and abroad.

The three pillars of the U.S. national strategy to combat WMD are seamless elements of a comprehensive approach. Serving to integrate the pillars are four cross-cutting enabling functions that need to be pursued on a priority basis: intelligence collection and analysis on WMD, delivery systems, and related technologies; research and development to improve our ability to respond to evolving threats; bilateral and multilateral cooperation; and targeted strategies against hostile states and terrorists.

COUNTERPROLIFERATION

We know from experience that we cannot always be successful in preventing and containing the proliferation of WMD to hostile states and terrorists. Therefore, U.S. military and appropriate civilian agencies must possess the full range of operational capabilities to counter the threat and use of WMD by states and terrorists against the United States, our military forces, and friends and allies.

Interdiction

Effective interdiction is a critical part of the U.S. strategy to combat WMD and their delivery means. We must enhance the capabilities of our military, intelligence, technical, and law enforcement communities to prevent the movement of WMD materials, technology, and expertise to hostile states and terrorist organizations.

Deterrence

Today's threats are far more diverse and less predictable than those of the past. States hostile to the United States and to our friends and allies have demonstrated their willingness to take high risks to achieve their goals, and are aggressively pursuing WMD and their means of delivery as critical tools in this effort. As a consequence, we require new methods of deterrence. A strong declaratory policy and effective military forces are essential elements of our contemporary deterrent posture, along with the full range of political tools to persuade potential adversaries not to seek or use WMD. The United States will continue to make clear that it reserves the right to respond with overwhelming force—including through resort to all of our options—to the use of WMD against the United States, our forces abroad, and friends and allies.

In addition to our conventional and nuclear response and defense capabilities, our overall deterrent posture against WMD threats is reinforced by effective intelligence, surveillance, interdiction, and domestic law enforcement capabilities. Such combined capabilities enhance deterrence both by devaluing an adversary's WMD and missiles, and by posing the prospect of an overwhelming response to any use of such weapons.

Defense and Mitigation

Because deterrence may not succeed, and because of the potentially devastating consequences of WMD use against our forces and civilian population, U.S. military forces and appropriate civilian agencies must have the capability to defend against WMD-armed adversaries, including in appropriate cases through preemptive measures. This requires capabilities to detect and destroy an adversary's WMD assets before these weapons are used. In addition, robust active and passive defenses and mitigation measures must be in place to enable U.S. military forces and appropriate civilian agencies to accomplish their missions, and to assist friends and allies when WMD are used.

Active defenses disrupt, disable, or destroy WMD en route to their targets. Active defenses include vigorous air defense and effective missile defenses against today's threats. Passive defenses must be tailored to the unique characteristics of the various forms of WMD. The United States must also have the ability rapidly and effectively to mitigate the effects of a WMD attack against our deployed forces.

Our approach to defend against biological threats has long been based on our approach to chemical threats, despite the fundamental differences between these weapons. The United States is developing a new approach to provide us and our friends and allies with an effective defense against biological weapons.

Finally, U.S. military forces and domestic law enforcement agencies as appropriate must stand ready to respond against the source of any WMD attack. The primary objective of a response is to disrupt an imminent attack or an attack in progress, and eliminate the threat of future attacks. As with deterrence and prevention, an effective response requires rapid attribution and robust strike capability. We must accelerate efforts to field new capabilities to defeat WMD-related assets. The United States needs to be prepared to conduct post-conflict operations to destroy or dismantle any residual WMD capabilities of the hostile state or terrorist network. An effective U.S. response not only will eliminate the source of a WMD attack but will also have a powerful deterrent effect upon other adversaries that possess or seek WMD or missiles.

NONPROLIFERATION

Active Nonproliferation Diplomacy

The United States will actively employ diplomatic approaches in bilateral and multilateral settings in pursuit of our nonproliferation goals. We must dissuade supplier states from cooperating with proliferant states and induce proliferant states to end their WMD and missile programs. We will hold countries responsible for complying with their commitments. In addition, we will continue to build coalitions to support our efforts, as well as to seek their increased support for nonproliferation and threat reduction cooperation programs. However, should our wide-ranging nonproliferation efforts fail, we must have available the full range of operational capabilities necessary to defend against the possible employment of WMD.

Multilateral Regimes

Existing nonproliferation and arms control regimes play an important role in our overall strategy. The United States will support those regimes that are currently in force, and work to improve the effectiveness of, and compliance with, those regimes. Consistent with other policy priorities, we will also promote new agreements and arrangements that serve our nonproliferation goals. Overall, we seek to cultivate an international environment that is more conducive to nonproliferation. Our efforts will include:

• Nuclear

  ◦ Strengthening of the Nuclear Nonproliferation Treaty and International Atomic Energy Agency (IAEA), including through ratification of an IAEA Additional Protocol by all NPT states parties, assurances that all states put in place full-scope IAEA safeguards agreements, and appropriate increases in funding for the Agency;

  ◦ Negotiating a Fissile Material Cut-Off Treaty that advances U.S. security interests; and

  ◦ Strengthening the Nuclear Suppliers Group and Zangger Committee.

- Chemical and Biological

  - Effective functioning of the Organization for the Prohibition of Chemical Weapons;

  - Identification and promotion of constructive and realistic measures to strengthen the BWC and thereby to help meet the biological weapons threat; and

  - Strengthening of the Australia Group.

- Missile

  - Strengthening the Missile Technology Control Regime (MTCR), including through support for universal adherence to the International Code of Conduct Against Ballistic Missile Proliferation.

Nonproliferation and Threat Reduction Cooperation

The United States pursues a wide range of programs, including the Nunn-Lugar program, designed to address the proliferation threat stemming from the large quantities of Soviet-legacy WMD and missile-related expertise and materials. Maintaining an extensive and efficient set of nonproliferation and threat reduction assistance programs to Russia and other former Soviet states is a high priority. We will also continue to encourage friends and allies to increase their contributions to these programs, particularly through the G-8 Global Partnership Against the Spread of Weapons and Materials of Mass Destruction. In addition, we will work with other states to improve the security of their WMD-related materials.

Controls on Nuclear Materials

In addition to programs with former Soviet states to reduce fissile material and improve the security of that which remains, the United States will continue to discourage the worldwide accumulation of separated plutonium and to minimize the use of highly-enriched uranium. As outlined in the National Energy Policy, the United States will work in collaboration with international partners to develop recycle and fuel treatment technologies that are cleaner, more efficient, less waste-intensive, and more proliferation-resistant.

U.S. Export Controls

We must ensure that the implementation of U.S. export controls furthers our nonproliferation and other national security goals, while recognizing the realities that American businesses face in the increasingly globalized marketplace.

We will work to update and strengthen export controls using existing authorities. We also seek new legislation to improve the ability of our export control system to give full weight to both nonproliferation objectives and commercial interests. Our overall goal is to focus our resources on truly sensitive exports to hostile states or those that engage in onward proliferation, while removing unnecessary barriers in the global marketplace.

Nonproliferation Sanctions

Sanctions can be a valuable component of our overall strategy against WMD proliferation. At times, however, sanctions have proven inflexible and ineffective. We will develop a comprehensive sanctions policy to better integrate sanctions into our overall strategy and work with Congress to consolidate and modify existing sanctions legislation.

WMD CONSEQUENCE MANAGEMENT

Defending the American homeland is the most basic responsibility of our government. As part of our defense, the United States must be fully prepared to respond to the consequences of WMD use on our soil, whether by hostile states or by terrorists. We must also be prepared to respond to the effects of WMD use against our forces deployed abroad, and to assist friends and allies.

The National Strategy for Homeland Security discusses U.S. Government programs to deal with the consequences of the use of a chemical, biological, radiological, or nuclear weapon in the United States. A number of these programs offer training, planning, and assistance to state and local governments. To maximize their effectiveness, these efforts need to be integrated and comprehensive. Our first responders must have the full range of protective, medical, and remediation tools to identify, assess, and respond rapidly to a WMD event on our territory.

The White House Office of Homeland Security will coordinate all federal efforts to prepare for and mitigate the consequences of terrorist attacks within the United States, including those involving WMD. The Office of Homeland Security will also work closely with state and local governments to ensure their planning, training, and equipment requirements are addressed. These issues, including the roles of the Department of Homeland Security, are addressed in detail in the National Strategy for Homeland Security.

The National Security Council's Office of Combating Terrorism coordinates and helps improve U. S. efforts to respond to and manage the recovery from terrorist attacks outside the United States. In cooperation with the Office of Combating Terrorism, the Department of State coordinates interagency efforts to work with our friends and allies to develop their own emergency preparedness and consequence management capabilities.

INTEGRATING THE PILLARS

Several critical enabling functions serve to integrate the three pillars—counterproliferation, nonproliferation, and consequence management—of the U.S. National Strategy to Combat WMD.

Improved Intelligence Collection and Analysis

A more accurate and complete understanding of the full range of WMD threats is, and will remain, among the highest U. S. intelligence priorities, to enable us to prevent proliferation, and to deter or defend against those who would use those capabilities against us. Improving our ability to obtain timely and accurate knowledge of adversaries' offensive and defensive capabilities, plans, and intentions is key to developing effective counter- and nonproliferation policies and capabilities. Particular emphasis must be accorded to improving: intelligence regarding WMD-related facilities and activities; interaction among U.S. intelligence, law enforcement, and military agencies; and intelligence cooperation with friends and allies.

Research and Development

The United States has a critical need for cutting-edge technology that can quickly and effectively detect, analyze, facilitate interdiction of, defend against, defeat, and mitigate the consequences of WMD. Numerous U.S. Government departments and agencies are currently engaged in the essential research and development to support our overall strategy against WMD proliferation.

The new Counterproliferation Technology Coordination Committee, consisting of senior representatives from all concerned agencies, will act to improve interagency coordination of U.S. Government counterproliferation research and development efforts. The Committee will assist in identifying priorities, gaps, and overlaps in existing programs and in examining options for future investment strategies.

Strengthened International Cooperation

WMD represent a threat not just to the United States, but also to our friends and allies and the broader international community. For this reason, it is vital that we work closely with like-minded countries on all elements of our comprehensive proliferation strategy.

Targeted Strategies Against Proliferants

All elements of the overall U. S. strategy to combat WMD must be brought to bear in targeted strategies against supplier and recipient states of WMD proliferation concern, as well as against terrorist groups which seek to acquire WMD.

A few states are dedicated proliferators, whose leaders are determined to develop, maintain, and improve their WMD and delivery capabilities, which directly threaten the United States, U.S. forces overseas, and/or our friends and allies. Because each of these regimes is different, we will pursue country-specific strategies that best enable us and our friends and allies to prevent, deter, and defend against WMD and missile threats from each of them. These strategies must also take into account the growing cooperation among proliferant states—so-called secondary proliferation—which challenges us to think in new ways about specific country strategies.

One of the most difficult challenges we face is to prevent, deter, and defend against the acquisition and use of WMD by terrorist groups. The current and potential future linkages between terrorist groups and state sponsors of terrorism are particularly dangerous and require priority attention. The full range of counterproliferation, nonproliferation, and consequence management measures must be brought to bear against the WMD terrorist threat, just as they are against states of greatest proliferation concern.

END NOTE

Our National Strategy to Combat WMD requires much of all of us—the Executive Branch, the Congress, state and local governments, the American people, and our friends and allies. The requirements to prevent, deter, defend against, and respond to today's WMD threats are complex and challenging. But they are not daunting. We can and will succeed in the tasks laid out in this strategy; we have no other choice.

Op-Ed Columns
Wall Street Journal

November 1, 2004; Page A15
"Setting the Record Straight on Tora Bora"
—By Michael DeLong

In recent days, John Kerry has repeatedly accused President Bush of having "outsourced the job" in Tora Bora to kill Bin Laden. Knight Ridder reporters concluded that in Tora Bora we "relied on three Afghan warlords" to catch Bin Laden, "ignored" warnings from own officers about incorrect methodology, and that we also relied on the Afghan warlords as our blocking forces, thus letting more than 1,000 Al Qaeda escape. As the #2 General at CentCom in charge of the Afghanistan War, I can say with certainty that all of these allegations are incorrect. It is past time someone set the record straight on what really happened in Tora Bora.

As I explain in detail in [A General Speaks Out], we strategized Tora Bora in essentially the same way we strategized the rest of the Afghanistan War: by using a combination of our elite Special Forces and CIA Agents, embedded with native Afghan troops. We chose this approach in waging the Afghan war for many reasons: it minimized the number of U.S. troops put in harm's way; it drew on the strengths of the native Afghanis who had been fighting in that terrain for years and who were adept at traversing the mountainous terrain on horseback; and it helped avoid the same mistake the Soviets made in Afghanistan, who had opted for a large troop presence and ended up with thousands of their troops killed. The fact that we took Afghanistan in a matter of weeks—a feat which tens of thousands of Soviet troops were unable to accomplish in a matter of years—proves that our strategy was exactly the right approach for Afghanistan. This was essentially the same strategy we employed at Tora Bora. Thus, to say that we "outsourced" the job by relying primarily on U.S. Special Forces and U.S. CIA Agents is absurd.

This is especially the case in Tora Bora. I said "essentially" the same strategy because in Tora Bora we did shift tactics. Instead of letting the Afghan warlords have command (as they had for the rest of the Afghan war), we put U.S. Special Forces in command. U.S. Special Forces conceived and executed the attack on Tora Bora, while the Afghan warlords took orders from us. We never "relied" on them: we were 100% in charge. Few people realize that Tora Bora began as a ground war, led by U.S. troops; bombing only followed later. Despite what some have said, no caves were too deep for our reach. We bombed nonstop for three weeks. We received many leads on Bin Laden's whereabouts, and had U.S. troops rush in only to find dry holes.

The Knight Ridder reporters claim that we let 1,200 U.S. Marines sit idly by in an air base 80 miles away from Tora Bora while the Afghans did the fighting for us. This is also not the case. General Franks, working with the Special Forces commander and consulting with the Secretary of Defense, all agreed that tactically it would be best not to use those 1,200 troops. It was a deliberate decision, because using them would have meant killing hundreds—if not thousands—of Afghan civilians, hostile to a heavy U.S. presence. A strong Afghan warlord presence was essential. We could have sent more U.S. forces in and killed everybody—but we may very well still not have gotten Bin Laden, and we would have definitely forever put the South at odds with us. Indeed, if we pursued such a strategy, the ramifications would be so great that it is quite possible there would be no stable Afghan government today.

The same holds true for the border region between Afghanistan and Pakistan, where Bin Laden likely escaped (if indeed he was there to begin with). The Knight Ridder reporters claim that we relied on the Afghan warlords to block the border for us. Again, this is incorrect. We relied on the Pakistani Frontier Forces—once again, because we had to. The U.S. could not go in to the border region with a heavier presence without sparking a war with the locals; indeed, the regular Pakistani army could not even go in there without sparking a war. The border area had to be blocked by Pakistani Frontier Forces if we didn't want to risk murdering thousands of civilians and making Pakistani President Musharraf's position untenable with his people. Such actions would have meant losing a strong U.S. ally in Musharraf, an ally who has facilitated the killing or capturing of the largest percentage of Al Qaeda in the world since 9-11.

Finally, most people fail to realize that it is quite possible that Bin Laden was never in Tora Bora to begin with. There exists no concrete intel to prove that he was there at the time. Most importantly, capturing Bin Laden was not our #1 priority. Our mission in Afghanistan was to topple the Taliban regime and rid the country of Al Qaeda. If we caught Bin Laden it would have been a major plus—but it was not our #1 objective.

One must remember that Tora Bora was a military operation and its execution was a tactical decision, which means that it was never run by the President, and never should have been—which makes this one less reason to hold the President directly accountable on this issue. If anyone should be accountable, it should be us. And we are more than satisfied with the way we handled the Afghan war—including Tora Bora. If we had to do it again, we would do it exactly the same way.

New York Times

April 16, 2006; Page 13
"A General Misunderstanding"
—By Michael DeLong

As the #2 ranking General at United States Central Command (CentCom) from September 11, 2001 through the Iraq War, I was a participant in all of the events that transpired, and I was the daily "answer man" to Defense Secretary Rumsfeld. I briefed Rumsfeld twice a day, and spoke to him more times than that, and few people had as much interaction with him as I did during this two year period. In light of the recent criticism of Rumsfeld by retired generals, I would like to set the record straight on what he is really like to work with.

When I was at CentCom, the people who needed to have access to Rumsfeld did, and he carefully listened to our input. That is not to say that Rumsfeld is not tough in his convictions—he is—or that he will make it easy on you—he will not. If you approach him unprepared, or if you don't have the full courage of your convictions, he will not give you the time of day. He will not give in easily, either, and he will always force you to argue your point thoroughly. This can be tough for some people to deal with. As I detail at length in my book, [A General Speaks Out], I witnessed many strong, professional conversations between Franks and Rumsfeld—but Rumsfeld always deferred to Franks on warfighting issues.

Ultimately, I believe that a tough Defense Secretary makes commanders tougher in their convictions. Was Rumsfeld a micromanager? Yes. Did he want to be involved in all of the decisions? Yes. But our professional civilian and military discussions made the decisions better. And Rumsfeld never stepped on toes and told people in the field what to do. It all went through Franks.

Rumsfeld did not like waste. He knew that many of the operation plans we had on the books dated back to the 90s (some even to the late 80s), and he asked us to examine whether we could update these plans with a more streamlined, technological force. He made the following request to all of the Commanders: "Can we do it better, and can we do it with less people?" Sometimes Franks and I answered Yes, at other times we answered No. When we said no, there was a discussion; but when we told him what we needed, we got it. I never witnessed him endangering troops by insisting on replacing manpower with technology. In both the Afghanistan and Iraq wars, we always got what *we*, the commanders, thought we needed.

The outcome and ramifications of a war, however, are impossible to predict. On March 17, 2003, two days before our invasion, Saddam opened his jails and let loose 50,000 Iraqi prisoners. The Iraqi police force walked out of their uniforms on the day we invaded, compounding domestic Iraqi chaos. We did not expect this. We also—collectively—made some decisions in the wake of the war which, in retrospect, could have been better. We banned the entire Baath party, for example, which ended up slowing reconstruction (we probably should have banned only a portion the party); we dissolved the entire Iraqi army (we probably should have retained a small cadre of the army, to enable us to rebuild it more quickly). We relied on the supposed expertise of the Iraqi ex-patriot Chalabi (and others) who assured us that once Saddam was gone, the three major Iraqi parties would unite in harmony. Their counsel proved to be disastrous, and the ex-patriot Iraqi army they rounded up was largely ineffective—but then again, Chalabi was the highest ranking Iraqi ex-patriot who was willing to come forward at that time with advice and counsel. Other members of the Iraqi ex-patriot community also predicted that a post-Saddam Iraq would unite in harmony. Obviously, they were wrong.

But that doesn't mean we didn't plan extensively for post-war Iraq, or that a "What's next?" plan didn't exist. It did. Franks drafted the plan, and the Joint Chiefs, the Department of State, the Department of Defense, the Treasury Department, the Justice Department, and a host of other departments—and all other cabinet members—had input on the plan. This plan was thoroughly "wargamed" by the Joint Chiefs of Staff. It was dubbed our "Phase IV" plan, and it was a thoroughly inter-agency plan, which incorporated input from all branches of government.

To step forward in retrospect and try to pin blame on one person is wrong. When distinguished individuals step forward and criticize a sitting administration, particularly one at war, the rest of the world watches—and it weakens the United States.

Acknowledgments

We would like to thank Richard Kane for believing in the merit of this paperback edition. Thanks also to the rest of the staff at Zenith Press and MBI Publishing.

We would like to thank Regnery Publishing for having faith in the hardcover edition of this book (titled *Inside Centcom*), in particular, Harry Crocker, Marji Ross, Harry Burton, Paula Decker, and Kelley Keeler.

We would like to thank General Zinni for his introduction; Newt Gingrich, General Franks and General Hoar for their support; Captain Shelly Young, Barry Hammill, Assistant Secretary for Public Affairs Larry DiRita, and Dan T. Morris, associate director of intelligence at CentCom, for their superb fact checking; Angela Carlascio for her after-work administrative help; Dave Pecchia for his generous photography; Mike Corbitt and Gus Russo for making the connection; and Major General Gary Harrell, for his generous time and contribution to this book.

General Delong: I'd like to thank the great community of Tampa/St. Petersburg. To mention a very few of the extraordinary people: former Mayor Dick Greco and Dr. McLintock Greco; Tampa's only royalty, Vivian Reeves; the Pope of Tampa, Monsignor Higgins; Eddie and Candy DeBartolo; the Lightnings' Ron and Mary Jane Campbell; the Devil Rays' Vince and Lenda Naimoli; Dr. and Mrs. Hashmi; Owen and Susan Roberts; George and Paula Wilson; and John and Susan Sykes. I'd also like to thank the Shaw Group—Jim Bernhard, Tim Barfield, and Diana Severs-Ferguson—for their foresight and forbearance, and Fred Hardwick for keeping me *alive*!

Noah Lukeman: I'd like to thank my family for their continual support.

Index

Lieutenant General Michael P. DeLong (Ret.) served as Deputy Commander, United States Central Command, from 2000 until his retirement in 2003. His history of team leading and building for over thirty-six years enabled him to lead a team of over three thousand personnel to help conceive and implement Operations Enduring Freedom and Iraqi Freedom, while assembling a seventy-member coalition focused on the global War on Terrorism. Currently, General DeLong is a senior vice president of the Shaw Group, Inc. and on the board of directors of Sykes Enterprises.

Noah Lukeman is author of the critically-acclaimed and bestselling books *The First Five Pages*, *The Plot Thickens*, and *A Dash of Style*. He lives in New York City and is president of Lukeman Literary Management Ltd.